Warming Up Julia Child

Warming Up
Julia Child

The Remarkable Figures
Who Shaped a Legend

HELEN LEFKOWITZ
HOROWITZ

PEGASUS BOOKS
NEW YORK LONDON

Pegasus Books, Ltd.
148 West 37th Street, 13th Floor
New York, NY 10018

Copyright © 2022 by Helen Lefkowitz Horowitz

First Pegasus Books paperback edition February 2023
First Pegasus Books cloth edition April 2022

Interior design by Maria Fernandez

Library of Congress Cataloging-in-Publication Data is available.

ISBN: 978-1-63936-368-1

10 9 8 7 6 5 4 3 2 1

Printed in the United States of America
Distributed by Simon & Schuster
www.pegasusbooks.com

To Julia Child's alma mater, Smith College,
an institution capable of transforming the lives of its students and faculty,
including my own and that of my husband, Daniel Horowitz.

CONTENTS

Introduction   ix

Chapter 1: Assembling the Initial Team   1

Chapter 2: Avis Comes Aboard   25

Chapter 3: Marseille   41

Chapter 4: Home Leave and Germany   62

Chapter 5: Washington   85

Chapter 6: Shifting Gears   103

Chapter 7: Waiting   124

Chapter 8: The House of Knopf   141

Chapter 9: The Launch   172

Chapter 10: The French Chef   194

Chapter 11: "Julia"   236

Endnotes   257

Acknowledgments   277

Illustration Credits   279

Index   281

INTRODUCTION

Julia Child was a person of great intelligence, drive, and accomplishment, but she did not work and achieve alone. This is a book about friendship and collaboration. It is a study of Julia and her relationships with those who assisted and enabled her work—and ultimately her enduring fame. Julia Child had a great capacity for friendship. She also possessed a keen business sense that carried an understanding of the importance of working with others and appreciating their help in achieving her goals.

Julia Child made friends easily. Vivacious and warm, she drew others to her, and by the early 1950s, as her culinary ambitions developed, she began to gather those who stimulated, nurtured, aided, and championed her. She and Paul, the man she married in 1946, were already partners, supporting each other through life's many challenges. He not only encouraged Julia as she became an accomplished home cook, teacher, cookbook writer, and television presenter, he aided her work as her photographer and man-of-all-work. In Paris in 1951, Julia met and formed an alliance with Simone (Simca) Beck, who first taught with Julia in their cooking school and then brought her into collaboration on a French cookbook for Americans. Simca supplied recipes, shared with Julia responsibilities for testing each one, and provided all recipe titles. A letter in 1952 led Julia to a close friendship with Avis DeVoto, who encouraged her and opened the door to Houghton Mifflin and a book contract. In 1959, when that publisher rejected the manuscript, Avis saw that it was immediately sent to William Koshland, the unofficial general manager of the publishing house, Alfred A. Knopf. Koshland carefully shepherded the cookbook manuscript through the publishing process, seeing that, from that point on, it was in expert hands and, in the many years that followed, that Julia was treated with every courtesy. Koshland put the manuscript in the hands of Judith Jones, who read and supported it and, with Knopf's acceptance, served as its careful and tactful editor. These key allies aided and abetted Julia on her path to *Mastering the Art of French Cooking*. With that achievement behind her and its promotion in mind, in 1962 Julia began to work at WGBH with Ruth Lockwood, a staff member of the educational TV station who became Julia's right arm in the production of *The French Chef*.

These six people helped Julia Child develop her gifts between 1952, when she began teaching at the cooking school and working on the cookbook, and 1966, when her fame was sealed by an Emmy Award for *The French Chef* and her portrait on the cover of *TIME* magazine. Without these six, Julia Child would not have become the "Julia" of fame and memory, and Americans would have lost an important new way to understand and enjoy food and the pleasures of the dining table.

Of course, there were many others in the background who made Julia Child's career possible. There were her prosperous parents, a loving mother and a financially generous father, who saw that their energetic and friendly daughter received the excellent education that fostered her organizational skills and lucid writing—first at the Polytechnic School, a private day school in Pasadena, California, then the Katharine Branson School, a boarding school north of San Francisco, and finally, Smith College in Massachusetts.

These parents implicitly contributed an awareness of business and its values as part of Julia Child's heritage. Her father, John McWilliams, Jr., was a real estate manager who became vice president of J. G. Boswell Company, a major land owner and developer of Southern California land during that region's growth years.[1] Active in civic affairs, in 1934 he became president of the Pasadenda Chamber of Commerce. Julia's mother, also Julia, held wealth from her own family's paper manufacturing company in Grafton, Massachusetts; her death when Julia was in her mid-twenties left Julia grieving, but also with a bequest that gave her independent means.

In early adulthood, although ambitious to become a novelist, Julia worked in advertising. Producing copy was unfulfilling, but the work fostered her self-discipline, developed her organizational skills, and enabled her to understand the important role of promotion. World War II offered the chance of meaningful service, and Julia joined the Office of Strategic Services (OSS), working first in Washington and then abroad. In that work she learned the importance of accuracy and proved to be extremely efficient and organized. In Ceylon and China she arranged and kept the agency's files, ultimately processing top-secret papers as head of the Registry.

This experience served her well in her later career, as in like manner she meticulously dated and filed recipes for the future cookbook.

During her World War II service, Julia met the most important person in her life, Paul Cushing Child. They met in Ceylon and then were separately transferred to China. There the two often escaped army food to eat in small nearby restaurants and enjoy each other's company. Their relationship deepened, and by the time of their return to the United States at the war's end, they were a romantic couple. After joining up in Pasadena, they traveled by car across country to Maine and the summer place of Paul's twin brother Charlie and his wife Freddie, where they announced their intention to marry. An auto accident failed to delay their wedding on September 1, 1946.

"Julia and Paul at Their Wedding," Schlesinger Library, Harvard Radcliffe Institute.

Paul got a job at the State Department, and they settled in Washington, D.C. Charlie, too, was in government service and lived with his wife nearby. This allowed Freddie to try to help Julia learn to cook. The shared life of the brothers and their wives in Washington wasn't to last, as both men soon learned that their jobs would be ending. Charlie decided to become an artist full time; Paul began to negotiate with the United States Information Service about a posting abroad. He got lucky, and in 1948, Paul and Julia departed for Paris, where Paul was assigned to the American embassy to be in charge of exhibits.

Making their way from Le Havre, where their ship landed, to Paris, Julia and Paul stopped to have lunch at a restaurant in Rouen. Once she took her first bite of a sole meunière, Julia was hooked on French food.

It was fortunate that Paul's work brought Julia to Paris. In the years following the Second World War, Paris was a mecca for many Americans. The great city attracted leading figures in the arts and letters, and they, in turn, gave Paris a special luster. This inspired many Americans to venture there, most simply to visit, but some to live. Interest in French cuisine had been growing for some time in the United States. Le Pavillon had opened in 1941 in New York City, to join the esteemed French restaurant nearby at the famed Waldorf-Astoria Hotel. American writers on food brought new attention to the quality of French cuisine and wine, and it became "at that moment synonymous with *luxury* food and wine."[2] This led to greater interest in French restaurant food in the U.S. and enhanced the desire to enjoy it in Paris.

Some Americans residing in Paris sought to reproduce restaurant dishes in their own kitchens. Among them was Julia Child. After she and Paul settled in their roomy Paris apartment on the Rue de l'Université and Julia had worked on her French enough to be able to converse with others, she set about exploring the city's food markets. With Julia's inheritance from her mother, she and Paul were able to enjoy many restaurants in Paris, from simple bistros to luxurious establishments. These meals helped inspire her to want to learn to cook well and reproduce such French flavors in her own kitchen. Since her service during the war, she had been missing a focus for her energies. She knew, however, that it would never again be an office job (or even hatmaking, after she looked at the results of her efforts). On learning about Le Cordon Bleu, the famed Paris cooking school, Julia signed up for its course of study and practical work.

Julia was fortunate in having Max Bugnard as her teacher, not only at the school but also in her home, where he gave her private lessons. Bugnard was a chef able to teach the living tradition of French cooking. As a restaurateur and chef in London before World War II, he worked for several years under Auguste Escoffier. Thus, Julia was only a single degree of separation from one of the greatest names in French cuisine.

"Julia Child and Chef Bugnard," Schlesinger Library, Harvard Radcliffe Institute.

In time, Julia absorbed additional knowledge as she acquired and read texts from the masters of French cooking, such as Marie-Antoine Carême, the eighteenth-century chef who codified grande cuisine in his many books.

She studied reference works, including *Larousse Gastronomique*, the comprehensive encyclopedia of French cuisine. The work that was likely the most important to her was *La Bonne Cuisine de Madame E. Saint-Ange*, as it was designed for the home cook that she was determined to be.

But it was a long journey from a cooking student with a desire to be a compentent home chef to bestselling cookbook author and cultural icon. One she did not make alone. As Julia Child made her way to co-authoring *Mastering the Art of French Cooking* and teaching culinary techniques and recipes on *The French Chef,* she acquired a remarkable set of close friends and co-workers. As each entered her world, Julia Child gained someone important in her life. And in distinct ways, each joined in enabling her culinary ambitions to grow beyond her own kitchen. I see them as forming Julia's team.

Julia appreciated the friendships that members of her team offered, while at the same time she understood each person's value as an ally in her work. She was also clearheaded, taking appropriate action when she understood that a potential alliance wasn't working. With her savvy business sense, Julia knew that in developing a product in a competitive market—in her case a cookbook—it was important to protect the work from theft. As she sent out recipes to others to try them out, she often used the words "Top Secret" in her correspondence, and she warned them not to let the recipe out of their hands or disclose their contents.

Julia's understanding of promotion was a key element in generating sales for *Mastering the Art of French Cooking.* She developed her own "launch" after its 1961 publication, traveling the U.S. from coast to coast with Paul and Simca. Following this book tour, she accepted invitations to give demonstrations to nonprofit organizations. All the while she tracked sales and the accompanying royalties. Then in 1963 came her most important promotional step. In what might today be called "branding," she created her own television cooking show, *The French Chef,* on Boston's WGBH. This came at a fortunate time, as educational television was coming into its own, ultimately uniting nationally into PBS, thus putting Julia's cooking methods and comedic talents in households across the United States. As each broadcast featured a recipe from *Mastering the Art of French Cooking*, the show boosted book purchases by its widening audience, causing sales to take off exponentially. By 1966, she was famous across the U.S. As the cover story in *TIME* magazine declared, she was on a "first name basis" with her American readers and audience. Julia Child was now "Julia."

There have been many books on Julia Child. Mine differs, for the story I have to tell focuses on the interactions between Julia and her team of six. It explores her deepening relations with each of them and their efforts for and support of her, and also sheds light on the extraordinary people they were. William Koshland and Ruth Lockwood in particular are two lesser known collaborators in my narrative, and I dwell on their biographies at some length, as each in turn offers insight into the inner workings of an important institution, publishing and educational television.

I have sought to develop this narrative in a special way, made possible by the rich archival record of correspondence in collections at the Schlesinger Library of the Harvard Radcliffe Institute and the Harry Ransom Center on the campus of the University of Texas. The letters between Julia Child and members of her team in these important archives have enabled me to offer a series of "conversations" via the written words exchanged between Julia and each of them during the critical years between 1952, when Julia began work on a French cookbook for Americans, and 1966, when she reached national renown. These conversations give Julia Child and her team members agency and allow entry into their specific interactions over time as relationships developed and changed. These written words evidence the substanial aid each collaborator gave, and they open as well an important window into Julia Child's own astounding personal and professional growth.

Chapter One

Assembling the Initial Team

I n the beginning, there was Paul. He was a key player in everything that Julia became. He loved her dearly, and an important way he manifested his love was to champion Julia in everything she chose to do. He was a remarkable human being. In addition to being a supportive husband, he was a gifted photographer, a determined artist, an amateur poet, and a great letter-writer. Much of what can be known about Julia's development as a cookbook writer and television host comes from his pen.

PAUL

Paul Cushing Child was born in New Jersey in 1902. He and his twin brother, Charles, were the second and third children of achievers in very different realms. Their father, Charles Tripler Child, was an electrical engineer, then working at the Smithsonian's Astrophysical Observatory; their mother, Bertha Cushing Child, had enjoyed an earlier career as a concert singer. When the twin boys were six months old, their father suddenly died. Bertha Child returned with the two boys and their older sister to the Boston area, where she successfully resumed her musical career. Paul and the brother he always called Charlie were close, although sometimes rivalry supplanted supportiveness. At age seven, Charles accidently blinded Paul in his left eye. Characteristically, Paul never blamed him.

Both boys were talented and became unusually cultured adolescents; but they had very different personalities. Paul was shy and seemingly pessimistic, while Charles was gregarious and appeared optimistic.[1] Charles, remembered by his grandson as "brawnier, louder, more charismatic, and less sensitive than Paul," got favored treatment that included the payment by Edward Filene, Bertha's lover at the time, of his full tuition at Harvard. In contrast, Paul was supported for one year at Columbia, likely in the School of General Studies.[2] In the years that followed, Paul found work in many places in the U.S. and abroad.

By 1930, he was in Cambridge, Massachusetts, teaching in private schools. He lived then with his first great love, Edith Kennedy, the mother of one of his students. Older and more established than Paul, she brought him into the broader intellectual world of Cambridge. She suffered a weak heart and edema, however, and died in 1942.[3] With the coming of war, Paul joined the Office of Strategic Services (OSS), and working abroad, he met and fell in love with Julia Child.

Paul found that the pleasures of life in Paris compensated for whatever frustrations were posed by his bureaucratic office work at the American embassy. Life there offered the right balance between his job's duties and his artistic work—painting and photography. As the years passed, bringing moves to different postings abroad and at home, that balance would cease to be possible, causing him much distress.

In Paris, Paul also relished the fruits of Julia's developing culinary skills. Writing to Charlie in early 1951, Paul told him of a dinner Julia prepared for their guests, "performing with her usual mastery on two pheasants."[4]

Julia enlisted Paul to add artwork to certain of her food preparations. For a cocktail party on January 11, 1951, in honor of Ivan Cousins, the fiancé of Julia's sister Dorothy, Julia sought Paul's efforts in designing the galantine decorative surface.[5]

That party may have been the most important moment in Julia's professional life. It is where Julia met Simone Beck Fischbacher—Simca. That is, if one believes the origin story of meeting Julia that Simca told.

SIMCA

In 1951, Simca was in her mid-forties and, unlike Julia, had many years of a cooking life. By her own account, she received her first culinary lesson at age seven when she escaped from her nanny and watched the family cook make a roux for a boeuf bourguignon. Toward the end of her life, Simca published *Food & Friends*, a book that combined autobiography and recipes.[6] It is a revealing work offering insights into not only her privilege and experience, but also her personal resilience. Baptized Simone Suzanne Renée Madeleine Beck soon after her birth in 1904, Simca was the daughter of a well-to-do family in Normandy. Their wealth originated with Alexandre Le Grande, her mother's father, the creator and manufacturer of Benedictine liqueur. Her father was an engineer who, at the time of the cook's roux lesson, was the owner of a factory that made a silicate powder used in the production of ceramic tiles. The large family house in Rainfreville, 24 kilometers [15 miles] from Dieppe on the Normandy coast, was surrounded by a stable, greenhouse, garden, and farmyard. The house alone was serviced by a staff of six. The English nanny was there not only to keep Simone and her older brother Maurice in line, but also to give them lessons and to enable them to be bilingual.[7]

With the coming of World War I, Simone's father entered military service, and her mother moved the family to Rouen. There, she and her brother entered a boarding school as day students. Later, when conditions required that she be a boarding student, she suffered from malnutrition that she later believed caused her scoliosis. With the influenza epidemic, she returned home, as did her father, ravaged after suffering from the poison gas used by the Germans at Verdun.[8]

In the years that followed, Simone was close to her father, who taught her to drive a car and to dance, even the tango. She accompanied him and Maurice on hunting expeditions. She, in turn, helped out, once even in the kitchen. At a time when the family cook was away, she prepared the meal for unexpected Americans, who had traveled to Rainfreville on business.[9]

Simone grew to be tall like her father, in her case 5 feet, 8 inches, a height unusual for a French woman. And she assumed the posture and something of the hauteur of a privileged bourgeois daughter. It was expected that she would live a conventional life, centered around family. With that vision before her, she married a man she hardly knew, Jacques Jarlauld. She wrote that he had come to stay as "one of our shooting guests," and after a few days, he asked her father for her hand. This took her by surprise. Her adolescence had been devoid of beaux, and she was unaware of her own needs. Her grandmother on her mother's side, living with the family at the time, urged Simone to accept. The desire to leave home overcame Simone's hesitations: Jacques Jarlauld lived in Paris.

The wedding came in June 1923, complete with a five-hour catered wedding banquet for forty guests in the Beck dining room. What followed was a wedding night on the train to Paris that was, in Simca's words, "a nightmare . . . a disaster." After the couple settled in Paris, Jacques spent his days at work and essentially left her alone. They gave cocktail parties, and she played bridge, went to lunch with her women friends, and had them over as well.[10] Once Jacques learned from medical tests that he was sterile, he no longer sought sexual relations. In retrospect, Simca wrote, "I realize that those ten years I spent with Jacques were dreary and fruitless but not desperately unhappy." A turning point came when she visited her dying father. He told her that she deserved a better life and persuaded her to leave her husband. She decided to file for divorce.[11]

Simone had tried bookbinding and mastered it, but at this point she chose to refine her cooking skills at the Cordon Bleu. The formal course was not satisfying, but it led her to the instructor, the great chef Henri-Paul Pellaprat, who agreed to teach her privately in her home.[12]

In 1936, with her divorce final, she took on salaried work for her father's company, now in the hands of her brother Maurice. Her job was to visit bathroom-supply manufacturers to tell them about the value of silicate for their products. And that is how, on a business call, she met Jean Fischbacher, a slightly younger man who was the assistant to the director of such a manu-facturing company. He was from an Alsatian family and Protestant, then something of a bar for a French Catholic woman, but two months later, she agreed to dine with him at a restaurant. When afterwards he escorted her to her car, he gave her its name, Simca. With Jean came romance and passion. The two wed in 1937 and sustained a long, love-filled marriage.[13] They established themselves in an apartment in Neuilly, a commune at the western edge of Paris.

Their good life began to unravel with the coming of World War II. Jean entered the military as a second lieutenant. Initially, Simca was able to visit him, but once the fighting between the French and the Germans began in earnest, she retreated with her in-laws to their home in Chinon. When she learned that Jean had been taken prisoner, she rushed to Paris first to gather food for him and then to the convent where he was interred. Even after he was moved to Germany, she managed to provide him with sustenance.

She retreated with her mother to Rainfreville, forced to share the house with Nazi occupiers. She became "an indirect *résistant*" after she was "cajoled" by a wealthy contact to lend her Neuilly apartment "as an occa-sional meeting place for resistance people." She ultimately learned that it had been "a drop-off point for letters" and likely as a place for "printing false passports and identity papers."[14]

The end of the war brought Jean's return, after five years, "his eyes and cheeks sunken, his clothes in tatters." His imprisonment had been long and difficult, with life-threatening days, and he arrived in Paris weighing "not more than a hundred pounds." Jean's conduct during his long internment merited him the Legion of Honor.[15]

As Simca and Jean resumed their life in Paris, he returned to his work as a chemical engineer at the perfume company that had continued his salary during his service and internment. And new possibilities opened for Simca. One of Jean's work colleagues secured a sponsor for Simca to become a member of Cercle des Gourmettes, a luncheon club founded in 1929. Simca described it as an "assemblage of women from a certain social class, to the manner born," who met to enjoy good food, wine, conversation, and handsome table settings. While the club hired professional chefs for the luncheons, its members were encouraged to venture into the kitchen as the food was being prepared—and even help out with some of the cooking chores. Simca became a "devoted member" and was given the responsibility of overseeing the woman who helped the chef choose the menus for the club's gatherings. Occasionally, she worked with the chef in preparing the luncheon meals.[16]

Simca had known Louisette Bertholle prior to the war. When meeting later at a cocktail party, Louisette told her of a visit to the United States on a business trip with her husband during which she spent time with an American friend, Lucille Tyree. After Louisette helped Lucille prepare dinner, her host suggested that Louisette write a cookbook about cooking the French way. Encouraged by Jean, Simca began to collaborate on "a small book for recipes for America, *What's Cooking in France*," actually more a pamphlet than a book, published by Putnam in the United States. Subsequently, during a period in which Louisette was preoccupied with family, Simca recalled that she "forged ahead" on her own. One result was Simca's authorship of a brochure in France regarding prunes and prune liqueurs.

Describing her life during this period, Simca wrote, "I went wild, becoming a workaholic as I frantically wrote down recipe after recipe to create a valid cookbook for Americans." She gathered from all the sources she knew, including her "mother's black recipe notebooks, . . . tips from chefs in restaurants," her memories of food cooked in her family's Normandy kitchen, and recipes from Aimée Cassiot, the female chef of the Gourmettes luncheons.[17]

After working on her recipe collection for a year or more, she used a powerful contact she had through Jean's family and sent a large batch of the recipes to Dorothy Canfield Fisher, a noted American author on the selection committee of the Book of the Month Club. The response was deeply discouraging. This respected authority candidly wrote back to Simca: "This is just a dry bunch of recipes, with not much background on French food attitudes and ways of doing things." Because Americans were used to much simpler cooking, the recipe collection needed to explain to Americans "the whole way the French do things in the kitchen." She followed, however, with the valuable suggestion: "Get an American who is crazy about French cooking to collaborate with you; somebody who both knows French food and can still see and explain things with an American viewpoint in mind."[18]

In *Food & Friends*, Simca related how these words led her to arrange a meeting with Julia Child in 1949. Not knowing such a woman, Simca got the advice and assistance of a knowledgeable friend who went to George Artamonoff for help. He was an American businessman who was in Paris at that time as the director of the Marshall Plan in Asia. Artamonoff told this friend that Simca should meet Mrs. Paul Child, and kindly issued an invitation to Simca to attend a large cocktail party where Julia would be one of the guests. Artamonoff let Simca know that at the party he would be too busy circulating with his one hundred guests to introduce the two. Simca should be able to spot her, however: "She's over six feet tall."

Spying a possibility at that party, Simca positioned herself behind a seated "handsome, curly-headed woman." Once she stood (and thus revealed her height), Simca introduced herself. "Mrs. Child? I've been looking for you . . . please call me Simca." With that, she told Julia of her hope to teach "French cooking to Americans through a cookbook and perhaps by giving lessons in Paris." Julia immediately invited her to come over to her apartment the next day.[19] In Simca's telling, their meeting happened because she had prearranged it for the specific purpose of furthering the cookbook.

Julia, however, told a different story of their meeting. It was part of the unpublished "Cooking Biography" that over a decade later, she prepared for her publisher, Alfred A. Knopf, Inc. The document was designed to be used for publicity purposes the following year when *Mastering the Art of French Cooking* reached publication. Julia wrote that she met Simca in Paris "at a lunch with mutual friends. We immediately began to talk cooking, and she asked me to attend a luncheon cooking session at 'Le Cercle des Gourmettes.'" Julia described this as "a group of French women who meet twice a month in Paris and work with a chef to prepare a grand lunch for the rest of the members of the circle." Julia continued that she later "met Louise Bertholle, and learned about the two French women's collaboration on a book of French cooking for the United States. We soon became good friends, and kept toying with the idea of starting a joint cooking school for Americans in Paris. In January 1952, our idle talk of a cooking school suddenly became serious when two friends of mine from California arrived to stay in Paris for several months, and demanded cooking lessons. We started up within a week."[20]

Julia's appointment book establishes the date of the Artamonoff party as January 11, 1951. She was certain to attend, for the event was held in honor of one of Artamonoff's assistants, Ivan Cousins, who was departing the next day for the United States with his fiancé Dorothy McWilliams, Julia's sister. Julia noted in her appointment book that she had prepared as her food offering for the party that elaborate galantine de volaille that Paul helped design. It consisted of cold chicken, pressed and served in aspic, and took over three days to make. Julia hoped it would have "magnificent results."[21] Later in her appointment book she added that the party was a "mad success." There was no mention of meeting the woman who would change her life. And, on the following day, she wrote only "See Dort & Ivan off on Liberté Boat Train. Buy pheasants." It reported nothing about a visit from Simca Beck.[22]

8

Julia's first mention of Simca appears in an undated reference in her 1951 appointment book, in an early section of the book where she jotted down notes to herself. In this case, the subject was a restaurant: "W. M Perronica ami de Fishbacher; Simca—Au Petit Peu." Perhaps the conflicting evidence about meeting Simca is only a matter of Julia's ignorance of Simca's effort to meet her for the purpose of enlisting her in the cookbook project. The two may well have first encountered each other at Artamonoff's party, with the restaurant lunch following. Julia's 1951 appointment book does state that on January 30, 1951, she was to "Meet French women cook—'Gourmette Club,'" and this may well have occurred at Simca's invitation.

In thinking about the divergent information on their first meeting, there may, however, have been something more afoot. In Simca's case, when her book *Food & Friends* was published four decades after the event of the two's first acquaintance, Julia Child had become famous as an American television host and instructor. Reading Simca's narrative, I see her as wanting to put on record her agency. The diverging accounts also suggest an important difference between the two women. Simca suggests her motivation was to wrangle an American collaborator for a French cookbook for Americans. By contrast, Julia put friendship at the center—both in her early relation with Simca and in the instigation for their cooking school's startup.

The important element is that when they met, Julia found a person who shared her passionate interest in French cooking. Simca Beck was rooted in the women's gastronomic world of Paris and was an important member of the Gourmettes. And most important for what would become their collaboration, Simca had lived French cuisine her entire life and brought a heritage of recipes from her wealthy, established family. The gain was on both sides. Simca found in Julia Child not only an American woman interested in French cooking, but a person who brought to their joint project, a French cookbook for Americans, a logical mind, well-honed organizational skills, advertising experience, and the ability to write fluidly and clearly. In addition, both women proved to be energetic, strong, and ambitious.

"Simca, closeup," Schlesinger Library, Harvard Radcliffe Institute.

Almost a year later, at the end of December 1952, Julia wrote out a somewhat different sequence regarding the evolution of the cookbook. It was a careful narrative, and, as a former worker in the OSS, Julia was precise about facts and dates. It was written to set the groundwork for a legal document regarding what would become her cookbook with Simca and Louisette, and both of her co-authors signed it. In this account, both Simca and Louisette were active from roughly 1948 in "writing their big book on French cooking." Visiting New York in 1951, Louisette had taken their joint manuscript (likely the one that Simca sent to Fisher). "It interested Sumner

Putnam," head of the New York publishing company Ives Washburn. The publishing house put out the pamphlet "What's Cooking in France" as a "teaser" to test the waters for the book. The two women lost control of this small collection of their recipes, as selection, translation, and editing was placed in the hands of Helmut Ripperger, a writer on food. Based on an understanding with Putnam, but no contract from the firm of Ives Washburn, the two women continued to develop their comprehensive cookbook. It thus seems likely Simca shared Dorothy Canfield Fisher's judgment with Louisette, and both French women realized they needed an American partner for this enterprise.

From Simca's perspective, Julia Child must have seemed perfect for the task. She was clearly an energetic and enthusiastic American, deep into learning French cooking. In contrast to Simca's telling in which she put all the cards on the table at Artamonoff's party, I see Simca working a bit more slowly—fishing in a stream, sizing Julia up, testing her, and then reeling her in.

Her first step was to bring Julia into Les Gourmettes, and as Julia's appointment book attests, she first attended a luncheon on January 30, 1951. By April she was welcomed as an official member. For the rest of her stay in Paris, Julia attended the luncheons every other Friday, and often visited with its elderly American-born founder, Paulette Etlinger.

Simca then introduced her to Louisette, and the three women began to see each other outside the club's biweekly luncheon gatherings. Writing of this early period of their mutual working relationship, Simca wrote, "We soon became a kind of triumvirate of cooking."[23]

Thus, much about Simca's account rings true. After working with Louisette on a French cookbook designed for American women in American kitchens, the two Parisians needed an American partner, and Simca snagged Julia. However, in the same memoir, Simca attempted to declare her chief role in the cookbook that they had developed together. She asserted in the creation of *Mastering the Art of French Cooking*, she was the "prime mover." She was, as she put it, "more of an authority on French Food, more of a 'boss.'"[24]

One can recognize Simca's importance—and the absolute fact that *Mastering* would not have existed without her—and yet see her role somewhat differently. She was the instigator who recognized that Julia could be useful to her cookbook project and snagged her. She (and, to a lesser extent, Louisette) supplied most of the recipes that she and Julia adapted for American cooks using American ingredients and appliances in American kitchens. And for the many years of development for their two collaborative books, Simca and Julia shared the hard work of experimenting with methods, testing recipes, and checking with the many established works on French cuisine. The two worked together as partners, always in touch with each other wherever their kitchens and books happened to be.

But in taking the credit for *Mastering the Art of French Cooking*, Simca failed to recognize that a cookbook is a book. It has a logic and organizational structure that Julia, albeit with Simca's help, hammered out over time. It also has a literary style. It was Julia's logical mind, organizational skill, and writing ability that played the critical role in *Mastering*, drawing readers in, providing instruction, and giving them the courage to try the recipes.

Finally, thinking only of the French recipes in her repertoire, Simca forgot all the other actors who helped bring *Mastering the Art of French Cooking* into being, foster its success, and broadcast it to an American audience.

From Julia's correspondence, one learns that she was beginning to hold ambitions beyond improving her domestic cooking skills. In April 1951, in a letter sent across the Atlantic Ocean to Freddie, Julia wrote of her rage after she flunked her Cordon Bleu examination. She laid that failure at the institution's head. From Julia's perspective, she had been treated unfairly. She had been a good student, studied hard, and learned to make complicated dishes. She had taken private lessons with Max Bugnard, her Cordon Bleu instructor. But instead of being examined on her advanced work, the head of the school demanded tasks so elementary that Julia was unprepared to be tested on them. With this rejection, Julia expressed to Freddie her growing ambition. She wrote, "The main thing, of course, is that I know how to cook. Chef Bugnard says I am pretty well qualified to be chef in a maison de la Haute Bourgeoisie. But I may need a better diploma from the CB sometime, for our restaurant or school."[25]

"Our restaurant or school"—in April 1951 Julia seemed to be referring to an aspiration that the sisters-in-law likely shared—that, once Julia was back in Washington, they might collaborate professionally. Julia continued only with the second option. Their school would be different from the Cordon Bleu. "Anyway, the Olive Avenue Cooking School [the location of Julia's Georgetown house] will be run on quite different lines; and the main idea of the school is, anyway, to make cooks out of people, and not to make money. . . . the school isn't to lose money, but it is definitely to be an establishemnt [sic] dedicated to learning and the enjoyment of cooking through friendliness and encouragement and professionalism."[26]

But then, quite soon, what seemed like a mere wisp of aspiration began to take form—not in Georgetown and not with Freddie. Reporting on a lunch, Paul wrote in mid-December 1951 of the guests, who included Louisette Bertholle. He described the latter as "an energetic and knowledgeable Gourmette (presently engaged with another gourmette named Simka [sic] Fischbacher in writing a cook book to be published in USA; both special pals of Jlie's). . . . Julie & Simka & Bert[h]olle are planning to start a little cooking-school, classes to be limited to 4 students, and to be held in Bert[h]olle's kitchen."[27]

In January 1952, Julia, Simca, and Louisette began their cooking school, soon to be named "L'École des Trois Gourmandes."[28] Although the original plan had been for the school to be at Louisette's residence, the renovation of her kitchen prevented it, and, for unknown reasons, Simca's home in Neuilly was not considered. Thus the school's location became Julia's kitchen on the Rue de l'Université.

Paul described to Charlie the hasty start of the school: "A 55ish Californian named Martha Gibson turns up, wanting lessons in French cooking.

Plenty mazuma [i.e., rich]. Also next day comes a Gibson-friend Mrs. Ward—then two days later, a third acquaintance who runs an Inn in U.S.A., whose [sic] been at Cordon Bleu & isn't satisfied w/ same. Suddenly the leisurely plans for a 'school' of cookery have precipitated out into the physical world (somewhat before the girls were ready . . .). Well, there they were, money in fist & wanting to start. <u>So it's started!</u>"[29]

Working with Simca, Julia carefully planned each session. Her 1952 appointment book demonstrates that she and Simca got together on many days of the week as they prepared for the classes—only occasionally joined by Louisette. Julia's early typed lesson plans demonstrate her orderly mind. Underneath the menu of the day, she laid out what each of the trio was to teach in sequence. Enjoying her new role, she typed "Prof." before Julia, Simca, and Louisette. Her handwritten comments for March 18 included both "Good menu" and what Julia planned to say to the students as she demonstrated the sauce for the crepes: "Discuss—Dogmatism—'the real bouillabaisse' . . . proof in eating."[30]

As time went on, Julia announced the school through the *Embassy News*, an informal newsletter for American embassy staff. The first page on June 20, 1952, for example, held what was essentially an advertisement: "INFORMAL LESSONS IN FRENCH CUISINE" that promised "a small, informal cooking class with emphasis on the cook-hostess angle."[31] The cooking school was the perfect medium for Julia at that moment. It was both social and serious. As they planned it, the three women would take in a small number of students at any one time, all of them American. Beginning at ten in the morning, as the students collectively made a midday meal, the trio would teach them according to French techniques. At 1 P.M., students and teachers would then dine on their creations together, using the occasion to criticize and discuss how not to make mistakes. The location of the school in Julia's kitchen enabled her to shape it in her own image. Envisioning it in sharp contrast to the Cordon Bleu, Julia intended her school's atmosphere to be "homey and fun and informal, and passionate pleasure from both pupils and professeurs."[32]

"Group portrait of Simone Beck, Julia Child, and Louisette Bertholle seated at a wooden table chopping vegetables," (left to right: Louisette, Simca, Julia) Schlesinger Library, Harvard Radcliffe Institute.

The trio quickly evolved into more of a duo. Julia's appointment book in the early days of the school reveals that preparation for the classes was essentially a partnership between Julia and Simca. Day after day holds the entry "J & S work." Initially, Julia didn't even know how to spell Louisette's name, and even after learning, it never evolved into "L" in the appointment book.

Louisette's name typically appears in ways that suggest she provided the social glue for the three instructors, hosting cocktails or dinners in her home. As teaching began, it was Simca who worked consistently with Julia to prepare and plan.

Energetic, precise, and knowledgeable, Simca was an excellent collaborator. Although at the time she met Julia she was enjoying the good life as the wife of a prosperous businessman in postwar Paris, she was also ambitious, seeking more than the life of a bourgeois Parisian matron. And, when the situation required, she was tough-minded, as her earlier personal history suggests. Most importantly, she was a trained, experienced, and enthusiastic cook.

Julia's letter to her sister-in-law Freddie written in spring 1952 offers a sense of Julia's appreciation of Simca and the duo's working relationship. Simca is, Julia wrote admiringly, "full of ideas on cakes & pastries—and has made some of the most delicious things with powdered almonds, sugar & egg whites." By then Simca had enlisted Julia in the cookbook project, the adaptation of French recipes for American cooks using American ingredients. Julia wrote to Freddie, "Simca and I are practicing by ourselves—which is very useful. Lately we've been doing pastry (pie crust). She [Simca] found, to her horror, that, using US 'Gold Medal' flour, all her proportions were off (fat vs flour)—so we've been doing the 'operational proof.' The French flour is much fatter & full of body, and seems to need as much as ⅓ less fat to make a nice crumbly 'short' crust. I suppose our flour, so that it will last indefinitely without turning, and be conveniently available at our super-markets, has to go through a lot of chemical processes which takes out some of the natural fats. And the French flour is more or less natural, & get maggoty after a while."[33]

Julia then wrote out for Freddie the measurements they were experimenting with, including many different combinations of butter, margarine, and Crisco. What was at issue for Julia in the outcome was not just texture, but taste. "The crisco gives an entirely different effect, certainly, and much more crumbly. But, me, I love the taste of butter in a crust."[34]

To Freddie, Julia assessed what the three women were bringing to their school. During this season, she wrote that Simca and Louisette brought the experience of "a lifetime in France, and having spent 3 years over writing a cookbook, and knowing nice little dishes and cakes and pastrys [sic]." Julia, however, was not modest about her own accomplishments. She stated that she had critical skills learned from "3 professional chefs," who taught her "good methods of cutting things up, handling the knife, cleaning and carving and saucery." In addition, she wrote, "I can also bring the practical side of being an American, and cooking with no servants anywhere."[35] At the same time, Julia's appointment books reveal Simca's important role. Not only had she been engaged with cooking from early on, studied with a great chef, and built a huge repertoire of recipes, Simca proved to be as committed and as hard-working as Julia.

During these early months of the cooking school, Simca extended invitations to Julia and Paul to visit at a number of her family homes, including the one of her childhood in Normandy. For this we have only Paul's grudging record, filled with complaints about the physical discomforts he experienced, the lack of taste in the house's furnishings, and in Normandy, the preference of cider over wine. What Paul gradually came to enjoy, however, was the company of Jean Fischbacher, Simca's husband.

As for the cookbook, it began to surface explicitly in Julia's jottings in her appointment book in late August 1952, a time when the cooking school was not in session. On Thursday, August 28, Julia noted, "Louisette, Simca & Book," and on the following day, "J & Simca work on cookbook."[36] A full record of this survives in the daily record that Paul, using the nickname he favored, labeled his "P'ski Diary." Paul came to write down each day his thoughts and activities, and he compiled these in a weekly letter to his brother, Charles. His entry of August 29, 1952 began by stating that the editor of "That famous cook book wh[ich] Simca & Louisette wrote for the American public, and wh[ich] was theoretically to have been published for the Christmas trade this Fall" had not happened. "So now Les Trois Gourmandes will have to do it. This means that the job of putting it into readable English will fall on Julie—and that aspect of it needs an immense amount of work—not to mention the re-writing of most of the original technical instruction (Louisette & Simca have not had professional training so, let's face it, even <u>that</u> isn't all it should be). It's a big book—it'll be a colossal job. . . . So Julie is girding-up her loins & spitting on her Underwood."[37]

Paul understood from the outset that Louisette with her "wonderfully vague temperament" was not fully on the team, and that the cookbook was really a partnership of Julia and Simca. In the days and months that followed, Julia marked almost daily "J works" or simply "works." On a few occasions she noted that Louisette was present. But for many days of 1952, it was Julia and Simca or more simply "S & J work." Once, a famed chef, Claude Thillmont, came to give them a lesson on cakes.[38] In these instances, it is not possible to know whether the two women were working on the cookbook or preparing for their classes. On one occasion, however, a Sunday in early December, Paul was there to observe, and wrote, "Julie and Simca are slugging away at their book."[39] And a month later, after dining with guests on the outcome of their labors, a garlic soup, Paul wrote to Charlie, "Julie & Simca are working on Chapter no. 2 of THE book. It's Soups."[40]

Julia shared many of Simca's attributes and had her own contribution to make—plus her unique vantage point as an American, versus a Frenchwoman who had been imbued with French culinary traditions her entire life. Julia brought her strong desire for scientific proof to recipes, her early experience in advertising, the organizational skills she had honed in the OSS during the war, and her communication and writing abilities. Once engaged in work on the cookbook, Julia's experience, logical mind, and literary interests enabled her to emerge as a lucid writer.

Equally important is the drive that propelled Julia, evidenced in the early days of the trio's cooking school. As her notation of her discussion points for the March 18, 1952 class suggest, Julia had an intense desire to demystify French cooking and replicate it in her own ordinary kitchen. Julia sought clarity and logical steps. She would take French cuisine away from the magic of the man in the white toque with a whisk, break it into elements that could be mastered, and teach the specific techniques needed to attain delicious outcomes for the table.

For this work Simca was just the ally Julia needed, and together Simca and Julia would prove to be a formidable team.

Once Simca was on the scene, Paul had an early reason to be grateful to her. After she brought Julia into the Gourmettes, Paul got the pleasure of dining "with the Prince Consorts Abandonés." He explained to Charlie that this group was composed of the husbands of the Gourmettes who met for a "fabulous lunch on [the] same day" that their wives were dining together. Paul described them collectively as "the group of civilized, witty, intelligent gourmets I've been looking for all these years."[41] Later in the spring, Paul raved to his brother about a lunch in which the Gourmettes and their husbands ate together at the restaurant in the building housing the Chamber of Deputies: "The food was really splendid. The whole mob (about 50) was first taken on a guided tour of the building to look at the place where the Deputies speak, at their wonderful old library, the murals & statues etc."[42]

Many months later came Paul's first description of Simca after she had come to lunch. He presented her to Charlie as "Mme. Fischbacher, a gourmette. . . . a flashy and charming Française of about 42."[43] In December he told Charlie of the plans for the cooking school to be conducted by Julia, Simca, and Louisette.[44]

Paul was able to see the school firsthand, because its location was in their kitchen. An astute observer, Paul came to understand the dynamics among the three women. Louisette, he wrote, had "a Romantic approach to cooking," i.e., she did not measure ingredients but used "instinct." By contrast, Simca and Julia were "hard workers & good organizers," and they had "more 'scientific'" and "measured quantities."[45]

Paul's work contributed in a direct way to the school's initial success. Not only did the American embassy's newsletter advertise its opening, Paul's work and wider social orbit likely helped bring in some of the women who came for lessons in Julia's kitchen. When the small class sat down at 1 P.M. to share the luncheon meal they had prepared, Paul was typically at the table, as his lunch break was long, and his office was only a short walk from their apartment. In his "P'ski Diary" of February 5, 1952, he noted that the gathering at the table was very "merry, self-congratulatory & fun."[46]

Behind the jolly lunch atmosphere that enlivened Paul's difficult workdays at the embassy lay a great deal of work. Julia and Simca were not playing—they were dead serious. On February 4, Julia wrote a full report on her teaching days to Freddie. The school began at 10 A.M. At 1 P.M., the teachers and students sat down to eat the meal they made, but the work did not stop. At lunch, "everybody must criticize anything, and if mistakes are made, we can discuss why and how to avoid them. And the atmosphere is just what we want it to be, homey and fun and informal, and passionate pleasure from both pupils and professeurs."

As for Paul, Julia wrote, none "of it could happen at all without him and his interest and good business sense (wouldn't his mother be shocked if she knew he was a good business man!). And having him for lunch lends a certain gaiety and tone to the event. Tomorrow he is going to give a little discussion on wines and the serving of. These gals have never really had good wine, and keep saying 'Oh red wine, I don't like it. Maybe I would like a really dry red wine.' So we are serving a fine bottle of Medoc 1929 tomorrow, to show them the difference."[47]

Julia worked hard in preparation. As she wrote to Freddie in March 1952, now giving the enterprise a name, "Have much too little time to write lately, as 'L'École des Trois Gourmandes' takes most all my time—even though lessons are only 2 times a week. It is a wonderful opportunity to get my hen-scratches into typewritten order. And every recipe I do takes hours of time, but I feel I've gotten the meat out of it at last, and it is, for the time being, 'definitive.'"[48]

Paul accepted the reality that the school's three teachers were working for love, not money. Julia explained the economic side to Freddie: "And so far we have made 7,000 francs [$20.20 or slightly less than $200 at the time of this writing] in three lessons, or 600 francs [$1.80 or slightly under $18] apiece per lesson (at about 25 francs [$.07; $0.69] per hours work). That includes everything, plus $3. wear and tear on our kitchen per lesson. As Paul puts it, per our remarks 'So, you are in business so you won't lose money'. But that's about it."[49]

More generally, with Paris in the 1950s an important gathering place for Americans, Paul had the opportunity in his work at the embassy to meet many leading figures in politics and the arts and letters from the U.S. When the teaching trio decided to widen the lunchtime circle, they invited a few outsiders to enjoy what the students had prepared. A fee of 500 francs (equivalent to $1.43, or $12.58 at the time of writing) helped to defray costs.[50] It may also have helped to develop the future reputation of their teachers.

Given his design talent, Paul embellished Julia's endeavor with what became an enduring image. In the early spring, he wrote to Charlie that he was at work "drawing a sort of 'trade mark' for the Trois Gourmandes to use on letter-heads, 'and other things.'" And with this, he let his comic imagination fly. "Well, they can decorate a cake w/ it when their first anniversary comes 'round—not to mention its obvious utility for sky-writing, banners, television, sand-painting, posters, title-pages, seal-rings, branding-irons, and for tatooing [sic] on the chest between the bosoms."[51] It remained a lasting contribution as what we would call today their logo, and it served to adorn their aprons and their stationery.

Paul's "trade mark," Schlesinger Library, Harvard Radcliffe Institute.

What about the project behind the cooking school that had brought the trio together, the French cookbook for an American audience? As Paul had noted, it began to appear in August 1952. By September, Paul's letters give a sense of what Julia's commitment was becoming and indicate that there would be little free time to roam the streets on weekends. On Saturday, September 6, 1952, he wrote, "J. works on her cook book revision. She kept it up all day." He, however, was busy then as well, for he was studying for an exam, a necessary step toward attaining a regular Foreign Service position.[52] But more than parallelism was at work. Paul had a genuine respect for what Julia was trying to accomplish.

Paul made up for his lack of formal classical training by intensive self-education. All of this served him well in understanding what Julia was up to. In early October 1952, as she was deep into work on sauces, Paul wrote that "Julie plugs away steadily at her cook book. Even so, Getting out of Sauces is as hard for her as it was for Christian to get out of the Slough of Despond. Everything is pretty Korzybskian. . . . [whose] Precepts of General Semantics are being put to practical use: 'The word is <u>not</u> the thing' was never better exemplified than Julie's refusal to believe what the books say without subjecting the theories to operational proof. All recipes are checked & counter-checked on the stove & in the stew pot, so are Old Wives tales."[53]

Paul then expanded to discuss Julia's work to turn French measurements of grams into the "American cooking vocabulary of spoonful, cupsful, 'medium-sized onions,' etc." In doing so, he applauded one of Julia's discoveries: the flaw in American cookbooks, even in the American standby *The Joy of Cooking*. She found that the recipe for Béchamel sauce had made a mistake in translating grams to spoonfuls: the fact that butter and flour weighed the same did not translate into equal volume. The book had given equal tablespoon measures when they should have been at a ratio of one tablespoon of butter to two of flour. "This may seem an arcane triumph indeed to outsiders, but it's an exciting discovery to our Wifelet."[54]

Paul also looked for books that might aid Julia's work. He bought her the 1,488-page, two-volume *Harrap's French and English Dictionary*, "whose sources are both England & America." He explained the utility of these sources as Julie worked on the cookbook. There were words such as "le carrelet which in English-English is plaice, but in American-English can be sand-dab, or lemon-dab, or lemon-sole."[55]

On October 20, 1952, Paul announced to Charlie, "Julie is wrestling w/ multifarious butters, the final chord in her symphony of sauces." Somehow, both Paul and Julia assumed that publication would come quickly and easily, for nine days later he wrote: "Julie just had to write the final draft of the SAUCES section of the cook book. It is shortly to be sent off to the publisher as a sample of style & method." Julia, he stated, had plans to send copies to her twelve cooking friends to test, the ones she called her "guinea pigs." Along with Freddie they offered "critical & helpful comments, many of which will be included in the ultimate, final-final-final draft for the printers."[56] Right after that, in Julia's appointment book for October 20, is an unusual entry: "S. comes at 9: work Louisette at 11:30 Do Beurre Blanc," followed by "S for lunch & Beurre Blanc. Work P.M. (sick of butter)."[57]

Julia may have been tired of butter, but for Paul there were more serious issues. In January 1953, after announcing to Charlie that Julia and Simca were now turning to soups, Paul continued, "Thank God we're out of Sauces, is all. Now my liver can get back to normal. We had a marvellous [sic] garlic soup today." Paul needed to be careful with what he ate, as he faced real health issues from the dysentery he suffered during his war service, and had taken medicine for it in recent years.[58]

As the cooking school began its second year, Paul described it to Charlie in glowing terms: "L'Ecole des 3 Gourmandes began its winter session once again this morning, w/ Chef Thilomont [Thillmont] holding the spoon-of-office. . . . a fine, honest, salty technician w/ a ripe & rapid accent, and a wonderful way w/ a pie-crust. When you watch him squeeze decorations onto a cake you can appreciate that famous utterance: 'There are only 4 great arts, Music, Painting, Sculpture, and Ornamental Pastry—architecture being perhaps the least banal derivative of the latter.'" After Thillmont offered Julia a modest compliment for the birthday cake she had made for Paul, "the Wifelet has been sparkling w/ pride all afternoon."[59]

In mid-January, Paul got word that he would likely be reposted to Marseilles. It meant for both of them the loss of Paris, and for Julia, the awareness that she would no longer be an active member of the teaching team Les Trois Gourmandes. But in the meantime, Avis DeVoto had come into her life, and the cookbook was beginning to loom larger in her mind.

Chapter Two

Avis Comes Aboard

S imca and Julia were roaring ahead, with Paul's constant support. But this was only the beginning. By summer 1952, only months after beginning her work with Simca, Julia found another great friend, the woman who moved Julia and Simca's collaboration on its forward path toward the publication of their remarkable book—Avis DeVoto. On receiving the first letter from Avis, written April 3, 1952, Julia entered into a correspondence that quickly grew into a deep friendship—one that not only altered her immediate plans for the cookbook, but also reshaped her life.

AVIS

When Avis wrote to Julia, she was forty-eight years old and living in Cambridge, Massachusetts. Born Avis MacVicar in Houghton, Michigan in 1904, Avis had a freshman year at Northwestern University in Evanston,

Illinois. At the end of that year, she married her English instructor, Bernard DeVoto, a man seven years her senior. Four years later, in 1927, they moved to Cambridge, where in the shadow of Harvard, Bernard's alma mater, he sought to become established as a writer and teacher. Except for a suburban move to Lincoln and two years in New York in the 1930s, the DeVotos remained in Cambridge. By 1952, they owned a grand house on fashionable Berkeley Street, and Bernard was a very famous man. He had published many books, including the Pulitzer Prize-winning *Across the Wide Missouri*. He wrote pieces in magazines, and he was about to publish *The Course of Empire*, a work for which he would receive the National Book Award. A person knowledgeable on the American West and an outspoken conservationist, he was the voice of the *Harper's* column "The Easy Chair."

In addition to running their large house, working in the garden, caring for their younger son Mark at home, and often worrying about their elder son Gordon, Avis served as Bernard's secretary, proofreader, and hostess of his regular Sunday cocktail hour. She was also responsible for giving the many dinner parties that formed the reciprocal rounds of Cambridge social life. For Avis, cooking was an important outlet for creative expression as well as a means to satisfy one of her primary pleasures, eating a good meal.

Living within the context of the early 1950s as the wife of a man very different from Paul Child, Avis seems to have seen herself principally as a helpmeet to her husband, sons, and friends. Understanding her place as an intellectually astute domestic woman, she used her gifts for language, precision, typing, and cooking primarily for others. Her rewards were her family, close friends, Cambridge life, and the pleasures that sprang from Bernard's fame. She was hardly the simple happy housewife of 1952 magazine ads, however. Ambition stirred within her.

Working with her writer husband, she was aware of her proficiency with words and relished clarity and precision. Bernard, or DeVoto as she called him, published with Houghton Mifflin in Boston, and that gave her important connections. Avis knew how to work her friendships, including that with Dorothy de Santillana, Bernard's editor. Given her good eye for talent, Avis conferred with de Santillana about prospective books, thus serving informally as a scout who steered manuscripts to Houghton Mifflin. She shared her husband's politics on the liberal left and engaged in small-scale fundraising for the Democratic Party candidates she favored. Julia knew little of this at the time, only that Avis responded warmly, was the wife of Bernard DeVoto, and was very interested in sharp knives and good French food.

In retrospect, it seems fated, but the friendship of Avis DeVoto and Julia Child came almost by chance. Had Julia not read "The Easy Chair" in *Harper's* November 1951 issue, expressing Bernard DeVoto's frustration with American stainless steel knives ("They look wonderful, but they won't cut anything"), had Julia not responded by sending him a "nice little French" knife as a "token of appreciation" for his words—and adding a brief description of her culinary work in Paris, and had Bernard not turned to his wife to answer such correspondence, Avis's important presence in Julia's life and Avis's invaluable contribution to the development and publication of Julia's *Mastering the Art of French Cooking* would not have happened.

On April 3, 1952, Avis DeVoto typed a letter to "Dear Mrs. Child." In contrast to Julia's short note, Avis wrote at length. After apologizing that she, not Bernard, was writing in thanks, Avis stated, "I am green with envy at your chance to study French cooking." With this she opened the conversation that the two would sustain for as long as Avis lived. "There are two dishes served at Bossu on the Quai Bourbon that I remember in my dreams, and if by any possible chance you know how to make them I would be forever in your debt if you would let me know." One was eggs, the other veal, both made with cream and fresh tarragon. Avis's awareness of taste and national differences must have been immediately evident to Julia when she read, "I probably can't get the right kind of cream for it [the egg dish] but I live in hopes. . . . Bossu probably has access to younger veal than I can get here."

A discussion followed regarding the abundant knives she and Bernard had received after his *Harper's* piece and the knowledge they had gained regarding the carbon steel knives manufactured for American butchers. Then Avis made a request: "I wish you would tell me how you sharpen your knives. Steel, hone, or what?" Here Avis told of her reliance on a professional knife sharpener as well as her own efforts to master the hone. Both gave evidence of her seriousness about her work in the kitchen.

She ended her letter expressing the pleasure of both DeVotos with Julia's appreciation of Bernard's column in words that revealed the zesty spirit she and her husband had in common with Julia and Paul Child: "Thanks again for the knife, which is a little gem. My husband, I regret to say, has snitched it for his own use—cutting the lemon peel the proper thinness for the six o'clock Martini—but it will be mine while he is in California."[1] Given Julia's nature, how could she resist?

"Avis DeVoto," Schlesinger Library, Harvard Radcliffe Institute.

She didn't. A month later, addressing Avis as "Dear Mrs. De Voto [sic]" Julia replied at great length. Nestled in her opening words of apology for her long delay, she announced "the sudden inauguration of 'Mrs. Child's Cooking School, Paris Branch.'" In the next paragraph she explained she was partnering with two French women in "L'École des Trois Gourmandes." Meeting twice a week with a maximum of five students, the trio aimed "to teach the fundamentals of French cooking to Americans." Now, after twenty-two lessons, she found she was "enjoying it immensely, as I've finally found a real and satisfying profession which will keep me busy well into the year 2,000 [sic]. But I wish I had started in when I was 14 yrs. old." Julia's zest and sense of resolution about attaining a professional career must have taken Avis's breath away.[2]

Julia replied fully to Avis's requests. First, a lengthy discussion regarding knives. Regarding sharpening, she wrote that her husband Paul, "a one-man art factory," went over their knives with a soap stone, and she used a large steel implement. Turning to cream, she explained how the French separator is set, making its cream richer. Avis could get a similar effect in the U.S. by beating in "bits of butter, a bit at a time." Julia added the clear instruction, "but never reheat to even under the boil again or the sauce will thin out or the butter will release itself. And you could get a slight sour by a few drops of lemon juice." Although Julia had never tried the two dishes at Le Bossu, she further explained why French scrambled eggs were distinctive: low heat, constant stirring, and a bit of butter added at the end. And she wrote out the full "method" for creating "Veal a la Crème, a l'estragon."

Julia's final words were about politics, a topic that she sensed she could discuss freely with the wife of the outspoken Bernard DeVoto. Julia distinguished her position somewhat from his. He had written a recent column railing against "the hopelessly antediluvian monsters" in Congress. Julia stated her more hopeful view that Republicans "need to 'grow up' to their responsibilities. I have faith that the nation is strong enough to withstand them and to teach them, though my faith is not without dreadful qualms."

As she closed in French language and idiom, she included Paul in sending best wishes to both DeVotos.[3]

When Avis replied at the end of May to "Dear Mrs. Child," she revealed a good deal more of herself. Julia had sent a second knife, and after abundant thanks, Avis wrote a lengthy disquisition on knives. She expressed her dream of going to England. Bernard might be sent to France to study the nation's industry and potential collaboration with other European countries, allowing her this side trip. Pulling back, she stated that this was unlikely, however, given his orientation to the American West, something Avis did not appear to share. She was looking forward to the summer with her twelve-year-old son in Annisquam on the North Shore in Massachusetts. (Attended by her maid, her husband and older son would stay in Cambridge, though Bernard would visit on weekends.) Avis then lustily described lobster feasts on the beach.

Avis duly thanked Julia for the veal recipe, noting, however, that she would not be able to find shallots in her market. She wrote of her own way of cooking vegetables with olive oil. In turning to eggs, she made it clear that something was still missing and hoped Julia would "eat the eggs with tarragon at Le Bossu, because there is some element there that I have not hit on." She also requested the recipe for pipérade, a spicy egg dish she had tasted in a Paris restaurant, whose name she had forgotten. It was good for the stomach after a night of wine drinking, or supposedly so. "Not that I ate it as a hangover cure: I have not had a hangover in fifteen years, thank you."

At the letter's close, Avis gave Julia important information about herself. In addition to her home duties and acting as her husband's secretary, she was correcting the proofs of his forthcoming book, and writing "a weekly newspaper column on detective stories."

Revealing herself in these ways must have been enticing to her new correspondent, but what must have really pulled Julia in were unprovoked words about Julia's own future. Avis asked, "Do you plan to come back to America eventually and set up shop here?" If so, Avis saw Julia's only competition as Dione Lucas, the British-born, Cordon Bleu-trained writer of a French cookbook "who at present is sweeping all before her, on radio, television, and in person." The Smith College Club brought her to Boston every spring to "mobbed" gatherings. "I must admit she is a very good showman, and I believe she is making a fortune." Avis posed this not as a barrier, but as an opportunity: "Plenty of room in the field for you, and a very good living."[4]

In these first two letters, Julia learned of Avis's deep interest in kitchen tools, desire for specific recipes, knowledge of products unavailable to Americans, democratic politics, and her sideline as a writer. All this augured well in a new correspondent. But what did it mean to have found a person who also envisioned a grand future in the U.S. for Julia herself? Hard at work in Paris, Julia must have perceived that this literate, playful, politically engaged American woman—with a deep interest in food, good connections, business sense, and a vision—offered a friendship worth having.

"Trial shot of Julie reading letter," Schlesinger, Harvard Radcliffe Institute.

Still writing to "Dear Mrs. DeVoto," Julia sent Avis the little cookbook "teaser" that Simca and Louisette's publisher had issued to build an audience for their larger work. In early October, still addressing "Dear Mrs. Child," Avis apologized for her long delay in answering, caused by a viral illness. With this came a tidbit of further enticement. Despite still under the weather, she had to close the letter to "dress to go to the Ritz to have dinner with Alfred Knopf, that great gourmet."[5]

As Julia's correspondence with Avis developed, Paul began to enjoy it as well. In his November 8, 1952 P'ski Diary, Paul wrote Charlie about finding the restaurant of Avis's pipérade and thereby introduced Avis. After summarizing how Avis happened to come into their lives via a letter of thanks for a knife sent to Bernard, Paul wrote, "Mrs. Devoto [sic] is damn near as good a stylist in her writing as her husband, so her letters are great fun. She must love to write because when she starts its [sic] like a Spring flood—she goes on for 5,6,7 pages. Well, seems she's always remembered a <u>piperade</u> (an omellette [sic] w/ peppers, tomatoes, bacon & onions) she ate once at the restaurant where we lunched today & she wondered how they made it. So we went there: to analyze the <u>piperade</u>." In a typical Paul comment, he added that the dish "<u>was</u> excellent, but we couldn't stand the restaurant. It reminded us of an American dog-wagon, complete w/ radio & rush."[6]

With Paul on board in this fashion, Julia threw caution to the wind. In a long letter that began with her consolation regarding Adlai Stevenson's loss in the November presidential election, she revealed to Avis that her California family were "Old Guard republicans of the blackest and most violently Neanderthal stripe," and that she was "persona traitoria" to them. Her second revelation, however, was not political, but culinary. "I am sending you with this letter a part of the Sauce Chapter from our forthcoming book FRENCH HOME COOKING. We are so steeped in it, we cannot look at it objectively, and need some intelligent American opinion."

She then inquired if Avis knew about the Ives Washburn Company, the presumed publisher-to-be of the cookbook she was now working on with her two French cooking school partners. The three were "sewed up morally (not legally)" with the firm, but Julia's ambitions regarding publishing their book had grown during the months she had been teaching, testing, and writing. To Avis, she asserted, "I immodestly think that this could become a classic on French cooking." With this, she gave her pitch. The book, she wrote, was designed both for "the novice" and the "practiced cook." It will offer "a complete re-studying of classical methods and recipes, in view of making them easier to do, and of bringing them up-to-date."

Wanting Avis's honest comments, Julia urged her to be "frank and brutal." But in a postscript, she showed her concern about protecting her product. She warned, "Please do not show this ms. to anyone. I think cooking recipes and methods are too easily stolen, and, as quite a bit of this is new stuff . . ."[7]

Avis's response—to "Dear Julia," not "Dear Mrs. Child," moved well beyond the task Julia had given her. After receiving Julia's letter on Christmas Eve, she wrote on Christmas Day, 1952, "I am wildly excited." Although she had not had time to "do more than dip here and there" and would leave a fuller report until then, nonetheless, she continued, "I most heartily approve the general scheme and am absolutely convinced that you have got something here that could be a classic and make your fortune and go on selling forever." And then, music to Julia's ears, Avis stated: "I want to grab this book for Houghton Mifflin."

Confirming her close relationship to the publishing house, she wrote that on the very day of writing, "Lovell Thompson who is Vice-Pres. and head editor is dropping in here today as he and his family always do, bearing bourbon, and I'm going to talk to him, preparing the way." Avis then asked for Julia's permission to let the press's "top editor," Dorothy de Santillana, see the manuscript, asserting that she "knows more about food than any woman." In contrast to the publisher Ives Washburn—"small, poor, and not well known," Avis testified to both the integrity and the strength of the Boston house. She also added inside information about the big advances that Houghton Mifflin was capable of offering, $12,000 (roughly equal to $105,600 at the time of writing) to Bernard for his *Course of Empire*.[8]

Julia and Paul were away in England, celebrating Christmas with close friends, when the letter arrived in Paris. It was thrilling to find Avis's letter on their return. As Paul wrote to Charlie, "We are excited by a letter from Avis de Voto (wife of <u>THE</u> DeVoto of <u>Harpers</u>). . . . She writes w/ style & vigor. An intelligent, humorous & sharply-edged personality emerges from her writing." After describing Julia's sending of part of her manuscript on sauces to Avis, Paul stated that Avis "thinks the manuscript has possibilities for being made into a splendid & useful book & has asked Julie to allow her to show it to Houghton & Mifflin (De Voto's publishers) for possible publication by them." Paul explained to his artist brother that this was "a thoroughly-established house w/ a great cooking expert on its staff." Dorothy de Santillana was a person "not only in a position to back up such a project w/ adequate funds," but also one who "will know how to evaluate the manuscript from a cooking standpoint." In addition, Avis conveyed that "H-M are <u>wonderful</u> to deal with, completely honest & generous, & she believes they would welcome the manuscript just now for certain internal publishing reasons." Paul closed his report with, "So <u>that's</u> why we're excited."⁹

Although Paul conveyed something of what receiving Avis's Christmas Day letter meant to the Child household, before Julia could reply to Avis, she had to get permission from her colleagues to proceed. On December 29 she wrote them a careful letter in the hope of shifting them away from publishing with Ives Washburn. Addressing Simca and Louisette as "Cheres Colleagues," she informed them that after sending Sumner Putnam, the head of that publishing house, the sauce chapter, she had not heard a word from him. In contrast, she had now received an admittedly "wonderfully exciting" letter from "Mrs. Bernard De Voto. . . . First appreciation of the book yet received; and her suggestion of Houghton Mifflin sounds dandy to me." In addition, the letter "confirms our suspicions about Ives Washburn."

Julia asked for Simca's and Louisette's permission to show the draft to Avis's "friend Dorothy." Then, if Houghton Mifflin made an offer, they might then compare it to Ives Washburn's. The three of them would also need to write a history of prior dealings with Putnam, in order to be up-front with Houghton Mifflin. In the future, there might be "delicate dealings with Putnam," but Julia's "great inclination would be to have ourselves with the HM Company, as they are one of the best, and furthermore, know about cook books . . . which is a great lack vis-à vis Putnam. I'm sure he is a trer-ribly [sic] nice man, but I don't feel he is able to bring up our baby the way the other chaps could." Eager for a quick resolution, Julia asked both Simca and Louisette to "Please telephone me right away!"[10] One sees working here Julia's carefulness, tact, clarity, and business sense.

Julia's letter to Avis, written the following day, came after both col-leagues gave their permission to let Dorothy de Santillana see the manu-script pages. Using now the more familiar salutation "Dear Avis," Julia began with a light-hearted version of her and Paul's reaction. "Your letter has thrilled us all (would say <u>excited</u>, which is my real reaction, but am learning not to use that word because of its more carnal implications in French!)." She then turned professional. Her lawyer, Paul Sheeline, "a fine, hard-headed young man, Harvard graduate" and Paul's nephew, had informed her that Simca and Louisette's publisher had a poor reputa-tion. However, he gave the advice of Don Moffat, an established author (and his father-in-law), that, as novices, the trio should accept "almost any deal." Julia asserted her own conviction "that if we can get the book into the hands of someone who knows about cooking, it will sell itself." She stated that the obligation to Ives Washburn was personal and moral on Louisette's part, not legal. Her own fear about Washburn arose from the trio's current thinking of publishing the book in sections. The house might fold while they were "in the middle of the series." Moreover the editor had already displayed poor judgment by publishing *What's Cooking in France* by Louisette and Simca.

Julia then sent Avis—to pass on to Dorothy de Santillana—"the full chapter." This included "the TOP SECRET recipes, which we'd love to have you try out and report on." Julia valued the possibility of having the reading by de Santillana, as an editor "who can evaluate a ms. professionally and give competent criticism." With her letter, Julia sent a raft of enclosures that included correspondence and the "history of our relations with Ives Washburn," the lot intended for Avis to use at her "discretion."[11]

On receiving this packet on January 2, 1953, Avis moved into high gear. Writing immediately after reading the chapter, she revealed the intensity of her emotional reaction: "I am in a state of slight stupefaction." But she was also "in a state of despair" about the slowness of publishers to "make up their minds." Attempting to give a realistic evaluation of her own connection to the firm, she wrote, "I am nothing to them except wife of one of their authors, friend of most of the executives, and occasional reader of ms. and consultant." But then, she let her knowledge and agency show. Eager to push things along even in the "horrible week" after the holidays, she had just tried without success to reach de Santillana. She was hoping on the following day to "spend a couple of hours with her" over the manuscript. She wrote of the firm's ladder to climb, that included not only Lovell Thompson, but the editor-in-chief above him. "But I will keep a finger on the pulse and am in a position to go in and scream at excessive delays."

After refusing to subject the manuscript to criticism, for that was to be de Santillana's job, Avis nonetheless offered some "small items" that dealt with language usage and the problems posed by differences in food culture in the U.S. and France. But mainly Avis poured out praise. The book was "going to be a classic—a basic and profound book. . . . I like the style enormously—it is just right—informal, warm, occasionally amusing." She nixed, however, any notion of publishing it in parts. "I would much prefer one big book and I don't give a damn how big or how expensive."

In the middle of writing the letter, Avis announced that she just reached de Santillana by telephone. "She is excited." Avis was going the very next day, a Saturday, to her house with the manuscript. The two women planned to visit before attending a party with their husbands. "We can have a couple of hours over it all alone." With that, Avis put down Sheeline's second-hand advice to Julia that she, as a first-time author, should be grateful for "any kind of contract from a publisher." She called it "phooey" offered by a man who, however experienced as an author, "couldn't have had any idea what kind of a property you have here." Although all would take time at Houghton Mifflin, "The next step is tomorrow when I go into a huddle with Dorothy."[12]

Avis's report the next day, January 4, 1953, was deeply encouraging. Dorothy read enough of the work to judge it as "a property which if properly handled would sell—perhaps not spectacularly but very solidly—for many years and bring you in a steady if not large income." After reading it thoroughly, Dorothy planned to take it to Lovell Thompson, who will "depend heavily" on both Dorothy's opinion as well as that of Avis. Dorothy agreed with Avis that Julia "must entirely give up the notion of having this published in parts. . . . It's got to be one big book, if it takes you the rest of your lives."

On Tuesday, Dorothy would try to see Sheeline, Julia's lawyer, in New York to "get his opinion as to the exact legal status of the property." Here she sent words of caution regarding Thompson: "Lovell will not take a step in the matter until he is convinced that there is no slightest chance that HM will be accused of pirating, or getting around another publisher." She warned that "Lovell also moves very very slowly" and even with "a green light, it may be some time" before he proceeds. With Dorothy now in the driver's seat, Avis wrote, "I will now bow out of the picture. . . . So watch and pray. I will be on edge until I hear from her one way or another."[13]

Beginning with that important Christmas Day, 1952, when "Dear Julia" replaced "Dear Mrs. Child," Avis became Julia's mainstay. She tested Julia's recipes, questioned Julia's word choices, asked for further discussion of ingredients, all the while offering continual encouragement. Julia responded with details about what she was trying and learning, always with an eye to the American cook. She discussed other cookbooks, such as the *Bouquet de France*, in this case with a combination of praise and dismay about its lack of explanation and instruction. As letters passed between them with discussions of frozen foods, equipment, and food preferences, their friendship grew.

Avis remained in conversation with Houghton Mifflin. In mid-January, she interrupted Bernard's phone conversation with Dorothy to learn that the powers at Houghton Mifflin saw no need for a visit to Sheeline, for Putnam held "no claims," thus Julia was "free to take any offer" she chose. It would require, however, further conversations at the press before Julia would receive a contract.[14]

A few days later, Julia responded that she was encouraged by Avis's words regarding Houghton Mifflin. It was good news, but it turned out that Houghton Mifflin would hold many conversations and move very slowly. It took almost a year and a half, but the will on both sides was there, and ultimately a contract for the cookbook was signed on June 1, 1954.

Filled as the two women's letters were with culinary discussion, publishing, and politics, they became increasingly rich with personal information. Each wanted the other to "know" her. Avis and Julia sent each other both photographs and descriptions of themselves and their husbands. Avis was not afraid to reveal her quirks and personal concerns to Julia. Perhaps that was one reason Julia trusted her so fully.

In January 1953, Julia wrote with the news of the move to Marseilles. Paul's job would involve dealing with cultural exchange programs across a wide swath of southern France, and this would require much travel. In writing to Avis, Julia tried to assess what this would mean personally and professionally. She first stated that leaving the cooking school was "a real blow" for "we three G's can't work closely together." Then she tried to strike a balance. A possible gain was that she could learn Provençal cooking firsthand. It was hardly an even exchange. Although Julia understood that, regarding the cookbook, "most of the main work we do separately anyway," she knew what she would miss: "It's the personal getting together and quick exchange, and experiments together that will not always be possible."[15]

A month before the move to Marseille, Julia visited there, giving her a first look at the coastal city in southern France. Writing to Avis, Julia expressed her sense that "the real work is about to begin." She would wrap her arms around the book and begin to "rough out the whole thing." With Paul's new job requiring fewer demands on her, she would be able to concentrate more fully on the book. At that moment she imagined she would have the whole manuscript ready in a year. Her first task was to give order to the soups and then "continue with the sections as outlined." She assured Avis that she would be very professional. "Each section will arrive in a neatly type-written state, all checked and proof-read." All this was in anticipation, for Julia knew that she first had to turn to the physical labor of the move itself. [16]

At this point Julia was rebelling against French culinary experts, dead and alive. She disliked the often-repeated quotes from epicureans of the past, and she was currently out of sorts with the octogenarian sage Curnonsky (Maurice Edmond Sailland), a food writer then all the rage. As she wrote to Avis, she called him "a dogmatic meatball who considers himself a gourmet but is just a big bag of wind." Along with Simca and Louisette, Julia had given him a recent dinner (the photo of which later became a publicity staple for the three). There Curnonsky insisted that beurre blanc had to be made over a wood fire with white shallots from Lorraine. Julia's reaction: "Phoo. But that is so damned typical, making a damned mystery out of perfectly simple things. . . . his dogmatism in France is enraging." [17]

Julia was determined to ignore all such directions and make everything possible using American ingredients in American kitchens. And she would use contemporary American technology and such equipment as the electric mixer and the new Waring blender to speed up the work.

Avis, an avid correspondent, cheerleader, and prod, encouraged this approach. She also pushed back against some of the advice from Americans that Julia was getting. From early on, Julia had sent recipes for testing and comment to her "guinea pigs"—trusted members of her family and old friends. Their recent responses to a draft were negative regarding Julia's explanatory introductions. Here Avis fought back: "Don't compromise— you know what you are doing. . . . This is a discipline, and it mustn't be watered down." She bolstered her position by telling Julia that the growing number of French restaurants in the U.S. gave the promise of stimulating Americans to try to cook French in their kitchens "to educate and enchant their families and to impress their guests." Avis reassured Julia that she had "a nice touch" and the "right tone" and should stick to her guns.[18]

These words make it clear that Avis was now fully engaged in Julia's work. She had become more than just a supporter; in many ways, Julia's project had become her own. Cooking, long an outlet for Avis's talents, merged with her literary gifts, her intimate knowledge of the publishing world, and her friendship with an important editor. Involvement in Julia's cookbook also allowed Avis to exercise areas of her own expertise, separate from that of her gifted and famous husband.

Nonetheless, while she was aware of her strengths and pleased with her seeming success in finding a home for the cookbook, there was a side of Avis that could be modest and even self-deprecating. When Julia wrote that she wished to dedicate the book to her, Avis demurred. She stated that although she would "expire with pleasure" at the dedication, she wanted Julia to "forget it. . . . For God's sake concentrate on writing the book, and see what happens to the relationship between you and me in the meantime. You may wind up hating my guts."[19]

Julia never did. Her friendship with Avis survived all her successive moves—to Marseilles, Bonn, Washington, Oslo, and ultimately to the place where Avis lived, Cambridge, Massachusetts.

Chapter Three

Marseille

W hen Julia Child left Paris in March 1953, her initial team was in place. Wherever she was to live, Paul, Simca, and Avis would be companions—in-person or through correspondence. Julia had a gift for expressiveness on the page, allowing her to hold intimates close, sustain relationships, and nurture new friendships even at a distance. During the years of working on her cookbook away from Paris, 1953 to 1961, she tested, researched, and wrote in four different places—Marseille, Bonn, Oslo, and Washington. In all these cities, Paul was by her side, Simca continued as an able and industrious partner, and Avis proved a loyal correspondent as well as a capable tester, editor, promoter, and intimate friend.

On March 2, 1953, Julia and Paul arrived in Marseille after driving from Paris. The move was momentous. The two would visit Paris often during their lifetimes, but would never again live there. For both of them this move involved change and leaving the city they loved. They became, as Paul put it, "ex-Parisians." While Paul continued to work as a cultural affairs officer, Julia could no longer teach with her two colleagues in L'École des Trois Gourmandes. As a result, the cookbook moved to the center of her work life.

"Rompillion," Schlesinger Library, Harvard Radcliffe Institute.

Although Paul's career determined where he and Julia lived, he nonetheless understood and supported Julia's commitment to her work. He loved her dearly. There must have been disagreements at times, but no word of this appears on the record. After so many years of living alone, Paul cherished Julia's companionship and their intimacy. Although he was an intellectual and an artist, he had to work for a living as a bureaucrat in an office. Thus he could understand and admire Julia's labor, not only for its good meals, but for its intellectual and literary side. This was expressed as he and Julia were packing for the move to Marseille. This required much heavy lifting on Paul's part. He wrote to Charlie that work on the book and "Julie's necessity for keeping at it" requires "pounds & pounds & pounds of textbooks, papers, file-boxes & so on. Two wretchedly heavy trunks full."[1] That didn't keep him from full support. When he wrote to his brother again, after settling into an apartment in Marseille overlooking the Old Port, Paul told him, "Here it is: midnight. Julie is woodpeckering her Royal Portable right next to me, jiggling the table like a tumbril on cobbles—but it's life, not death, that this tumbril symbolizes—so I can stand it."[2]

In late April 1953, Julia and Paul had to return to Paris to empty the Rue de l'Université apartment of their possessions and restore it to the taste of the owner. Paul, despite his frequent levity at Julia's expense, was now fully invested in her project. He used this opportunity to photograph the three authors in situ. Reporting to Charlie and Freddie, he wrote that Simca and Louisette came into the cold apartment at 9:30 A.M. with a range of ingredients "to be photographed in our not yet dismantled kitchen." He took pictures of the "3 G's at work" and then rushed with the negatives to his favorite developer.[3] Those photos, taken for publicity purposes, became part of the lasting public record of the trio's collaborative work at their L'École des Trois Gourmandes. As time went on, Paul's role as photographer became even more important to the cookbook. It was his photographs that later served as the basis for the illustrated drawings of the published book.

Although Paul could fully accept Julia's hard work, he found socializing with Julia's co-authors could, at times, be hard. At lunch with the three after that photography session in their old kitchen, he felt frozen out. He exercised his clever wit to complain to Charlie that he had been "as isolated as a Thibetan hermit by the non-stop chatter about Cookery-Bookery-Contractery-Saucy-Blanchy-à la je ne sais quoisy."[4] On a later visit with Simca and her mother at one of her mother's homes near Grasse, Paul saw the elder Mrs. Beck, then age seventy-nine, in action. He found her "opinionated, kindly, super-talkative, ego-centric, dogmatic, emotional, generous, snobbish." He went on to complain that Simca and her mother spoke in French "twice as loud & twice as fast as necessary & it is wearing for me to be with either for very long."[5] Nonetheless, at the same time, knowing how important the cookbook was to Julia, Paul fully accepted her work with Simca. In words that read like bragging, he then reported to his brother that following this visit, "Julie has put herself in 'an absolutely rigid' schedule: Mornings are for marketing & house-work and afternoons for Cookery-Bookery. This announcement was made a few days ago."[6]

As Julia settled into life in Marseille, away from Simca and the cooking school, Avis became increasingly important to her. Avis was more than a soul mate with whom Julia could discuss politics and family matters in her letters. Avis became Julia's American assistant. To ensure that Avis would be well armed for the task, Julia sent her key source books, such as *Cuisinière Provençale* by Jean-Baptiste Reboul, useful as Julia's work turned to the many variations of bouillabaisse.[7] When Julia later sent her *Larousse Gastronomique*, Avis let Julia know her delight: "The damn book is like popcorn, you can't stop reading it."[8]

Looming large in their correspondence were issues of cooking tools, recipes, spices, and methods. For both women, these were not just technical matters involving work: both Avis and Julia dealt with these facets of cooking in the high-pitched language of enthusiasms. Very real objects moved back and forth as well. Julia needed to know what dried herbs were available in the U.S., and Avis procured and sent them to her.[9] In the case of one of them, fennel, Avis could only find it in a pharmacy.[10]

Avis began to advise on publicity, and Julia sent photos taken by Paul. Despite how she felt about Curnonsky, Julia included Paul's photo of herself with Simca and Louisette surrounding the famous man at the dinner they had given him.[11] Avis suggested *Vogue* and *Harper's Bazaar* as magazines where Julia might place articles in advance of publication. Although Avis had no knowledge about compensation offered by these periodicals, she felt "fairly certain that they would jump at an article, or series of articles from you." Something that might likely pay off big was Simca's letter from Dorothy Canfield Fisher endorsing the forthcoming cookbook. When Avis received a copy, she sent it to de Santillana at Houghton Mifflin, thinking it might lead to "a nice plumy blurb." Likely imagining the possibility of the Book of the Month Club taking it, even though she couldn't "see them choosing a cookbook," Avis regretted the fact that Fisher was no longer on the club's board, for her "pronouncements on books carried great weight."[12]

Many of Julia's and Avis's letters in this period are chatty—discussing domestic matters, appliances, recipes, books, clothes, sex, travel places enjoyed, politics, and persons in their respective worlds. Life was complicated for Avis. She had a famous author as a husband who clearly commanded much of her time and energy, but she was a loyal wife, and these letters hold no negative word about him, other than making it clear that she would rather travel abroad than to accompany him to the American West. She had a promising young son, Mark, living at home whose talents in many areas boded well for his future. Her older son Gordon, with a more complicated and less successful life, was currently serving in the military and was about to be sent to fight in Korea. One senses that, in contrast to her own situation, Julia's life—living in France, having fewer domestic responsibilities, and focused professionally on French cooking—gave Avis vicarious pleasure.

Julia, in turn, valued Avis for her window into the United States. Julia, ever alert to the commercial prospect of the cookbook, was trying to keep up with what she hoped would be its market. She let Avis know during this time that she was buying and reading contemporary American cookbooks and trying out some of their recipes. She was also reading American magazines and viewing all the new kitchen equipment becoming available in the U.S.

Goods came to pass both ways. Julia sent fresh French herbs and many more knives; Avis provided Julia with flour from the U.S., as well as a meat tenderizer and canned clams. Avis continued to praise the cookbook sections that Julia sent, with the reassurance that "Certainly I will tell you when I don't like the way you express something. But you are a good stylist, too."[13]

Julia and Paul knew that they could not meet Avis in person until they received home leave, the period of time in which those in the diplomatic corps serving abroad returned to the United States for an extended stay. With this delay in mind, they arranged a meeting by proxy, a brief visit in late April 1953 by Avis to Charlie and Freddie at their home in Lumberville, a small village in eastern Pennsylvania. Paul admonished Charlie to write to him about Avis. "The more we know her through her letters, the better we like her." He added, "Please do take numerous photographs of all of you together, plus numerous single portrait studies of each individual."[14]

After Avis's visit, Charlie did as Paul asked. Much in his letter was complimentary enough for Julia to send Avis a long excerpt. It included this assessment: "An intelligent woman, hard outside, soft inside, real sincerity, real warmth, real integrity, real idealism, a person who yearns and believes and loves and is hurt."[15]

When Avis replied, she wrote, "I'm kinda stymied about this hard outside soft inside thing." Was it that he prefers curly hair? Or that, nearsighted as she is, she applied too much lipstick? Or was it, after living with her "reasonably profane" husband, that she swore too much? In any case she liked Charles and Freddie very much and wished they lived nearby.[16]

Julia had not mentioned the significant blemishes in Charlie's report on Avis. One, Paul simply brushed aside: "that harsh Mid-Western voice & that fake mouth."[17] The two brothers, though identical twins, were different in many ways, and Charlie's letters demonstrate the ways he frequently vied for the upper hand. Paul may have felt this when he chose to comment to his brother regarding Charlie's more serious mention of Avis's "neuroticism barely held in control." Paul's reply gave Avis's psyche a different spin. He wrote that although he and Julia had recognized Avis's tenseness, her liberal politics, and her "belief in & need to be directed by her husband . . . the little fears didn't peep out at us from between the lines. Or the big ones either. Just her basic niceness showed, and the fact that she's riding on many of the same beams that we're riding on most of the time. This gave us a v. friendly feeling toward her." Paul concluded, "I suspect that Julie may be a trifle upset to learn that this piece of golden crystal is really amber (w/ a fly in it) after all, but it affects me another way: I feel as though we can appreciate the jewel better now that we know it isn't topaz."[18]

Avis, for her part, had high praise for the house in Lumberville and the way that Charlie and Freddie lived. She reported that she and Freddie "took a shine to each other." She continued, "I would confess that with one or two exceptions I really <u>like</u> women better than men. I think my sex has a higher percentage of really terrific people than the opposite one has. Don't go away mad, Paul."[19] When Charlie wrote directly to Avis, it set her off. She stated to Julia that she had London friends who "both write and talk that way and it is disconcerting." She preferred not to get more letters from him, hoping that in the future he would only communicate through Julia.[20]

Perhaps it was knowing the "fly" in the "amber" that allowed Julia to trust Avis more fully. On April 10, Avis had written to Julia that she was now going to "crack the whip," for she expected three chapters of the book by late September.[21] But at that moment, Julia was stalled. Now in the aftermath of Charlie's report, Julia confessed her personal distress to Avis. At this point, Julia and Paul were fully settled in Marseille. In what suggests an unusual experience of uncertainty, Julia stated that insecurity was delaying her work. "There is so much that has been written by people so much more professional than I, that I wonder what in the hell I am presuming to do anyway." With that, she wrote an answer to herself. Theirs was not to be a book for experts, but rather an interpretation of that work "for the home cook." Slowing her down was her need for certainty. When faced with a seemingly simple question such as "what are, really the good cuts to use as stewing beef," she was "physically incapable of bluffing . . . a terrible handicap, either in political or gastronomical conversation."[22]

In this case, Avis tried to reassure her by telling her that she didn't have to strive for such certainty. After weighing in on her preference for beef shank in a stew, she wrote, "But sweetie, comes a time when you are writing a book when you have to take a firm grip of yourself and stop asking, 'Do I really and absolutely know that fact?'" Avis testified that she and others had worked with her husband on that very issue to get him to start writing his *Course of Empire*, the book that had just won the National Book Award.

"You can't know everything, and you can't know many things absolutely, and if you went on researching you'd never write a line."[23] Avis had the ability to combine tact and great kindness with the need she felt to urge Julia forward.

At the time that Avis and Julia were getting to know each other through letters, Julia had another important correspondent: Simca. The two women were now separated geographically, but Simca remained critically important to Julia as co-worker and friend. Although they would find ways to get together for work and pleasure, this future could not be known at the time that Julia and Paul decamped to Marseille.

It is extraordinary to realize how little time the two women actually had to work consistently side by side in a kitchen. In 1956, Simca wrote a note to herself about the sequence of their work thus far:

    1952 - Sauces
    1953 - Soups
    1954 - Eggs
    1955 - Poultry

She then followed it with all the categories, including meat and fish, that remained to be developed.[24] What this note reveals is that Simca's on-the-scene collaboration with Julia in Paris involved only sauces and the beginning of soups; and that, except for occasional and relatively brief visits, their working together in a kitchen ended with Julia's move to Marseille.

Yet that was enough for these two determined women, both with a stake in the cookbook they were building. And because—beginning in Spring 1953—much of their work was done through letter-writing, their correspondence has left a rich written record. Although Julia's kind note in 1952 of condolence on the death of Jean's mother exists, it was only after she moved to Marseille in 1953 that her close friendship and working relationship with Simca is revealed on paper.

"Julia Child silhouetted in Marseille apartment window with boats in the background,"
Schlesinger Library, Harvard Radcliffe Institute, copyright: Julia Child Foundation.

Initially Julia was deferential, for she saw her work as somewhat subordinate to her French colleagues, especially Simca. The recipes were largely Simca's. Julia's job was to adapt those recipes for American cooks who worked with American ingredients in their American kitchens. In October 1953, Julia made this explicit as she sent both Simca and Louisette a new version of a recipe for each to try out separately: "Let me know immediately if there is anything wrong, can't understand, etc." This was important, she added. "After all, this is most definitely a joint book, and just because I am official translator, does not take away from the fact that we all three must absolutely agree on all points."[25]

But of course, Julia was more than a translator, and this proved critical to the evolution of the cookbook. Yes, she was translating—and adapting— French recipes provided by Simca. But Julia's logical mind began to see patterns and relationships that would ultimately help define their cookbook as it was published—the "master recipe" followed by "variations."

Beyond her own need for logical development, Julia was at heart a teacher who wanted to convey what she had learned. French cooking was not a magical element that could only be produced by French chefs. Julia sought to break through the mysteries of French cooking for American readers. She was working on a cookbook that would demonstrate that behind many an important French dish or sauce was a core recipe that held ingredients and techniques that needed to be understood and perhaps practiced. And each of these basic recipes could be altered in ways that offered variety and distinctive tastes.

Thus, just four days after she had limited her role to "translator," Julia wrote Simca regarding béarnaise sauce and revealed what was working in her mind. "The point is to show that Beranaise [sic] is no different than Hollandaise, as it is only the flavoring that changes." Despite a slight alteration (in this case, the need for using an additional pan), she continued, "I think that making too many suggested changes in methods would be confusing to the reader, and would break down the 'family relationship.'"[26]

Prodded by Avis, Julia began to focus on an important aspect of American life that separated her audience from the world of her French collaborators—the relative lack of servants. Julia wrote to Simca that Avis was eager for casserole dishes, explaining that an American woman entertaining in her servantless home "wants to have cocktails with her guests, but have everything ready to serve and eat whenever she wants." Thus, it should be an important aspect of their work to give directions about "how and what can be prepared ahead of time." They shouldn't just think of casseroles but should extend such directions to other dishes—for example, roast chicken. As Julia then expanded, she showed her awareness of her potential market: "I think, if we can be really clever about this cooking and re-heating, we will do something that NO OTHER COOKBOOK HAS YET DONE. And that alone will make it sell to a large public, as it is the large public there that has no cooks, and no waitresses."[27]

Julia herself wanted to work on roast chickens—with delay and keeping warm in mind. Simca clearly was on board and immediately sent Julia her directions. Four days later, Julia wrote, "Will honestly and truly get a chicken for Sunday, and try out your system."[28]

As Julia took a stronger role in the process of developing the recipes into a book, Simca clearly needed reassurance. Despite her hauteur, she also had insecurities. In late October, after making her structural suggestions, Julia picked up a clue to this. Writing back to Simca, Julia responded, "if you are fishing for a compliment on your intelligence, there aint no fish in these waters. You know perfectly well that you are an extremely clever girl!"[29] When Simca replied with a self-evaluation, Julia responded by stating that she thought it "very good and true" as far as it went, but that "I think you are cleverer than you think. . . . What you have, which is wonderful, is a tremendous energy for work, and you can work fast. As for intellectual, I am never quite sure what that means, but I presume it implies a cerebral and philosophic approach [to] the things. I am not either, but would like to be!"[30]

Perhaps Julia wasn't, but she lived with Paul who certainly was. And thus she was able to add certain philosophic terms in her letters. For example, she had written Simca about the three of them as engaged fully in developing their cookbook, "It is rather like Existensialism [sic], I suppose, that we alone are responsible for how this book turns out."[31] Now, in this letter, as she turned to the untrustworthy recipes that existed in books and magazines, she wrote to Simca, "We must be Descartesian, and never accept anything unless it comes from an extremely professional source, and even then, to see how we personally like how it is done."[32]

The bulk of the letters between Simca and Julia during this period document their collaborative work. After getting the initial French recipes from Simca, Julia—working with only ingredients and tools available in the United States—tested them in her Marseille kitchen. She wrote questions to Simca about processes, timing, and ingredients. Simca also tested the recipes in her own kitchen, reported to Julia, and answered her questions; and both cooks frequently retested recipes over and over again. Julia also checked existing recipes in print from her growing library of French culinary books. Her holdings included Escoffier and Larousse, but the source that came closest to being a model for Julia is a 1927 book written for the home cook: *La bonne cuisine de Madame E. Saint-Ange*. In spring 1954, Julia wrote to Simca, "I think it is an extremely good book, and is, actually, doing just about what we are. Very careful and full explanations on how to do things."[33]

At times Julia asked Simca to consult with two chefs: Max Bugnard, Julia's former teacher and culinary adviser, and Claude Thillmont, important to Simca as the chef for luncheons of the Le Cercle des Gourmettes. All the while, Julia wrote and rewrote, and as she did she developed the structure of each of their cookbook chapters.

One can see this process beginning to take shape in Marseille. In early January 1954, as Julia was working on a section on eggs, she sent a rough draft to Simca for scrambled eggs. About three weeks later, Julia reported on her egg work. She had tried the recipe for shirred eggs, but "found that without question, the oven makes a tough egg and just should not be used at all." Responding to Simca's suggestion regarding the use of French names for all their methods and her correction of Julia's recipe for omelettes, Julia accepted both. Thinking on paper as if in conversation, Julia wrote that she was worried about the order of these egg recipes, but then she reversed herself: "it makes little difference, as long as the recipes are done, they can be placed anywhere we like. It is an impressive dossier, Chere Chef Supreme!"[34]

Three days later, Julia changed her mind about her opposition to oven-cooked eggs, peppered Simca with questions about eggs in ramekins, and began to figure out how to organize their egg recipes in the chapter that she was hoping to send to Houghton Mifflin. She wanted Simca to ask Thillmont about "stale egg whites for beating": "Does he think it is easer to beat fresh or less fresh eggs."[35]

On the very next day, Julia wrote a letter—unusual in the archival record of these years—addressed to Louisette. Julia was reading Escoffier and noted that "he suggests making the Beurre Noir first, then cooking the eggs in it. . . . a very good idea, as it saves on pans and bother." Julia added, "how delicate some of these operations are if they are to be impeccable. That, I am sure is where the excellence of French cooking lies." Julia let Louisette know that she saw her job for the book as striving "to make the operation as simple as possible." One of Julia's other important tasks was to organize the recipes, and she did so by categories. She demonstrated this after she received a new recipe from Louisette, writing that she would "put mushrooms and shallots under Other Cooked Garnishings, p/3, very good idea."[36]

As back and forth the women worked through the sections of their cookbook, normally Simca and occasionally Louisette offered recipes. Then both Simca and Julia tested and retested, checked written sources, and occasionally asked questions of the two chefs. Finally, Julia wrote the text of the recipe and placed it in a chapter.

Paul had a firsthand look at Simca and Julia at work on the egg chapter on May Day 1953. Simca came to visit Julia in Marseille, and the two women spent half of a day working on their book. Paul wrote to Charlie, "Julie & Simca have been hotly & relentlessly talking & typewriting all day about eggs." After giving some details, he quipped, "It would discourage any normal hen if she knew what these two mad creatures were plotting to make out of her hard-working craftsmanship."[37]

One senses that it was in Marseille that Paul became deeply invested in Julia's cookbook project. As a photographer and painter, he was looking to engage in more meaningful activity than he had found in the Foreign

Service. Already during that short return trip to Paris in spring 1953, Paul saw a new possibility for his future life with Julia. He wrote to Charlie, "If job folds I & J think we may just git out of Govt. ent-irely; & set ourself up in the world of Cookery—freezery—bookery—sellery—teachery."[38] This isolated hint of what was on his mind is curious. But it likely had a basis in a private talk with Julia, one she had revealed on the previous day in a letter to Freddie. Julia believed she and her co-authors could deliver the cookbook manuscript to Houghton Mifflin in a little over a year. She wrote, "We are aiming to try and get it done before we come home on leave," assumed by Paul and Julia to be slated for the summer of 1954.[39]

Paul, however, was doubtful of this. He understood that the cookbook was growing into a long book that would not be ready by the year 1954, as specified in the Houghton Mifflin contract. As early as 1953, he thought it might require seven hundred pages and that delivery would be delayed for a year. As he described the process of both women testing and Julia writing, he wrote to Charlie, "Drafts, suggestions & criticisms are sent rushing back & forth from Marseille to Paris & return." In a letter filled with wisecracks and witticisms, he concluded, "It's aimed at Everybody, like bird-shot from both barrels, from Brides to Guides and from Sophisticates to Wistful Mates. We don't care who they are as long as they come up to the book-store-counter w/ 5 mucks in their mitt & a look of anticipation on their mug."[40]

Paul reported his increasing engagement in the cookbook project when May Day brought Simca to visit Julia in Marseille. Working with Julia, he wrote biographical sketches of the trio, "as a basis for H-M's future publicity."[41] Amid the holiday tumult outside, "The 2 Gourmandes spent half the day working on their book & the latter half cooking & arranging tonight's dinner."[42]

By early June, at the point when Avis was getting organized for travel with Bernard on their long-planned Western trip, Julia had much to report about the progress of the book. She discussed the uses of the pressure cooker, fish research, and her life as Paul's hostess wife. Then she asked a battery of questions about the availability in the U.S. of sausages and salted ham, the way that white beans came in cans, and the nature of string beans. Avis's reward was "Simca's garlic sauce for roast lamb (a deep secret!)"[43] To this, Avis responded to each question at great length.

Upon her return to Cambridge in early September, Avis sent a quick note that she had found the entire line of spices sold by Spice Island in Missoula, Montana, and bought them all.[44] Putting on her editorial hat, on September 12, she wrote more fully: "I am extremely anxious to see your soup chapter." Despite not cooking soups in her current life, she would "read it with avidity." Then came her admonition: "Hope to God Simca and Louisette don't tear it to pieces and you have to start all over again. This you must fight. Comes the time, as I have told you, when you have got to send your child out in to the world no matter how many flaws remain to be corrected."[45]

The chapter on soups came before the month closed, and Avis gave it her full attention. After speaking with Dorothy de Santillana, who had read it as well, Avis wrote, "We're both extremely pleased. . . . You have achieved thoroughness and maintained simplicity." She suggested a typing change, one that would involve the entire book, based on the feeling of "vague discomfort" on reading the recipes. Because one normally read left to right, the ingredients that the cook must assemble should be on the left, with the preparation method on the right. Avis offered other editing advice, for example, "I don't quite like 'madly extravagant'—'very' will do." Regarding clams and mussels, she raised the issue of their availability in much of the U.S. and the possibility of substituting canned for fresh ones. She judged the "quick country soups" to be "ghastly . . . Are these actually good?" In contrast, both she and Dorothy were ready to try the garlic soups which "sound marvelous." The overall judgment of the two was that the soup chapter was "an absolutely bang-up job" with impressive clarity, thoroughness, and "infinite care for detail." They were "thrilled at the prospect of such a book and more than ever convinced that it will sell very well and for a long time."[46]

Julia and her collaborators waited for over a month to hear directly from Dorothy de Santillana, their Houghton Mifflin editor. In her letter of early November 1953, de Santillana confessed that she knew she had been a bad correspondent, but she explained that this was "partly because I have the cozy feeling that Avis (DeVoto) is back and forth across the Atlantic several times a week." With that stated, she wrote that she, too, was delighted with the chapter on soups, regarding it as "absolutely wonderful." After giving a number of technical suggestions regarding preparation of the final manuscript, de Santillana continued, "It is tantalizing whenever sections of this cook book appear on my desk. It makes me want to run home to the stove."[47]

In late November 1953, Julia and Paul moved to a different apartment in Marseille. In the seeming nightmare of unpacking and resettling, Julia wrote Avis that "judging from kitchen equipment [and 200 bottles of wine], one would think this was going to be a restaurant." Facing her many roles, including the entertainer expected as a consular wife, Julia worried about the slow progress with the cookbook and feared Avis and Houghton Mifflin would become discouraged. She resolved once again to maintain a regular schedule similar to Simca: "5 solid hours of bookery a day, no matter what happens (Sunday excepted)."[48]

During this time, as the letter from de Santillana revealed, Avis held an important, albeit informal, role at Houghton Mifflin, making her useful as a provider of information and reassurance to Julia. Avis may have served as one of Julia's "guinea pigs," but she was one who talked back with her own ideas. For example, after Simca followed Julia's instructions to send Avis their recipe for veal Orloff, Avis gave it a try and prepared the dish. In her careful comments, Avis wrote that she had found it difficult to get the recommended cut of veal from her butcher, even in her sophisticated and relatively wealthy section of Cambridge. And since her cooking was interrupted by attending a cocktail party, she related her way of preparing ahead of time by first making a stock and then placing the roasted meat in it to cool. As a result the veal was "perfectly tender and quite juicy." That led her to generalize that, "It can't just be my imagination that by leaving these things [including salmon and shrimp] to cool in their various stocks they keep their juiciness." With this, she offered instructions, implicitly recommending her technique, and she repeated the need for the cookbook to have directions about what "can be done ahead."[49]

A few days later, Avis wrote her thrill in reading the egg chapter that Julia had just sent: "Swept off my feet." Avis found it "Masterly. Calm, collected, completely basic, and as exciting as a novel to read." It should cause "the famous pros like [Dione] Lucas" to "be green with envy." This long letter continued with a wide range of topics. For reheating, she suggested using foil, celebrating its many uses and promising to send it to Julia if it was unavailable in France. Since she couldn't reach de Santillana, she put on her own editing hat. She discussed ingredients that were generally not available in the U.S., such as sorrel, as well as American products, such as Canadian bacon, that were good substitutes for ham. She questioned some of Julia's word choices ("unctuous" was an example); reminded Julia that tomatoes had no roots, only stems; and asked, in writing of "canned peppers," if Julia had meant pimentos.[50]

In contrast to Julia's fulfillment in her work, Paul was becoming increasingly uneasy in his. One cannot know for certain what was on his mind, but it is likely that reports of the anti-Communist crusade in Washington were taking its toll on his psyche and his career expectations. Anxiety was mounting in diplomatic circles, as Senator Joseph McCarthy, the chairman of the Senate Permanent Subcommittee on Investigations, was going after putative Communists in the State Department. It pained Julia to learn that her father supported McCarthy. As Paul put it, "Poor wifelet! She had the pitiful face of a daughter who has just learned that her mother owns & runs a brothel."[51] In his letters to Charlie, Paul often dealt with his work frustrations and uncertainties by focusing on the fine wines he was drinking and the treats he was enjoying. One was a grand dinner that Simca organized at the famed Baumanière in Les Baux, where Paul noted, "The food & wines were perfect."[52]

As he observed Julia, Paul expressed increasing admiration, writing to Charlie repeatedly of her efforts. Sprinkled throughout his daily accounts are such statements as "Julie is working, working, working, on the SOUP chapter. Regular schedule, just like me." "Julie is plugging & plugging at her manuscripple. A hard and conscientious workess: The Bookery is growing w/ the sloth (but I think the strength too) of an oak tree." "Julie's Soup Chapter is finally first-drafted, which really means every part of it has been gone over about twenty times."[53]

Paul engaged his playful side in a letter in September 1953, when he suggested possible titles for the cookbook. The title "BALLS!" he wrote, "is designed as a psychological come-on to attract not only the formal dance crowd, but the golf-crowd, and the ball-bearing crowd. Maybe we can cream-off some of Kinsey's mob." Opening the book would lead people to buy it "in order to compensate for their sense of guilt in having peeked." He next put together the preference of Americans for simplifying cooking by merely warming up canned food with their fascination with Parisian night life to arrive at a "title that ought to appeal to pretty nearly <u>everybody</u>,"— "<u>The Paris Can-Can</u>."[54]

As the year turned to 1954, Julia and Paul began thinking of their impending home leave. It would bring Julia and Avis face-to-face for the first time, and thus the visit with the DeVotos in Cambridge began to enter into Julia's and Avis's correspondence. Avis had long been looking forward to having them as houseguests. In February, in the midst of a discussion of a veal dish and a critique of the egg chapter came Avis's thoughts on the explorations she hoped to make with Julia—to her butcher to talk about cuts of meat, to stores to look at the new oven-proof dishes.[55]

At this point, as Julia and Simca were shifting their focus to poultry, a chapter they found to be arduous and slow in development, Simca's voice (in French) begins to appear in the archived correspondence, rather than filtered through Julia's responses. In March 1954, Simca had in hand the chapter's 115 pages and realized the work was still incomplete. Writing to Julia, Simca asked a number of questions, such as would preparation in advance for chicken be the same for turkey, goose, and duck? Simca also conveyed her confidence and independent judgment. In discussing foie gras with Chef Thillmont, she mentioned poaching it in water. When he responded that such a procedure did not exist in "la cuisine fine," Simca called his words nonsense. She wrote that each chef had his own method ("je crois que chaque chef à sa méthode").[56]

A few days later, Simca wrote something self-disparaging. This led Julia to insist on Simca's essential role in their enterprise. "This is a joint work if I ever saw one and quite literally neither of us could do it alone. . . . we have both worked like dogs. And who knows better than I, your American digestive tract, the recipient of all your work, what a remarkable girl you are!"[57]

Simca came to visit Julia in Marseille in spring 1954. Judging from Julia's letter following Simca's departure, it seems that some tension had arisen between the two during their time together. Julia wrote that she had been reflecting on their working relationship. Although she believed that they generally worked together effectively, Julia was concerned that Simca was giving in too much. "We are both people of strong convictions, and I well realize that I am not the easiest of people to work with because of my violence of temperament."

What was on Julia's mind was a conversation in which Simca spoke of their recipe for "Sauce à la Rouille as 'a Rouille Julia.'" This was, for Julia "a SHOCKING remark." It meant that Simca had allowed a recipe by only one of them, a "popote [dish] Julia," into their book. Julia here insisted that one of Simca's important tasks was "to see to it that such a thing does not happen." They were "equal partners in a joint enterprise" with "equal responsibility." Julia recognized that she could be difficult to convince, but it could happen if Simca offered sources and her own experience. Julia admonished Simca, "So assert yourself. Even if this is not in the tradition française, you must, or the book will suffer."[58]

Although Julia and Simca did not discuss Louisette in writing, Paul did. As he watched Julia work alone and with Simca, he understood that the cookbook-in-progress was the work of only two of the trio. In a letter to Charles in early autumn 1953, Paul wrote, "Julie's book (I imagine the Fischbackers call it "Simca's Book"!) has got to have 3 authors, because it's legally set-up that way, so psychologically necessary. Julie is really to be congratulated on her diplomacy in this connection. I don't think these things are ever simple & easy." At this point, future royalties were to be split three ways, "& for the sake of good working relations everyone must maintain the fiction that there are 3 authors, sharing equally in the work, the knowledge & the drudgery, a female version of Brahma, Vishnu & Shiva—where each goddess has her part & all are equally important."[59]

As she approached home leave, Julia had mixed feelings. She would be leaving Marseille and France, but there would be time in Cambridge with Avis. Being in the United States could be useful for getting reacquainted with American ingredients and tools. Away for eight years, Julia knew she needed to become aware of changes in American cooking practices, such as those brought by the emergence of frozen foods. She would be an ocean away from Simca, but hoped, as she wrote to her, that Simca would come to the U.S. to visit and cook with her.[60] As the leave approached, Julia let Simca know that it was important that the two remain "very hard on each other, and very critical; and always extremely frank and direct. And this means that YOU must be just as hard on me, ma chère."[61]

Julia and Paul traveled to Paris in late March 1954, and there they learned the bad news regarding new U.S. government rules limiting the number of years that Foreign Service officers could live in any given country. That meant that after home leave, Paul would be reassigned to a posting outside of France.

Julia would now need Simca more than ever to supply the recipes for their cookbook. While the classic works of French cuisine were known in the U.S., at least among chefs and cookbook writers, their joint work would be special because of each one's unique contribution. Writing to Simca, Julia stated, "So it will be up to you, my dear to continue furnishing personal recipes, or out-of-the-way ideas. I think our system of making the classical recipes the basic ones is very good. But also, good new recipes, always very French."[62]

A later letter from Julia to Simca reported that Paul had been given a choice of Germany or Japan, and, despite his own personal preference for the latter, he chose Germany. As Julia put it, Paul "has graciously and sweetly concluded that it would be terribly difficult for me to do cookbookery if we were that far away and in such an entirely different atmosphere."[63] If true, this was an important instance of Paul's many personal and professional sacrifices to foster Julia's work. It is my guess, however, that Paul did not think of the decision in this way. A man of many talents and wide-ranging interests, often frustrated by elements of his job, by 1954 Paul was fully invested in Julia's cookbookery both for her sake and his own future.

Chapter Four

Home Leave and Germany

In 1954 Julia and Paul left Marseille for the United States. During this home leave—in this case lasting through the summer and fall—they intended to spend most of the months in Washington, D.C., where they had lived before moving to France. First, however, came extensive visits in Cambridge, Massachusetts, and in California.

Although Simca's role in keeping the book "very French" remained important in the many years of the cookbook's development, there was a second side of the work of the two authors. Julia's job was to adapt French cuisine to American ingredients and tools in the hope that the cookbook would be published by an American press for an American audience. Thus Julia's stretches of time in the U.S. proved very valuable.

As promised, Julia and Paul pulled up to the Berkeley Street home in Cambridge of the DeVotos in July, and Avis and Julia met in person for the first time. Julia passed Bernard's martini test, and the two women got along splendidly. After departing, Julia wrote Avis in the unembarrassed words of female friendship that before their visit, "it did not then seem that love on paper would not blossom into love in the flesh, and it certainly did with an all-embracing bang. . . . You were exactly, I think, though now I can't be sure, our 'Dear Avis,' perfectly familiar."[1] And Avis replied in kind: "All I can say is, it's mutual." She and Julia could have found each other intolerable once they met, but "Instead, all this fine love at first sight. God is good." Avis had never had anyone stay at her house who was "so completely effortless and easy, and whom I was so eager to see again." And, for once, Bernard was on board, as well. "There is no mistaking his whole-hearted acceptance of the Childs and more than willingness to see them again."[2]

Julia conveyed her feelings to Simca, beginning in French, that "the visit at the DeVotos was exquisite. She is an adorable person, full of generosity, of good will—absolutely a good nature. We found ourselves old friends right away—after this long correspondence." ("La visite chez DeVoto était exquise. C'est une personne adorable, pleine de générosité, de bonne volonté—tout à fait, une bonne nature. Nous nous sommes trouvée de vieilles amies tout de suite—après cette longue correspondance.")

Finding she couldn't go on in French, Julia wrote of Bernard DeVoto. She described him as "a most impressive and moving person. His whole life is devoted to American history, especially to the pioneer days, the voyages of discovery, the great treks across the plains. He is also deeply interested in land conservation, public forests (Yosemite, Yellowstone, etc[.]). And is very active in politics, is a great friend of Adlai Stevenson, etc. He looks academic, and is; yet is earthy—and is complicated. A fascinating man—I quite fell for him."

During the visit, Avis invited to the house some important persons from Houghton Mifflin. Julia cooked for them a variety of dishes from her repertoire. "Everyone thought everything was wonderful and in view of the general state of American cooking, it was indeed."

Julia then described two sessions with de Santillana at the publishing house. "She is extremely nice, very professional and a femme du monde." Though overweight, she "has a very pretty face, and is very chic." She told

Julia to "take all the time you want, but make it good." They went over some details and got her approval. Basically the message was "We may do anything we want." Julia ended with a summary: "H.M. is expecting this to be one of their 'important books' . . . and a definitive work on French cooking methods for the average cook. (As do we)."[3]

Simca's role in keeping the book "very French" remained important in the years of the cookbook's development that were to follow, especially during the adaptations that Julia would make when factoring in American ingredients and tools. Julia first expressed this Franco-American give and take after leaving Cambridge, when she and Paul were traveling in California to visit with members of her family. Somewhere between San Francisco and Pasadena, she wrote to Simca, "I wish you were here—we need to market together. I want you to see American life, etc. etc. It is <u>very</u> different, in that living is so informal."[4]

Julia and Paul returned to the DeVotos for a brief stay. In anticipation, putting on her book-promotion hat, Avis tried to set Julia up with the editor of *Woman's Day*, who was visiting with Bernard. (He wrote for the magazine under a pseudonym.) In a letter to Julia, Avis stated that she talked to the editor "about you and your book" especially the soups from southern France, and she "wants you to come and see her when you are in New York. . . . I think it would be good promotion for the book."[5] In turn, during a late-August visit to Maine with Charlie and Freddie, Julia wrote Avis that she hoped to use part of the return visit in Cambridge to see the Houghton Mifflin people "to talk over book layout and illustration . . . to get some final plan of attack which we can follow out for the rest of the book."[6]

Soon afterwards, Julia also wrote a description of Avis to Simca, beginning with her appearance: "She is small—about Louisette's size, dark hair which she wears pulled back and into a bun. She has an odd way of adding extra lipstick above her upper lip, to make it look bigger, I guess—but one gets used to it. She is of a passionate temperament, with strong loves and dislikes (she just loathes Republicans—she just thinks our book is the only book that will ever be of any importance). We both love her—but she is rather a whirlwind—and, as such, stimulating to be with. How lucky we are to have her as 'mar[r]aine,' I think—and as friend."[7] With that French word, Julia dubbed Avis as the "godmother" to the cookbook in progress.

In Maine, Julia had the leisure to elaborate on how she saw American cooking practices. While she was finding that there was "definitely much more interest in food and cooking here since the war," it was not accompanied by knowledge. "So there is great need of FUNDAMENTALS, as far as I can see." In addition, except for the very wealthy, American women did their own cooking, using simple recipes that required little time and few pots and pans. This meant that the recipes introducing sections of their book needed to be "the very simplest, even with no garnishing." They should then follow that base with "various complications" and thereby "not scare off our audience. We just have to remember that we are writing for a very unshcooled [sic] audience, but a willing one."

At the same time, with her eye on the market for the book, Julia observed that there was something new afoot in the United States that could herald future sales, the budding development of a "doing it yourself" interest. "So there is good reason to believe that this interest in doing things will also reach out into the kitchen, as a good hobby to indulge in."[8]

A follow-up letter from Julia suggests that Simca misunderstood Julia's words about simplicity. In early September, writing about "COMPLICATED RECIPES," Julia tried to explain. "I don't mean 'to suppress them,' but to give the simplest first, then the more complicated ones afterwards." She wanted Simca to think of their book as a "school . . . so that any complicated recipe may be done after the backgrounds we have given, as our 'pupils' techniques will be sound."[9] These insights proved key to both the organization of the book and its usefulness to its readers.

Following their sojourn in Maine, Julia and Paul returned to Cambridge for a visit that included Julia's conferences at Houghton Mifflin. Julia reported to Simca that she learned that their publisher now saw the book as a household's "'second essential cookbook,' Joy of Cooking or the Boston always being the first American guide."[10] The book could thus command a high price, $6 (roughly $53 at the time of writing).

Julia did realize that hurdles lay ahead. In the U.S. in summer 1954, she had a publisher and a dear friend, but she was unknown as a writer or expert on food, and she had no idea how to discuss or promote the forthcoming book. Commenting on her trip with Paul to New York, she confessed to Simca that while she was in the city she chose not to meet anyone from the cooking world. "I think the less they know about us the better until the book is done. They are a very closed and gossipy and jealous little group; and I don't think we are ready, yet to tackle them."[11]

It was around this time that Simca made Julia aware of her health problems. During the summer of 1954, at her request, Julia began sending her sleeping pills.[12] In typing her letters to Julia, Simca began to add a new return address: Barbotan-les-Thermes. It was a location in southwestern France where she was taking "the cure." In the years that followed, Simca's seeming strength was punc-tuated by many such repeated periods when she sought to restore her health.

After the summer of visits, the remainder of home leave was spent in Washington, D.C. From the housekeeping apartment in a hotel where she and Paul were residing, Julia again conveyed her appreciation of Avis: "I have never known anyone so selfless and so generous, and so creatively kind as you are."[13] She reported on her visit to the New York office of *Woman's Day*, where she had been treated with courtesy but understood that "Anything for them would have to be good and simple and elementary." She saved her praise for the Bazaar Français, a store that sold all the equipment that "anyone could want," by which she clearly meant for cooking in the French manner. "Most of their French knives have Dione Lucas's imprint stamped on them. What a girl!" she remarked with, likely, a twinge of envy.[14]

In her postscript, Julia told Avis of her gratitude. Avis was her "business manager/promoter" who had done "wonderfully." She really liked Houghton Mifflin as a company and those she met there. "They, HM, represent the good, solid, ethical way of doing things that I am fighting for. . . . Thank you, dear Avis."[15]

It was in late September that Avis first wrote that she wanted Julia and Paul to move to Cambridge. "How I wish you lived around here, and here is where you must be when you finally return. When you read DeVoto in Holiday . . . you will realize that this is where you belong."[16]

Washington, D.C., offered preparation for the Childs for the next posting in Bonn, where Paul was to oversee the Amerika Houses in West Germany. Although Bonn would keep Julia in Europe, not that many travel hours from Simca, and Paul's position there as exhibits officer offered him an important assignment, Julia harbored deep reservations. Even before embarking on home leave, she had written to Avis that she had "a horror of Germans and Germany." World War II had ended in 1945, then only nine years in the past. Remembering it and the Holocaust, Julia could "smell the concentration camps and human soap factories." As a result, both she and Paul were "sick about this move."[17] However, as the two began to take German language lessons, Julia admitted that she was responding warmly to the German woman who was teaching them. This raised for her the question many Americans faced in these years: "How can Germans, who are, as I know, monstrous people, be lovely people? Or are they not monsters. If not, who made people in lampshades and soap? What would WE have become had we been Germans."[18]

In mid-October, Avis came to New York to be with Julia for two days before the Childs departed for Germany. In her letter before this final visit, Avis revealed one of her many facets. "Bought me a new hat and a new bag, and I will just have to do for NY. It is the one place that makes me feel dowdy and Bostony."[19]

BONN

In autumn 1954, Paul and Julia settled in Bonn, Germany. Paul's posting there would prove a difficult one for Julia, but this was less because of

Germany's past than her domestic present. They moved into a housing development in Plittersdorf, the diplomatic compound in a Bonn suburb; Julia found this location and the quarters to be isolating and sterile. Nevertheless, time there proved productive of much work with Simca on the book.

At this point Simca was giving cooking classes, and Julia thought they would be a good venue for testing their recipes. As she resumed her own work, Julia somehow felt the need to remind Simca of her role in their joint enterprise. "Once again, I must stress that you and I must consider ourselves absolutely on an equal basis. . . . your research and previous preparations, are the basis."[20]

The two collaborators were living very different lives. While Julia was in Plittersdorf, working alone on chickens in her kitchen and writing at her desk, Simca was in the thick of things in Paris. She was teaching with Louisette in the L'École des Trois Gourmandes. (The cooking school kept its name after Julia's departure.) Simca had also assumed responsibility for planning the luncheons of the Gourmettes, putting her in close touch with chefs Thillmont and Bugnard as they prepared the dishes for the group. In addition, Simca had access to recipes offered by some important chefs in the restaurants where she and her husband dined.

Simca was able to balance her many responsibilities and continue to contribute as an equal partner with Julia on their cookbook, but that wasn't true for Louisette. Paul had recognized this as early as 1953. Nonetheless, as signed, the contract with Houghton Mifflin made Louisette an equal author with Simca and Julia, and thus she was to have an equal share of the future book's royalties. Julia wanted this to change.

Standing in the way of altering the contract was Julia's knowledge of Simca's history with Louisette. The two women had been close friends for a long time. They had worked together on their cookbook for Americans and were now continuing as teaching partners in the cooking school. Nonetheless, Julia wanted to push on. In a March 1954 letter regarding Louisette, Julia wrote, "I have a strong feeling that this book we are doing is not at all the kind of a book that is her meat. I think she is more temperamentally suited to a gay little book, like What's Cooking, with chic little recipes and tours de mains [hand tricks], and a bit of poesy, and romanticism." Julia realized, however, that Louisette could be very useful in publicizing the book as the "wonderful, the cute, darling little French woman."[21]

Over the next months, Julia and Simca struggled with the issue, and in November 1954, Julia sent Simca a draft of a letter to Louisette to review. In it Julia wrote of her understanding of Louisette's life and the fact that she could not contribute the same time and effort as her cookbook partners. Emphasizing the positive, Julia wrote, "You can put in a certain amount of time in cooking school and in reading over and criticizing what we have done. You can also keep up a general promotion and publicity for the book, and at this you are very gifted."

With that, Julia outlined the different roles of the trio, offering details about their working days. She stated that in developing the book both she and Simca put in forty hours a week. Simca divided her hours as "30 hours at desk; 10 hours in kitchen." Simca was responsible for "Primary research and preparation of first (French) draft of each chapter for submission to Julia" and for "Editing and kitchen-testing of all finished recipes in second (English) draft, as submitted by Julia." Julia's forty hours had five fewer ones at her desk, spending more of them testing in the kitchen. In addition to being the banker and the go-between with the publisher, Julia's tasks were "Re-editing and kitchen testing of first draft of each chapter as submitted by Simca" and sending them on to Simca and Louisette, as well as the "Preparation of final draft, to be submitted to publishers, with OK by Simca and Louisette" and the "full responsibility for correct <u>American</u> aspects of the book (terminology, ingredients, equipment, etc)."[22]

Simca approved of Julia's statement but deleted two elements that Julia had put in regarding Louisette's mere nine hours of work per week. Interestingly, this made the separation of their respective tasks even clearer. Offering no reason, Simca insisted that Louisette's duties should not include either "Contribution of various ideas and recipes" or "Testing out of various recipes, as needed." Simca and Julia then suggested a new division of the earnings from the book: 10% for Louisette, with the remaining 90% to be divided evenly among herself and Simca. In addition, they sought to lessen Louisette's role in the most public way—on the book's title page:

FRENCH COOKING IN THE AMERICAN KITCHEN
By
Simone Beck & Julia Child
With
Louisette Bertholle

In the midst of this conflict came news from Avis in Cambridge that added a new dimension to Julia's understanding of her correspondent and dear friend. From its contents, one cannot know the extent of Avis's conversations with Julia during their Cambridge visits about her older son Gordon, but clearly the young man and his troubles had been on her mind for a very long time. At the beginning of November, Gordon returned home from serving in Korea. Avis wrote that he was in terrible physical shape, having lost four of his teeth and with acne leaving scars on his back and chest, making him look "like a thug." His friends were "the odd ones . . . misfits" as their beards indicated, and their girlfriends were "very queer characters too." At the moment of writing, she felt that both she and Bernard had "failed him terribly." She feared that Gordon might never be "able to make a life for himself."

Avis let Julia know that this was not a new problem. Gordon had been seeing psychiatrists since he was a child, but, according to Avis, nothing had worked. "They couldn't reach him. He fails in school. He fails at jobs. He gets fired. He can't live with us. He can't live without us." Avis noted that Gordon was "What the psychiatrists call 'a hostile dependent.'" As a result, Avis felt heartbroken. "I can't eat, or sleep without dope, and I feel as if I'm carrying around a thirty-pound weight in my stomach. I think Benny is too, but he puts up a good front."

After going through Gordon's various failures, including not finishing college at Boston University, she ended with an explanation: "I wasn't a very good parent, being far too snarled up in myself until I got analyzed. . . . I didn't grow up until several years after he was born." But nonetheless she didn't feel guilty, as she had done the best she could. She closed with these words: "I shouldn't unburden all this on you, except that I haven't spoken or written freely to anyone about it, and it has been piling up."[23]

During this crisis, Avis conveyed a lot of information about herself. In the past, she had gone through psychoanalysis to learn about herself in a way she believed had made her more mature. Nonetheless, when troubled, she took medication (her term was "dope") in order to fall asleep. And her relationship to her husband was such that she could only "think" that he shared her concerns about their elder son; she hadn't sought to penetrate his "good front."

By mid-November Gordon was being treated at a veterans' hospital, and Avis was more hopeful about his future. At this point she turned to the Louisette issue and treated it lightly. She wrote, "Poor Louisette sounds just like me. A peripheral character," and applauded Julia's efforts at a new agreement.[24]

However, once she learned that Louisette was refusing to discuss Simca and Julia's letter, she changed her tune to weigh heavily in Louisette's favor: "Your getting the book done is more important than strict justice in the way of credit. It's your problem, and you are you and Simca is Simca and Louisette has a lawyer and a tough husband. . . . Publishing the book is all and it would be better to bow to the inevitable and let L. have her third than to hold the book up for even a month."[25]

Then, in mid-January 1955, Louisette, traveling in the United States, paid Avis a visit, and she was smitten. Avis wrote Julia that Louisette "came to call last Saturday morning, and is she ever a cutie." Although Louisette had hoped "to meet HM folks," she had not allowed enough notice for that to happen. Avis continued, "However, we have at least met, and taken one another's measure, and liked what we saw, and now I know two of you."

Avis found Louisette to be "sweet, and amusing, and warm, and I liked her thoroughly."[26] Avis could easily be persuaded by charm.

This clearly upset Julia, but she kept her cool. Writing directly now to Simca, she only said, "That's all . . . Wonder what they talked about? Avis knows the full story of our relations, as I sent her all the correspondence. . . . Well the old girl is charming, as we both know very well, and a good publicity piece of Frenchiness for the book." Julia's important words came in the next sentence, directed now at Simca: "I am glad that you are determined to be firm. And I am with you. But I well realize that you are in a most delicate position, as you have been so close, and really love each other like sisters."[27]

The terms of the contract with Houghton Mifflin remained an issue fought over many months. As the language and terms of a revised contract went back and forth, Louisette demanded 20% and full credit for authorship. Ultimately Julia and Simca had to bend. In late February 1955 the settlement was reached, and, after some delays, signed. Louisette's name remained as co-author; but her take was reduced to 18% of the book's future earnings. And by early April, Julia could write that she was happy that Simca's "good relations are again established with Louisette."[28]

As Julia settled down in Germany, correspondence between Julia and Simca continued to reveal the nature of their working relationship as they developed their cookbook. Simca was the precipitant, proposing recipes; Julia was the reactor and often the cheerleader. On January 7, 1955, for example, after receiving a recipe and congratulating Simca, Julia wrote, "It sounds like a wonderful recipe, and very original. I shall make this very soon, too. Good for you. These special little recipes will give the book a great deal of value."[29] Simca was also responsible for the names given to each dish. In one case, on a letter in which Julia suggested the name "Boeuf Persillade" [beef with parsley], Simca wrote that it wasn't appropriate.[30] In accepting Simca's judgment, Julia agreed that the term must be "correct and in la bonne tradition, of course of course."[31]

Both Julia and Simca also paid special attention to Avis's judgment, for in addition to being their most important American tester, Avis was their promoter and editor. She gave clear reports on many recipes, including such matters as how long it actually took an American thirty-pound turkey to reach a safe temperature. In the background were Simca's consultations with chefs Bugnard and Thillmont, as well as the two authors' cookbook collections.

An important letter from Julia to Simca provides a critical background element, the careful way Julia organized and kept their files. With her experience in the OSS, especially as chief of the Registry in China, she understood the importance of system and was meticulous about dating and filing each recipe and communication. Julia was thus able to keep the many strands of their cookbook manuscript organized and accessible throughout its long process of development during which she lived consecutively in Paris, Marseille, Washington, Bonn, Washington a second time, and Oslo.

In an important letter of January 12, 1955, Julia summed up her understanding of their joint work of three years. Simca had obviously challenged Julia's insistence on testing in ways that Julia now paraphrased, "when a recipe is a [à] point, why fool around[?]" Julia's response to Simca was clear: "The question is, be it à point for me too, and for others?" This led Julia to state her belief in "the value of having us both testing things out, as well as having the wisdom of the ages, in book form, at our sides." As she expanded on this, Julia conveyed the way that her ambition for their joint mission was soaring. She wrote that she intended their book "to be a masterpiece; and in everything major that we go into, a real re-studying and profound and immensely intelligent and brilliant as well as scientific presentation of method. . . . a book that will have a profound and lasting value." Certain of her predecessors offered inspiration: Mme. St. Ange, who had "studied and worked deeply"; Escoffier; and Careme, "who was so impassioned by his metier." In closing, Julia expressed her growing commitment to developing basic recipes that could be adapted for many dishes. If such a basic recipe "can be, so to speak somewhat universal for its type, it is an education in cookery."[32]

Simca's husband, Jean, usually in the background, at this point objected. He had challenged Simca and Julia's efforts at creating basic recipes, stating that the two authors were "not Escoffiers." (One of the elements of Auguste Escoffier's contribution was his creation of five "mother sauces" that served as the basis for all others.) Although accepting that she and Simca should not be compared to the renowned chef and culinary writer, Julia defended to Simca their project in terms that Jean, an engineer and businessman, could understand: They must beat the competition by making their book "better and more explicit than our competitors" and this meant explaining "the whys."[33] Given Julia's own keen business sense, beyond a statement meant for Jean, Julia's words were likely part of her mental arsenal of marketing points for the future cookbook.

Simca's written response is not in the record, but her actions that followed make it clear that she accepted Julia's basic strategy for their book and its soaring mission.

Julia and Simca and were both happily married and childless. There were, however, significant differences between Simca's life and Julia's. Julia lived in a twosome with Paul, in contrast to Simca and Jean who remained deeply enmeshed in family. There were often elderly family members living with them in their Neuilly apartment, with some needing care. As a couple, the two traveled often in France to properties held and occupied by members of Simca's family. Simca typically had a dog who commanded much of her attention and affection. During this period, Julia and Paul seem to have had little or no household help in contrast with Simca who had a maid on hand to serve and clean up the kitchen. As a result, Julia occasionally had to remind Simca that they were preparing a cookbook for servant-less Americans.

And, of course, Simca lived in France. She and Jean resided in Neuilly, a commune adjacent to Paris's 17th Arrondissement, near the Arc de Triumph. Living now in Germany, Julia often felt isolated and missed France and her life in Paris. Paul's current job gave him broad responsibility for exhibits throughout Germany that necessitated pressured work, long hours, and frequent travel. Given Paul's successful efforts in cultural diplomacy, in April 1955, when he was called back to Washington on short notice, both he and Julia hoped for news of a promotion. Instead, Paul faced a frightening and humiliating interrogation. The mid-1950s was the era of Senator Joseph McCarthy, whose accusations and subsequent FBI investigations wrecked the lives and careers of many Foreign Service officers. In Washington, Paul had to submit to grueling questioning about his ties to Communists and spies. At one point, he was even asked if he was a homosexual. Paul bore up well and kept his position.[34]

Nonetheless, the suspicions that led to this inquisition may have affected judgments of him, for, despite his effective work over many postings, until very late in his service, Paul never received a promotion. How the grueling 1955 interrogation played in his mind cannot be fully known, but it likely contributed to his thinking about leaving the Foreign Service to give his all to assisting Julia's work and potential career.

When Paul was away in Washington, Julia took herself to Paris to work with Simca. The in-person collaboration proved reassuring. As Julia wrote to Avis, "I have had three fine sessions with Simca. We are really working like a team, now, and it is most satisfactory, NAH, inspiring. . . . .It has taken us a long time to jockey around to a joint conception, but I think we have finally gotten it. We both want each chapter to be a 'monument in quintessence.'" This required both of them to gain a full understanding of each subject "from one end to the other."[35]

Julia was also beginning to imagine a new and important role for Simca. It began with her realization of the need to attest to their credentials, both to establish legitimacy and to promote sales of their future cookbook. Aware that she was unknown in the American food world, Julia turned her focus on Simca. As early as July 1955, Julia wrote that public knowledge of Simca's contact with Thillmont was "good advertisement." More generally,

Julia was eager for Simca "to make a 'name' among those professionals who count in France."[36] One avenue was Simca's position in Le Cercle des Gourmettes. The group had become dormant for a while, and Julia encouraged Simca to take a stronger role in its revival. "You are the logical person to be on the board, and in charge of Les Cours. I think cold bloode[d]ly it would be a good thing for our book if Les Gourmettes became active again, and really respected, by the time our book came out. Then you could be known publicly as one of the leading members, in fact tha [sic] mainspring."[37]

On Sunday, November 13, 1955, Avis DeVoto's life took a terrible turn. Bernard DeVoto, age fifty-eight, died in New York City. At the height of his fame as a writer, he had traveled to New York to appear on television. Bernard's death, away from home and with no warning, shocked Avis to the core. She had built her life around him. As she wrote to Julia, "the house was run to suit him, our friends were mainly the people he wanted to see, his remarks over the papers at breakfast told me much of what I wanted to know about the world and politics, when he relaxed over his evening martini and a half he opened up and discoursed and I learned, how I learned."[38]

With her life suddenly turned upside down, Avis was on her own to work out how to live without her "B." Her many friends rallied and did what they could, but only Avis could work through her grief and reshape her life.

Julia, far away in Germany, learned of his death from the straightforward words of Charles Child's telegram: "BERNARD DEVOTO DIED TODAY, HEART ATTACK, CHARLEY."[39] Julia did the one thing she could do for Avis. She offered to pay airfare for her to come to Europe. Avis planned for a trip in late spring 1956, but in the meantime, she had to face the difficult practical problems of life as a widow.

In France and Germany, life and work on the cookbook went on, and the division of Julia and Simca's labor continued. With Simca having the last word about recipe names, Julia checked with her. For example, after shortening the method for demi-glace, Julia requested permission to call it simply "Brown Sauce," explaining that the change was necessary so "we cannot be criticized." Simca marked the request with "yes-ok."[40] More importantly, Simca resumed sending Julia recipes. One of them for chicken provoked this encomium from Julia: "A beautifully written recipe, my dear. COMPLIMENTS."[41] Both women spent many hours a week testing the recipes for inclusion in the book. Julia added research, including getting information from U.S. government agencies. For example, she wrote a letter to the "Nat[ional] Turkey Fed[eration] about cooking methods," in this case seeking important information regarding food safety.[42]

Julia had been encouraged by those at Houghton Mifflin to think of American periodicals that would print some of these recipes and thereby lend authority as well as advertisement for the future book. She sent to Simca a long list of journals she might aim for. Ultimately a single French publication that Julia had favored, *Cuisine et Vins de France*, took Simca on as a regular contributor, raising Julia's hopes that their cookbook might gain credibility in the American food world.[43]

As their fifth year of work began, Julia assessed not only what she and Simca had accomplished—sauces, soups, eggs, and poultry—but also what remained to be done. In a handwritten note, on the back of a letter from Julia, Simca gave this list of "Reste!" [remaining]:

Hors d'Oeuvres
    (Chaud et froid)[Hot and cold]
Entrees
    Luncheon dishes
    Fish-Shellfish
    Meat: beef
        Mutton lamb
        Veal
        PORK
    Rice-Noodles
Vegetables & Salades
Dessert?[44]

This was a tall order that likely was deeply discouraging both to write and receive. It provoked both women to think about ways to become published cookbook authors sooner than the many years more of work still ahead to accomplish their comprehensive cookbook. They began a new discussion about dividing the task into a series of cookbooks. They both had Dione Lucas's most recent cookbook limited to "Meat & Poultry." Simca proposed a book on "Sauces, Soups, Eggs, Poultry and Game." Julia agreed and suggested that they might follow with "Meat, Fish and Vegetables." She sensed that once she sent to Houghton Mifflin the whole poultry chapter, their publisher "will see how enormous the WHOLE is going to be." In the meantime, she thanked Simca for sending new recipes "which look good."[45]

Simca became discouraged at times. When, after making some minor mistakes in typing, she expressed feeling inadequate, Julia explained that her own typing had been shaped by experience in advertising and in the war "where mistakes meant death and disgrace . . . and that helped to train me." Moreover, Simca should not worry about her typing for Avis was an excellent proofreader. Julia then reminded Simca of her important role in their joint work: "you are the inspiration and the recipe gatherer for the book." All in all, Julia assessed, "I think we are very good together, as we each complement so many things in the other."[46]

Avis was, in these months, facing many difficulties. During Bernard's lifetime she had believed that, in the case of his death, he had taken care of everything for her future; but his executor informed her that she would need to find income in order to keep her house and pay the bills. Her first move was to take in boarders to live in Bernard's former working space in the upper-floor rooms. She had an initial hope that Julia and Paul might come and live there and wrote them to inquire; after they didn't accept, Avis treated her desire as only a fantasy. The rooms became a living place for graduate students.

To make the space available, Avis had many tasks to accomplish, including selling Bernard's equipment and, more taxing, dealing with his massive papers. When the archives of Stanford University agreed to purchase them, Avis plunged into detailed paperwork, telling Julia, that this was "going to drive me mad."[47] It did prove difficult, but Avis was ultimately rewarded by a check of $20,000 from Stanford for the papers [almost $195,000 at the time of this writing].[48]

Avis began to get steady work in February. Alfred Knopf, after visiting with Avis in Boston, wrote her about "a job as literary scout for New England" for his publishing company. When she replied and explained her situation and needs, he followed with an offer: a six-months' trial at $250 a month [almost $2,500 at the time of this writing] for part-time work to involve writing letters, reading manuscripts, and checking out magazines. Avis called the Knopf offer "a nice little boost to my faltering ego."[49] This meant that, with the exception of the cookbook, Avis had to relinquish her volunteer work for Houghton Mifflin. The press agreed to pay her two dollars an hour [roughly almost $20 at the time of this writing] both for reading the manuscript of the cookbook and for trying out its recipes in her kitchen. Houghton Mifflin also covered the cost of ingredients required for recipe testing.[50]

When Julia learned that Houghton Mifflin had essentially put Avis in charge of their manuscript, she was at one level "comfortable," but at another, felt that with de Santillana no longer focusing on the cookbook, she and Simca would get "no real criticism of a profound nature." Bracing herself, Julia wrote Simca that the two of them were now forced "to stand on our own feet, and be our own judges . . . gathering as much information as we can from all the professional sources we can reach." Simca had been consulting the working French male chefs she knew, but Julia saw that these men were not interested in "the 'why's' and 'hows.'" Julia also let Simca know that Avis had written that "she didn't know about publishing in two volumes, and that we should take it up with HM when we send in the poultry chapter."[51]

As spring came, Julia began careful preparations for the Paris leg of Avis's trip to Europe. Her visit was particularly important to Julia because Avis and Simca would meet in person for the first time. Previously, whatever knowledge they had of each other had all been filtered through Julia. Thus, when Simca arranged for the annual fête of the Gourmettes to take place during Avis's visit, Julia expressed her delight: "I was so anxious for OUR friend, Avis, to see something of the Gourmettes . . . Bravo." As Julia continued, she revealed what was on her mind. "I feel we should use a little 'sang-froid' or 'calcul,' to show in a subtle way that we (you, principally), move in the world of the gastronomes. She [Avis] thinks, enthusiastic body that she is, that we are wonderful people . . . but it would be also good, as she will report back to HM, that we are to be taken with great seriousness as two of the most well-informed . . . and greatest amateur/professional cuisinieres that it has ever been the luck of anyone to be acquainted with . . . much less to edit a book for."

Julia wanted Simca to see that one of their goals for Avis's visit should be to educate her so that she could better present their case to Houghton Mifflin. Julia contrasted Avis's amateur culinary knowledge with their own: "She knows very little about the depths of professional cooking; very little about French cooking. So she needs a bit of education on the subject, for her own use, as well as so that she can evaluate us a bit more astutely."[52] Julia hoped to arrange times for Avis to meet and watch Bugnard cook in Louisette's kitchen and for Avis to cook there with Les Trois Gourmandes. Julia's 1956 appointment book chronicled Avis's days in Paris. Both it and a photograph Paul took give evidence that Julia was successful in realizing these plans.

Julia's program for Avis also conveys an important aspect of her relationships to those who were both friends and co-workers. Amid all the affection and warm words, Julia understood each person's usefulness, and she could be calculating as she advanced her goals. Along with all her other attributes, what emerges here is Julia's business sense. Knowing Avis would be a strong advocate for the cookbook, in planning for her visit, Julia instructed one member of her team how to work effectively with another.

"Paris; Chez Gourmette's school, [Avis and Julia]," Schlesinger Library,
Harvard Radcliffe Institute.

The day after Avis departed, Julia summed up for Simca all that they had
accomplished. Their lunch with her in Rouen, Avis's two working days with
chefs Bugnard and Thillmont, the cake lesson, and the luncheon with the
Gourmettes "certainly gave Avis a look into our cooking life." In addition,
Julia commented, in ways to cement the bond between Avis and Simca,
"she really loves both you and Jean. She is a darling person, I must say." A
final note to Simca makes it clear that Julia also used the time to have a
serious discussion with Avis about the growing length of the manuscript.
Both Julia and Simca were hoping that Houghton Mifflin would see their
work as involving more than one volume. Julia wrote that it was "a relief"
that Avis seemingly agreed to stop the book at vegetables.[53]

"Portrait of Julia Child and Avis DeVoto seated outdoors [Rouen],"
Schlesinger Library, Harvard Radcliffe Institute.

Julia returned to Plittersdorf and wrote Simca frequently in the summer months that followed. Julia continued to work on poultry and urged Simca to send all the material that she and Louisette had on chickens. She then took up soup and prepared to focus on what she hoped would be their final chapter, vegetables. Once again, relying on Simca for material, Julia asked her if it wouldn't "be sensible, in the forthcoming vegetable work, for you to write down any recipes you find that seem interesting or unusual, whether or not you have experimented on them. Then we can work them out together." Once again, Julia also reminded Simca of the need for secrecy. Simca must not discuss with Thillmont their work with all-purpose flour, for "I still fear his discussions with other Americans who are our rivals!"[54]

In late August, Julia had another surprise. She learned that Paul was likely to be transferred to Washington in November. Word of this coming move came at a time when she was finally learning to appreciate aspects of Germany, partly from the course she was taking at the University of Bonn on twentieth-century German literature. She then turned upbeat and repeated what she had said just two years before: this move would be good for their book, for it would enable her to refresh her understanding of products available in the United States.[55]

In the meantime, there was travel in Germany with Paul and cookbook work to do. In September Julia wrote from Berlin to Simca, who was then in Normandy following her injury from an accident that required a partial leg cast. Julia told of her labors with the poultry section of the book, but also conveyed her reliance on Simca as the initial editor of her prose. In response to Simca's negative appraisal of a passage on ducks, Julia wrote that she would change the language because "if it confuses you it will confuse others." In her reading of Julia's drafts, Simca could be picky. She did not like the sound of "½ minute," and Julia agreed to excise it in a rewrite. Surprisingly, Louisette was still in the picture. Julia conveyed to Simca that she would write Louisette to review Simca's copies of the goose and duck recipes "for her OK."[56]

Once October came, Julia made it clear to Simca that her life revolved around the work necessary for the move to the United States. Julia had been through this upheaval enough times to know what it required. Stepping back, she wrote to Simca, "I must say this is a horrible way to collaborate on a cook book. . . . but if we hadn't chosen this life, I would never have met you! So there is that great shining merit to it!" Julia planned to spend her last European days in Paris with Paul and expressed her hope to cook with Simca. She wanted to work with her on confit, a French cooking method of low temperature cooking, "as there are so many points we should commune over jointly."[57]

Twelve days later, writing to Simca as packers were working in their dwelling, Julia's thoughts moved in a different direction. Believing now that she and Paul would be in Washington for a posting of four years, she didn't want to spend her Paris time in the kitchen. Rather, she wanted their visit to focus on enjoying the city, visiting museums and old streets, and wandering with Paul. Julia did, however, have one bit of business before leaving Europe: a mutual check to be sure that both of them had the complete existing manuscript.[58]

Chapter Five

Washington

In mid-autumn 1956, Julia and Paul left Germany for the United States. On this return, Paul was assigned to the Washington office of the U.S. Foreign Service, a division of the State Department. Because his job would not begin until January 1957, before settling in, Julia and Paul went on a round of visits to family and Avis.

In late November in Cambridge with Avis, they had many tasks to accomplish. One was the cookbook, and at this point much remained unresolved. Julia's editor at Houghton Mifflin, Dorothy de Santillana, had accepted Julia and Simca's plan for the cookbook to end after the chapter on vegetables. Now, more than two years past the delivery date specified on the book's contract, de Santillana clearly sought closure. She wanted the completed manuscript by the following October, a date that would allow the book to make the Christmas market. Interestingly, in writing to Simca, Julia realized that she was unclear regarding the year de Santillana was specifying.[1]

Paul had his health needs met by a series of appointments with Boston doctors. The reason for this cannot be fully known, but it was likely back trouble. Unfortunately for the historian, Paul's voice goes silent during several critical years, not because he was actually so, but because, as he later wrote in a note to accompany the collection of his letters, "There is a letter-gap (unexplainable) between October 1956 and May 1959." Thus, what we can know about him in that important interval comes mainly from Julia's letters.

Avis had her own agenda. She had long dreamed that Julia and Paul would move to Cambridge. As early as spring 1955, after reading Julia's letter with information regarding Paul's harrowing interrogation in Washington, Avis had exclaimed, "Well toots, if they get you, or if you resign in a blaze of glory—anyway if you come back to this country, you better come to Cambridge and I will move heaven and earth to get you a house or an apartment."[2] Now, a year after Bernard's death, having Julia and Paul live nearby may have felt more urgent. Writing to Simca, Julia gave a hint: "We keep looking at some of the beautiful old wooden colonial houses here."[3]

In late December Julia and Paul returned to Cambridge. At this point publishing took a different turn. When Julia met again with de Santillana to pick up the manuscript, she learned that the editor had set up an appointment with the general manager of the press, Lovell Thompson. Julia reported to Simca that Thompson "was not too enthusiastic about having a book that was not the complete thing, and is thinking of the possibility of publishing our book in several separate volumes! (Our old idea, but I didn't say so.) Thompson suggested six with the possibility of more; each was to be printed on good paper with illustrations and to cost about $5; but he had to talk to his salesmen before making a decision." Julia seems to have encouraged this plan, writing that she had responded to Thompson that she "would let them play around with what they wanted to do, but in any case we would not be able to finish

fish and meat for a good five years (to keep them from thinking about
the possibility of one complete book!)." With that, Julia let Thompson
know that, in collaboration with Simone Beck, she would "finish the
poultry and have it typed up in final MS form with the illustrations."
As she explained to Simca, "It would seem to me that the first volume
should be an important one, such as on Poultry, to give things a good
send-off."[4]

Over the holidays, Julia and Paul visited with Charlie and Freddie at
their home in Lumberville.

"Lumberville; Sacramento delta [Christmas, Julie singing carols],"
Schlesinger, Harvard Radcliffe Institute.

Members of Paul's family came to Washington for the wedding of Charlie and Freddie's daughter, Erica, to Anthony Prud'homme.

"Erica's Wedding [five people in kitchen during cake decorating]," Schlesinger Library, Harvard Radcliffe Institute.

During these early months back in the U.S., Paul was likely anticipating his job with little relish, for it involved work that held slight value in his eyes. Without his letters to Charlie, it is difficult to learn what his position entailed, but by late February, Julia reported that he was in Exhibits; oddly, he was the head of a branch that consisted only of himself. One bit of success came outside his bureaucratic work. *Holiday* magazine published his color photograph of Carcassonne, paying him $200, a princely sum worth over nine times that amount at the time of this writing.[5]

When the photograph appeared in *Holiday*, Paul was able to mount a small one-man exhibition of his photos at a gallery connected to a Washington bookstore.[6] Avis took it upon herself to promote his work and had some minor success. She reported to Julia that Herbert Weinstock, music editor at Knopf, was eager to purchase some of Paul's photographs. As the months went on, Avis moved into an amateur role as "agent" for his photographs. In November she wrote that she had recently taken Paul's photos of cats to New York "to show them to a couple of cat-mad editors," and for this she was "obstinately hopeful."[7]

When Julia and Paul returned to Washington at the beginning of January to reenter their Olive Street house, they realized that, after many years of renters and neglect, it needed extensive repairs. Renovation brought disruption and distractions during the 1957 winter and, for a time, Julia's loss of her kitchen. In late January 1957, thinking ahead, Julia began writing encouragements to Simca to visit her and see the United States for the first time. With the working assumption now that their magnum opus would be divided into successive volumes, Julia wrote Simca that a visit in February 1958 would come at "just the right time, and we should be having the MS for the first volume all ready." If the expense of the trip was a concern, Julia wrote, "We can perfectly well lend you whatever you need, and then we can take it out of the proceeds from the book."[8]

Simca and Julia were then hoping that "after the first volume," Louisette could be dropped as co-author, and Julia agreed to inquire into the possibility. Simca provided material on vegetables that to Julia seemed "a masterful presentation and very complete." She added, typically, that they could always add to it, if they had "any additional interesting recipes."[9]

When March came, Julia's kitchen allowed work on the cookbook, but she faced many distractions. One arose from her judgment that she now had to help Paul with his stalled career by becoming a proper helpmeet. That meant entertaining his associates. She wrote to Avis that failure to attend to this responsibility in the past was likely "one reason why his career has lagged until now. But it is such a bore! Trouble is, if he doesn't get himself up in grade, he doesn't have a change [chance] at the interesting jobs, and he has had enough of playing second fiddle to a bunch of boobs."[10] After complaining to Avis of having to entertain many unexpected guests, limiting her worktime, Julia added, "However, we are always ready for you, dear, as you are not people."[11]

Once again Julia took returning to the United States as an important step for the cookbook, enabling her to experience recent changes in products, food markets, and cooking in the U.S. Supermarkets in the late 1950s, often in large new buildings, offered a great number of goods. In remembering frequent trips then with my mother to the recently built supermarket in our neighborhood, I recall canned and packaged goods in abundance, taking up many aisles and featuring major national brands. With the exception of containers of dried pasta, ethnic foods so prominent in today's grocery stores were absent. One saw no butcher; meat was wrapped in cellophane; fresh fish was unavailable. There was considerable space given to large bins of fresh fruit and vegetables, but these items were generally limited to seasonal availability. Frozen foods had their own small section in the supermarket. Most shoppers, however, had only limited space to store them. A separate freezer in a home was then unusual. Moreover, refrigerators were typically smaller than today, with only a little compartment at the top for frozen foods. This allowed for only a few items, such as ice cream, popsicles, orange juice concentrate, and perhaps a vegetable such as frozen peas.[12]

During a visit to Charlie and Freddie in Lumberville, Julia wrote Simca about new devices for food preparation. She hoped to send Simca an electric skillet and scouring powder for copper.[13] Later in the spring, she encouraged Simca to visit with these words: "I just can't wait for you to come here and to go shopping. These vast super markets are too wonderful, and one of the best things about them is that there is so much sale that the turn over is fast, and everything is very fresh indeed. It is so heavenly to go to the asparagus counter and pick out each individual spear yourself; or each single string bean." Focusing on the asparagus, she wrote, "This is the season where they come by rapid transit from California, and are great fat green spears, sweet, tender and perfect." She added, "They have lovely young fresh turkey here. . . . The meat is tender, and it can be cooked just like chicken, using our chicken timing."[14]

During this period Simca was working hard to develop vegetable recipes in anticipation of the separate second volume. After Julia tried the recipes, she offered Simca many compliments. For example, she declared her gratin dauphinois (a la crème) to be "absolutely delicious, nothing curdled, and could not, I think, have been better. CONGRATULATIONS, ma cherie. That was a long haul, but you have succeeded."[15]

Avis and Simca had bonded since Avis's time in Paris and were now corresponding. In May 1957, Avis reported on a visit with Julia in Washington, where she stopped during a scouting trip for Knopf. Avis raved about the practicality and beauty of Julia's new kitchen, for which she gave Paul the credit. She did note that Paul and Julia's social life kept Julia from the level of cookbook work that she had sustained in Germany. She also let Simca know that Paul was unhappy with his work in Washington: "He is such a perfectionist that he won't be content until he knows exactly what it is all about and can run it with his usual efficiency." She ordered more knives from Simca, who had come to provide many of the wedding gifts that Avis now gave—pepper grinders as well as sharp knives.[16]

Avis's job as a scout for the Knopf publishing house involved locating potential authors and wooing them to the point of a book contract. By January 1957, she was relishing her work. She wrote to Julia that heretofore, she had lived her adult life "in the shadow of a great man," and had lacked confidence in her own powers. But now, she had snagged a new author, and her contract was renewed for another nine months. With this boost to her ego, she planned a trip to New York City to hang around the Knopf offices and find "out what makes the wheels go round." Summer would bring scouting at writers' conferences, including Bread Loaf, the famed one in Vermont.[17] There was, however, a serious downside. Her job at Knopf wasn't secure, and it didn't yield enough money to pay her bills.

It did, however, bring her to Washington to visit seven prospects. Avis carefully planned her time with Julia. Her main wish was to cook dinner in Julia's "dream kitchen and linger over the results" with Julia and Paul. She also named those she wanted Julia to invite as guests, promising to use her Knopf expense account to help pay for the dinners.[18]

The visit went well and gave Avis great pleasure. It was a welcome contrast to her life at home in Cambridge, now somewhat fraught. Her older son Gordon, still without a job, was living in her house, and Avis worried more than ever about his present and future. In Washington, Avis relished her time both in Julia's home and in her presence. Invested as Avis was in the cookbook's progress, she gained a good sense of Julia's working life, now that her cooking work had returned to normal. This was jarred somewhat by a letter following the visit, informing her that Julia had started a Monday cooking class in her new kitchen for wives of the Washington elite. Julia bragged to Avis that "they said they never ever had such a good meal. . . . they'd love to be guinea pigs for recipes."[19] Avis's comment on this latest venture offered both encouragement and concern regarding the cookbook's progress. She wrote that the school "should be a nice focus for publicity when the book comes out. When oh when?"[20]

Perhaps as a way of encouraging Julia, on a later visit Avis brought her Bernard DeVoto's typewriter as a gift. Responding, Julia wrote, "Am loving this machine, not only because of its history. . . . and am eternally happy and grateful to you for letting me have it."[21]

Avis was clear-eyed as she observed Julia and Paul, and sensed Paul's despair during her April visit. After returning to Cambridge, she wrote in a letter to both Paul and Julia that she realized "very clearly just how Paul feels up against a new job, not in command of routine and details, not clear about people, and pressed constantly by the thousand things that are screaming for attention." Cheerleading, she addressed him directly, "Paul my angel," to tell him that she believed he could handle the work, for he was "just a thousand percent better as a general bill of good, all around, every aspect, than any man I can think of."[22] What we know beyond Avis's description of Paul's state of mind is that he was isolated in a department of one and had been passed over for promotion. He had earlier expressed to Charlie thoughts about retiring from diplomatic work; but he linked this move to the publishing of the cookbook, and that remained in the unknown future.

A formal "Efficiency report" in Paul's papers, dated August 1957, suggests that at this time Paul was undergoing another review of his work. Although the report enumerated many positives, it explained that Paul held a rank well below his responsibilities and abilities possibly because he "may well have been impatient with certain administrative details and also because of a tendency to be self-effacing." Among the positives listed was his "intelligent and charming wife who is an asset to him professionally as well as representationally." The report went on to list his strength in "cultural phases." It noted that he had been "underrated," and should be promoted "immediately." Pulling together the different strands, the report's summary stated, "Mr. Child is a complex person who can easily be misjudged." He is "a man of many parts and exceptional ability." Although Paul had difficulty adjusting himself in the agency at times, in his present post he brings "great assets" of "intelligence and ability." This report was written by Ed Stanbury, chief of the division. He ended with the comment that Paul had substituted for him and could well serve in that position.[23]

At the same time as this evaluation was being prepared, Paul was finally receiving recognition. In June, Julia wrote to Avis, "After 8 years at an absolute standstill, he has had, actually, 3 promotion[s] in 5 months."[24] Nonetheless, this period remained difficult for Paul, as politics were intervening and the larger Foreign Service was endangered by budget cuts.[25] Julia later tried to help Avis understand the bureaucracy in Foreign Service in the State Department, explaining that although Paul was currently serving as "deputy chief of the Exhibits Division," he was "far from being head of the agency." Given the complex structure of the Foreign Service, she explained, he was not "top brass."[26]

Whatever was happening with Paul at his office, he remained Julia's mainstay. And, as always, he used his artistic talents to aid her. Later in the summer, in describing her labors in preparing duck, Julia told Avis of Paul's work on her behalf. "The new duck is now in the oven, having been duly photographed from all sides. She looks even prettier than the last, as Paul suggested and executed the decoration, a Nero's crown of oak leaves. Pretty sharp!"[27]

As Avis had perceived, work on the cookbook was only creeping along. Julia wrote in mid-June that although she was again putting in her usual working hours, "the work goes so terribly slowly!" At moments, even Julia became discouraged. Learning that Houghton Mifflin was now trying to get the *Ladies' Home Journal* to serialize the book, she wrote to Avis, "Suppose nobody wants the damned thing."[28] Within days Julia learned that the food editor at the magazine "found the recipes too involved." That judgment she could accept. "Well, they are involved, not getting away from that." Given this, she wondered if *House & Garden* might be a better possibility. Julia then did an about-face and wrote Avis that she planned to travel to Philadelphia to give cooking lessons there to a Mrs. Almy and her friends, passing it off again as potential publicity.[29] Given her earlier comment about a similar venture in May—"When oh when?"—Avis likely worried again about what Julia's new teaching stint would mean for the manuscript.

More distractions followed, leading to delays in the cookbook's development. To promote the future book, Julia was eager to publish in an American magazine. Her hopes rose when she learned that Martha Bacon, an acquaintance who worked at *Harper's Bazaar*, was coming to visit her in Washington for a feature on how people entertain. Bacon was enthusiastic about Julia developing a statement of her cooking philosophy. "So in fear, trembling and horror I am whipping up a trial piece for her." Of course, as she noted to Avis, this caused Julia to delay "typing up of the final draft of my turkeys."[30]

Julia understood that *Harper's Bazaar* offered an important opportunity to reach desired future buyers of the cookbook. She informed Simca that the magazine was "seen in all the homes of the well-to-do, and all the best beauty salons, and is considered 'le chic par excellence.'"[31] As she anticipated Bacon's visit, Julia wrote and revised what she thought might later serve as the cookbook's introduction, a statement of her cooking philosophy. Along with Paul, Simca had a hand in revising this essay, in Simca's case suggesting that Julia move its first paragraph to the end of the piece.[32] The magazine slated the article for its February 1958 issue.

Julia was also pushing Simca to gain a public presence in France. As she explained, Americans regard "anybody who is French . . . to be an Escoffier." Thus, "it would be most useful for our book if you could be touted as SIMONE BECK, who is becoming more and more well-known as a cooking authority, and has published many articles in recent French magazines."[33] She later suggested that Simca approach *Réalités*, *Vogue* (France), and *Cuisine and Vins de France*.[34]

Julia well understood the difficulties in obtaining such notice. "This is not going to be easy for either of us," but she saw "no reason at all why we should not be in the top range of cooking authorities, and so recognized, as there are few people who have our experience. It is just a question of getting the ear of the editors, and their confidence." And with that, she offered Simca the unnecessary advice that it was best to invite a magazine editor for a home-cooked dinner.[35]

In her own way Simca was seeking to publicize their work. She reported giving a talk at a women's club and told of her plans to speak to air force women. Nonetheless, Simca saw the primary task to be the cookbook itself, developing and testing recipes for future volumes. She also reported her success in getting Chez Marius to give her the recipe for one of the restaurant's dishes.[36] Since Simca's testing required American ingredients, Julia helped procure them through her contacts at the American embassy in Paris.[37]

In late August, Simca received news that she regarded as an insult, one that made her so angry that she was thinking of resigning from the Cercle des Gourmettes, the elite women's dining club in Paris. She had not been awarded their Honorific Diplôme des Gourmettes. Responding to this, Julia offered Simca a bit of tough advice. She should stick with the Gourmettes, for the lack of the award of recognition was not "worth your demission [resignation]."[38]

Soon, however, Julia would be facing her own professional hurdles. November 1957 proved to be a terrible month for her. Her hopes for pre-publication publicity were dashed when Martha Bacon returned her *Harper's Bazaar* article. It could not be published, because the death of Christian Dior on October 24 changed the magazine's entire content of its forthcoming February issue to focus on him. Even more distressing was the letter on November 19 from Dorothy de Santillana suggesting that the plan of successive small volumes, each to appear every year or two, had somehow vanished at Houghton Mifflin. The editor wrote, "Since this volume contains only sauces and poultry it is difficult for us to see how the other volume can encompass the whole other range of food."[39] Somehow Julia and Simca's cookbook was now to be a two-volume one. After clarifying her earlier understanding of a multivolume work with de Santillana, Julia rolled with the punches and let her editor know that she might expect the first of the now two-volume work in February 1959.[40]

Given the unforeseen future, one purchase by Julia and Paul during the summer of 1957 proved to be significant: "Finally we succumbed and bought ourselves a TV set, a 14" portable." She explained to Avis that she had done so only for the news and programs like "Meet the Press. Otherwise, judging from the daily programs, there has been nothing I would submit a dog to. What a bunch of drivel, and how depressing it all is, with those fake voices and situations and those endless commercials."[41] Avis replied to this in kind: "Certainly agree with you about television—hate it more and more. But couldn't do without it for campaigns, and things like the McCarthy hearings."[42]

A casual statement in a summer letter from Avis carried an importance that Julia had no way of anticipating: "And last week Bill Koshland, who's been with K[nopf] for 23 years and handles all the contracts, domestic and foreign, came up for the long week-end to stay with relatives, and I had a nice long evening with him."[43]

Early in 1957 Julia had begun to encourage Simca to visit. Learning in November that Simca planned to come in February 1958, Julia wrote, "It is just wonderful that you are coming, not only for you to see the country . . . but so that you will have some idea what America is like gastronomically! I can't imagine what you are going to think of it all, and imagine it will [be] something of a shock to you at first."[44]

Unfortunately, Julia's enthusiasm came at a time when Simca was not doing well. She was very tired and had what she called "La Tension!"—an early note of what would reoccur with increasing seriousness. Julia was sympathetic but could only give the anodyne advice to relax and rest for a half hour each day.[45] Ten days later, she added, "it is not necessary to do everything as though your life and honor depended upon it. . . . When you feel yourself tensed up, sit back, take some deep breaths, and force yourself to calm down."[46]

Houghton Mifflin now requested to see the manuscript of Julia and Simca's cookbook by mid-December. Julia planned to send it, telling Simca, "I do not have any deep inquietudes, and feel they will accept the book when they see the MS. Anyway, we shall know during your visit." She expected Simca to charm those at the publishing house, "especially when we have them for a soigné dinner, and they meet a real genuine French woman cuisiniere par excellence."[47]

Charm was unlikely to work its magic when what was at issue was the manuscript's slow development. Julia copied Simca an excerpt of a letter received from de Santillana. "Lovell Thompson feels that the most essential thing at the moment is to have at least 100 pages of completely finished manuscript. He says in a memo, with proper Thompsonian simile, that what we have seen so far is 'huge gobits [bits and pieces] of an as yet inanimate carcass.'" Julia's transcript continued, now with de Santillana's words (and Julia's bracketed response). "The idea of a long series of books is new to me [HAH!], but just as Lovell can't authorize the styling and illustrations until he has the book, so the editorial idea can't complete itself until there is in our hands a finished manuscrpt [sic] of what you feel is correctly 'a book.'"[48]

Copying Simca, Julia replied that she would send, as planned, the "completed manuscript of what we feel to be a 'book' around February 1st." A section of it would be "marked for layout and type-style," with commissioned illustrations to convey "a full idea of what he [the illustrator] and we have in mind."[49]

As Julia was awaiting Simca's visit and preparing the manuscript for presentation to Houghton Mifflin, she confessed to Avis that she was "deeply depressed and gnawed by doubts." At that moment she felt that all her work with Simca "may just lay a big rotten egg." While she was focusing on the opus coming out in separate topical volumes, she worried that "If the recipes are physchologically [sic] horrifying, who is going to do them? . . . or buy the book."[50] Avis, fearing that Julia might "bastardize" her book, responded, "You are <u>right</u> and you must be stubborn." In the meantime, she urged Julia to "try not to be too depressed." Now working for Knopf, Avis could no longer influence Houghton Mifflin; her role for the moment had devolved into lending Julia encouragement.[51]

Simca's long visit in the winter months of 1958 offered her a varied taste of the U.S. She arrived near the end of January and first stayed with Julia in Washington. They immediately turned to work, with Simca proofreading what Julia had written, and Julia redoing the section on sauces. They hoped all this would be finished prior to their late February visit with Avis in Cambridge, when they would present the manuscript to the press. Julia wrote Avis that she and Simca planned to "take the attack position" with the publisher: "That this is the type of series of books we plan to do, and that Volume II will be ready well within a year of the publication of Vol. I," with the subsequent volumes coming at an even faster rate.[52]

Jean Fischbacher, Simca's husband, would be arriving on February 7, staying with the Childs for the weekend, and then going with Simca to New York City until his February 13 departure. Julia then planned to join Simca in the city on February 18, when they would meet with *Harper's Bazaar*. The magazine was now planning an August issue that would include "the Child house, kitchen, and dinners" later to be photographed.[53] After giving a cooking lesson in Philadelphia, the two would arrive in Cambridge on February 20 to stay with Avis. As Julia prepared Avis for this visit, she gave important information about her co-worker. Simca was now "a little bit deaf." Julia gave the advice to Avis that she should speak to her "slowly and loudly and use somewhat simple language."[54]

When Julia informed Avis of Simca's plan to cook for company during the visit—with one dinner to include Dorothy de Santillana—Avis immediately replied, as instructed by the editor, that "anything that seems like social celebrating should be postponed until after decisions have been made." Thus there could be no dinner party that included de Santillana during Simca's visit. Anticipating that she would work with them on their manuscript, Avis promised to keep herself free from outside social commitments during the time Julia and Simca were with her.[55]

That February trip to Cambridge came and went, not as Julia had planned, but as Avis (and de Santillana) ordained. A waiting period followed. Julia returned to Washington. Simca traveled to Detroit to visit Lucille Tyree, a wealthy woman now residing in suburban Grosse Pointe. She was the one who, on a visit by Louisette, had made the original suggestion of creating a French cookbook for Americans, and in 1952 had been an early student at L'École des Trois Gourmandes.[56] Avis had a scouting trip for Knopf, going as far south as Chapel Hill, North Carolina, and planned at its close to spend time with Julia in Washington.

Julia let Avis know that Simca was "having wonderful time in Detroit. Giving cooking lessons. 2 interviews with reporters and photographers. Banquet in her honor." By contrast, this period of waiting on Houghton Mifflin's response was difficult for Julia: "As to the book, I seem to have nothing to say."[57]

On March 14, Avis gave a hint of her fear that Houghton Mifflin might reject the manuscript. She wrote not from knowledge coming from the publisher, but rather after sobering advice she had received from William Raney, an editor at the publishing house Rinehart & Company. Avis wanted to be sure that if Houghton Mifflin's response was negative, Julia should make no compromises. Julia should not "butcher that manuscript, and negate all the work . . . done." If the American housewife was deemed not ready for Julia's book, it could "wait until the times are more propitious." Avis wrote that because Julia had money to live on and did "not have to rip the guts out of this book to keep yourselves in groceries" she could "afford to wait until the right publisher comes along, which he will." Given that Julia's work was "so completely logical and unassailable," Avis was convinced that ultimately "some publisher is bound to agree with you."[58]

The conjunction of Simca's visit with the presentation of the manuscript to Houghton Mifflin turned out not to culminate with the happy celebration desired by Julia and Simca. After holding their work without response, on March 24, just before Simca was to return to Washington, Julia learned that Houghton Mifflin had rejected the manuscript in its current form. "I really dread to tell poor old Simca this news," she wrote to Avis. "I am sure she won't quite understand why and so forth. Any [And] my heaven, how long she has worked on 'a cook book for the USA.' She just backed up with the wrong horse."[59]

After Julia and Paul called Avis immediately with the bad news, Avis was distraught. On the following day, she wrote Julia, "I had to take three pills to get to sleep last night. . . . I can understand H-M's side of the question—the state of business and the increasing expense of publishing anything, plus the enormous hurdle of bucking the ordinary cook-book trend and really reeducating the American cook. When you send me the copy of Dorothy's letter I will study it for clues." For now, she planned to stay put, "Too emotional."

Avis proceeded to tamp down an alternative plan that she and Julia had clearly discussed. "I am perfectly positive that this is not the time to take it up with Knopf," she wrote. The reason was Avis's knowledge of a conflict at the publishing house regarding the June Platt cookbook that had, for a time, fallen to her to edit. She explained to Julia that Knopf was a family firm. Pat Knopf, Alfred's son, had pushed the Platt cookbook. "If the book flops, there is going to be a really ghastly family row—Pat against his parents."

(Familial conflict—or perhaps a son's desire for independence—became public when "Pat," Alfred Knopf, Jr., left his parents' firm to found Atheneum Publishers in 1959.) Moreover, Avis continued, given that the Knopf family meals were prepared by Blanche Knopf's cook, neither she nor Alfred had any understanding of a good cookbook's value.

In addition, Avis faced a barrier in communication at Knopf exacerbated by "Alfred's intensely gloomy convictions about business these days. . . . Alfred said yesterday that we are publishing far too many books, and they are not selling." Avis did mention that she had thought of approaching Bill Koshland and Herbert Weinstock. She had gotten to know both men, mainstays at the Knopf publishing house. She added they "cook themselves" and thus offered her "a chance of receiving some kind of sympathetic understanding." However, at this dark moment for the company, she couldn't. Moreover, she feared she might be let go by the house in September.

Avis also had considered Oxford University Press, but she did not feel ready to make an approach. She planned, however, to continue to consult with Bill Raney, the Rinehart editor whose advice she valued. "If Bill advises cutting down in size, I think you'll have to face to that."[60]

Writing for Houghton Mifflin in a carefully worded letter, Dorothy de Santillana made it clear that she recognized that Julia and Simca's manuscript represented a "most careful labor of love," a labor she called "gargantuan." However, the press had contracted for a single volume work and anticipated one that would fit the American market.

As she continued, de Santillana revealed the wide divergence between the publisher's aims and those held by Simca and Julia. A cookbook needed to have "a logical sequence of presentation following in the way the natural sequence of the meal, such as soups, sauces, eggs, entrees, etc." Moreover, a cookbook for an American audience required "a rigorous standard of simplicity and compactness, certainly less elaborate that [than] your present volumes, which, although we are sure are foolproof, are undeniably demanding in the time and focus of the cook who is so apt to be mother, nurse, chauffeur, and cleaner as well."[61] Her words dealt a very harsh blow to the two collaborators.

Julia's reply stated that "Both Mme. Beck and I are sorry that your collective eye cannot use our monstruous [sic] masterpiece in its present form." Nonetheless, she wrote, "we are not unduly surprised as it is indeed not the book you contracted for." And with that, Julia bounced back to propose that they would turn in a different manuscript suited to the trend in the U.S. for "speed and the elimination of work." They would develop "a short and snappy book directed to the somewhat sophisticated housewife/chauffeur. This would be about 300 pages or so of authentic French recipes." In it there would be a compendium of recipes to fit the American cookbook market.

Julia was at this point clearly compromising the standards that she and Simca held dear. She continued, going even further, to state that the future book would include "the pepping up of canned and frozen vegetables, a few cold dishes, and some good, easy desserts. Everything would be of the simpler sort, but nothing humdrum. The recipes would look short, and emphasis would always be on how to prepare ahead, and how to reheat. We might even manage to insert a note of gaiety and a certain quiet chic, which would be a pleasnt [sic] change." Julia promised to deliver within six months "a completed manuscript in your hands."[62]

For Avis, cutting the manuscript was one thing, but sacrificing principles was quite another. After she received a copy of Julia's letter to de Santillana, she first called it, "a fine wry dignified statement." But then came a terse retort: "But Gawd, don't go too damn far toward canned and frozen simplicity."[63]

When she was again at home with Simca in Washington, Julia demonstrated her resilience. She wrote to Avis, "My, Simca and I are busy. Trying out all sorts of recipes for the new book, and typing them out, and about to go over the whole gamut of what we intend to put in." She stated that de Santillana had set them on a better course, "a much easier book than our magnum O; and we don't have to worry about Careme [sic] and Escoffier turning in their graves, which realeases [sic] much of the pressure. Nor do we have to worry about being complete and exhaustive and immortal."[64]

Chapter Six

Shifting Gears

I

As life experiences build in a marriage, a couple may begin to imagine a different future and work toward realizing it. As Julia and Paul neared the end of their time in Washington, they started to see their life ahead in new ways. This altered Julia's relations with two members of her team. A reading of Julia's correspondence with Simca and Avis suggests that in the year between Simca's departure in early spring 1958 and the move to Paul's next posting abroad in April 1959, Julia and Paul began to shift gears. At work were two elements—a push and a pull.

First was the push—Paul's state of mind. He had hoped to be made chief of exhibits or given some other important position at the USIA, but this was dashed in late July 1958 when he learned he had once again been passed over. Now age fifty-six, he regarded himself as too old "to get into something else." Julia reported to Simca that he was in a "bad frame of mind."[1] As the specter of another foreign posting loomed, Julia tried to put it out of her mind: "They can't in all conscience, send us out again when we've only be[en] home a year and a half with expectation of 3–4 years."[2]

A few days later, after Paul had made many inquiries to try to understand his situation, the couple came to a new resolve. Julia wrote Avis that "Unless something really interesting is offered, we shall resign. We are so damned lucky to have my inheritance! Otherwise it would be out of the question. We would have to live in a much more modest way without job but we could make out perfectly well." Left by her mother, who died when Julia was a young woman, these funds in the past yielded a supplement to Paul's salary that allowed some luxuries, such as expensive restaurant meals. Julia made it clear that they now provided the two of them with enough regular income to live on. The fact of the inheritance, along with their thoughts that they might stay in the United States until the book was finished, were secrets she did not want Avis to reveal.[3]

Julia put it differently to Simca. In early August 1958, after she and Paul had returned from a short trip to New Haven, Paul found no word regarding a promotion. "So," Julia continued, "we are in a state of flux. He is really so fed up he is thinking of leaving. . . . Perhaps he will decide to take another foreign assignment, or perhaps he will just not work for anyone at all. I don't know. At any rate, he is going to hold off things, such as leaving here, until I get this book done! (Unless he has to be moved overseas.)"[4] It seems that at that moment Julia was not facing up to the very real prospect of being posted abroad, although just a week earlier, she had told Avis that such a posting was likely.[5]

By August 7, Paul had received definite word of his new position. Julia expressed her relief to Simca: "our future has been settled, and rather nicely, we think. Paul has been offered the post of Cultural Affairs Officer in Oslo, with 6 months of language training" in Washington. "He has accepted, and I am delighted." They would thus stay put until March, and "This means that I will have time to finish our BOOK, thank heavens!"[6]

Julia was speaking for herself, however. As Paul and Julia embarked on a month's vacation to Canada and Maine, Paul was in low spirits. In an early September letter to Simca, Julia wrote that, after the month away, he "looks well, seems rested, and is in <u>much better</u> humor." With that, she confessed, "He was really in a terribly depressed state when we left." Thus, one side of the shift in perspective—the push—was Paul's dissatisfaction and unhappiness in his work.

"Julia and Paul Child seated indoors reading at a table. Lopus [Lopaus], ME," Schlesinger Library, Harvard Radcliffe Institute, copyright: Julia Child Foundation.

The pull was a house in Cambridge. Since 1954 Avis had been quietly encouraging Julia and Paul to think of Cambridge as the place of their future home. On one visit Avis had driven them around to admire the town's older houses. Once they were in Washington, the drumbeat continued.

In late 1958 Avis's life was in transition. During this period of shifting gears, Avis also faced redirection. In July 1958, she learned that her scouting job at Knopf would terminate at the end of August. She needed a steady income to stay in her house and support herself and her two sons, and on July 28, she put in a formal application for a job at Harvard. She let Julia know that her goals were modest: "Went over yesterday and filled out forms at Harvard, for some kind of job. Don't know yet what there will be to suit me. I don't really want more than $250 a month, at least not right away—I don't want much of any responsibility, as I am not feeling very gifted or capable at the moment, but once I find I can do whatever job I get, feel I will get a bit ambitious."[8]

Working her network close to home, she soon had an eye on a job in the Harvard houses. These were (and are) groups of student dormitory buildings along the Charles River in Cambridge, with rooms for 350 to 400 undergraduates. Each house had a Master, typically a senior Harvard professor, who lived within the complex, and, along with a younger colleague with the title Senior Tutor, had responsibility for the running of the house and the supervision of students living within its quarters. Each Master had a secretary, the position Avis chose to vie for. In preparation, she signed up for a secretarial course to hone her skills, and by late September, her typing was up to speed and she was learning shorthand.

She landed the position at Lowell House, under the legendary Elliot Perkins, a friend of her late husband. It was all very chummy and settled over tea. The regular job was to begin in January 1959, but in the meantime, she was to be farmed out elsewhere at the university.[9] As Julia wrote to Simca, working at Harvard offered many advantages. Avis would get all college vacations, the salary she needed to stay in her house, a secure job that was essentially for life, and a pension when she retired.[10]

Despite all her work preparing for her new responsibilities, Avis continued to go over Julia's new efforts and encourage her. After seeing a sample, she wrote, "I think it is nifty—clear, simple seductive. . . . You are learning and improving all the time." She suggested that Julia send her more of the draft, adding, "I don't think there is <u>anything</u> frightening about this sample. Au contraire, think explanations of the pastry and so on would lure people into trying them, and with success."[11]

Even after Avis was hard at work at her new Harvard job, she continued her role as a primary reader of Julia's manuscript. "When you send your four big chapters up to HM Co.," she wrote, "are you going to have a copy for me? . . . I just feel I have a vested interest in this book, is all." She even gave her hope that at a later point she would proofread during her evenings.[12]

At this point, Avis was eager to help with Julia's writing and hoped Julia might someday live nearby, but she could no longer be Julia and Simca's publishing godmother. Or so it seemed.

On December 3, 1958, a Wednesday, Avis called, telling the Childs to "drop everything" and rush to Cambridge. After a dearth of desirable properties on the market, Avis had just learned through her grapevine that a storied Cambridge house on Irving Street built for the late Harvard philosopher Josiah Royce (and next door to what had been the home of William James) was about to go on the market. Paul and Julia boarded a train that afternoon and arrived in Cambridge late that night.

The next day—during a winter storm—they visited Irving Street, with its handsome houses. Seeing the one at 103 from the inside convinced them to put in an offer on the spot. It was, as Julia wrote to Simca, "just perfect, with plenty of room for our various activities" plus a full apartment on the third floor that could be rented. Currently owned by a "well-to-do widow," the house had been completely renovated and was in perfect shape. The only minor complication was that its purchase required their taking out a mortgage on their Washington house; but this was a matter soon resolved. After what she confessed was "an emotional week," Julia continued, "it is nice to know we have established a real root, and to know what we will do in the future."[13]

"103 Irving St.," Schlesinger Library, Harvard Radcliffe Institute.

The future it would have to be, for although 103 Irving Street became theirs, occupying the house would have to wait until they were free to live in it. In the meantime, they arranged to rent it back to its former owner until their return. But for now, Julia and Paul at least knew the location of their future life. And it would be in Cambridge, just a mile from Avis.

Avis was thrilled. After speaking with the seller, she wrote to Julia, "It all seems like a dream—best one I've had in ages. I can't tell you how much it means to me to know that you'll be around when we're all getting grey-haired and wobbly."[14] Once all was settled regarding the house, Julia gave her own hopes for 103 Irving Street: "I really don't think Paul should go on in the Gov't after his twenty years are up, as it would be a shame to move there when he had gotten so old he couldn't enjoy it. I feel that when we move in there, life will be beginning. Now, we must all plan to live through the year 2000."[15]

To Paul, 103 Irving Street in Cambridge meant more than an expectation of living in a large and lovely old house. It linked his future to his past. He had lived in Cambridge for many years (unmarried) with his first love, Edith Kennedy. Some of his students from those days were now prominent Cambridge citizens. One senses that for Paul, the prospect of moving to Cambridge felt like a return home.

II

Changes in Julia's perspective came gradually and in small steps. Initially its signs were her growing realism about her work and a more independent stance in her relation with Simca. The first inkling came in May 1958 when she wrote to Dorothy de Santillana regarding the professional cooking world in the U.S. that Julia was hoping to join. She had learned from the New York literary agent representing James Beard that in America "the professional cooking authorities operate in a fairly closed syndicate into which it is difficult to penetrate." With that stated, she asserted, "It is, however, our intention to break into this group on a permanent basis. But it will take time and some careful manipulation. I think we shall be in a better position to do so after our manuscript is completed and we have something concrete to show." Thus she would not undertake to establish herself as a cooking authority until the book was done. Simca, however, "is going to get herself known in France, although she finds, naturally enough, that the same exclusive corporateness applies there also."[16]

With this, Julia gave Simca her marching orders. After dutifully letting her know how much she missed her, Julia wrote that making herself well known in Paris "must be your main function, while I scurry around with the new MS. I don't know how you are going to do it, but I know you will manage, as it will be wonderful if you can emerge as 'the famous Simone Beck la Cuisiniere de Paris!'"[17]

Simca was, however, at that moment in no position to do this; she was at La Brise to take the "cure." She did not respond to the command but simply answered in French, complimenting Julia's perfect letter to de Santillana and stating her own vision of her job as providing "the best explained and well experimented recipes."[18]

In the months that followed, both women worked on the cookbook and wrote to each other regarding family life and recipes. Simca faced distractions resulting from her own health problems and her need to visit her elderly mother. Julia went on a vacation followed by a family wedding. A chance for some publicity came to Julia on her return to Washington, as she learned that *Harper's Bazaar* would try again for an article focused on her. They photographed her at home for two days. She prepared food for them, gathered the needed recipes, and provided them with pictures of Les Trois Gourmandes and the insignia designed by Paul. Julia wrote to Simca that she hoped they would "mention all our names, mention the book, etc. etc." But, having been burned once, she wasn't certain where all the effort would lead. "Now the question is," she wrote, "will anything at all appear in the magazine[?]"[19]

After this distraction, Julia returned to work on the manuscript. As she prepared a section for final typing, she sent it to Simca to approve. At that point, she put in writing each of their responsibilities. "American phraseaology [sic], grammar, etc," was Julia's task; to Simca she assigned "CORRECTION of the completed series of a section . . . the final word on French terms, French spelling," as well as "agreement on method and ingredients for recipes."[20]

When Simca informed her of the conflicting advice she was getting from the chefs with whom she was working, as well as information garnered from the great published authorities, Julia asserted her growing toughmind-edness: "I consider ourselves just as much AUTHORITIES as any one else, including . . . Thillmond and Escoffier. After all, this is our life-work, we have spent years and years upon it, and what we find and do and discover are valuable contributions to La Cuisine. If we agree with authorities, that makes the authorities still up-to-date. If we do not, we do not, and we have our reasons."[21]

Julia, however, was not always consistent. When it served her to argue a point with Simca, Julia herself turned to "authorities," most importantly the work of St. Ange. On one occasion, she turned around and demanded that Simca cite her authorities. Writing to her in late July, Julia stated, "IN GENERAL. It would be a help to me in the cases where you deviate from the classical proportions or methods of anything, that you make a note for me where you did so and why. Also useful to quote sources, just so I will know, as I like to know."[22] To this demand Simca fought back. She refused to agree to enumerate all the sources of her recipes, explaining, "the taste is our idea, and the method is good, we have no need of others."[23] Facing this assertion of authority by Julia, Simca did not give ground.

Because this created a potentially serious conflict, Julia wrote "LA METHODE J. CHILD" to provide Simca with a full explanation of her approach to their joint project. On receiving a recipe from Simca, before trying it out, she examined all recipes "on the same subject." From them she sought to learn everything she could. It was important for both of them to know "that it is La Veritable Cuisine Francaise, and not just La Cuisine Simca/Julia." While Julia would no longer demand sources, she needed "some comments" from Simca in order to know "why you are doing something which is different from the usual methods."[24] It is clear that Julia no longer felt that Simca had the last say about a recipe. She had warned Simca in 1954 that she was not to allow a "popote Julia"; now she was applying that standard to Simca's recipes. Nothing in their cookbook was to be idiosyncratic: all needed to be within the larger repertoire of French cuisine.

Nonetheless, Julia understood that they had to be selective. To do that she needed to rein in Simca regarding encyclopedic completeness. When Simca insisted on the many recipes for quiche beyond the popular quiche lorraine, Julia reminded her that "this is not a book on Quiches." Rather, it is a "personal selection of recipes" allowing the two authors to "put in and leave out whatever we wish."[25] Looking over the span of the six years that they had been working together, it is clear that by the summer of 1958 Julia had ceased being deferential to Simca. They were on an equal basis, and, at times, Julia believed she needed to be in control.

As she confronted the instructions from Houghton Mifflin, Julia found new strength. Going against what she had earlier written to de Santillana, Julia wrote Simca that their book should not "compromise on the techniques of making this taste the way they should taste." Americans had been sold that ease and convenience were more important than taste. "Our book is on how to make things taste the way they should." Simca should give her all the detailed instructions, even if they did not include them in the end. "People must say of this book. A MARVELOUS BOOK. I've never been able to make cake before, but now I can."[26]

What Julia and Simca were attempting to accomplish was indeed difficult, given that they were living so far apart. In mid-July came this cry from Washington: "WHY DID WE EVER DECIDE TO DO THIS ANYWAY? But I can't think of doing anything else, can you?" What followed was Julia's memory of the time in Paris when the two began their collaboration: "I keep wishing we could be working together, and having our Messiers being the double critics together."[27]

Along with Julia's new assertiveness with Simca regarding their cookbook, she began to write about her political positions. As Julia did so, she increasingly revealed the political divide that existed between the two cookbook collaborators.

May 1958 was a turbulent time for France: the crisis in Algeria ended the Fourth Republic and brought Charles de Gaulle back to power to head the Fifth. These events engaged Simca, causing her to write Julia of her strong support of de Gaulle and his commitment to keeping Algeria as part of France. Julia, politically on the liberal left, initially sympathized with Simca regarding the turmoil in her country. In a later letter, she attempted to avoid conflict and, at the same time, separate herself from Simca's politics by stating that her only issue regarding France was the need for it to remain an American ally. At this point Simca seemed to want the last word: "We must maintain the hope of a new and strong France, and de Gaulle's pro-gramme is measured and full of good sense." And with that, the discussion of de Gaulle stopped.[28]

Julia's willingness to distance herself from Simca's conservative views did not end, however. After Simca told her that the Gourmettes luncheon for which she had the responsibility was held in the grand Château de Vouzeron, Julia commended her for her labor and wished she had been there "to see all that Nobless." Julia then added, "Well, as for myself, I would have been in the front ranks of the mob who stormed Versailles, I believe."[29]

At this time, Julia's business sense was becoming more evident. In November 1958 she began to warn Simca that they must protect their cookbook's contents from intellectual property theft. Remembering that Simca had taught one of her American pupils how to make beurre blanc, she wrote, "I hope you cautioned her NEVER TO TELL ANYONE HOW TO MAKE IT. This is really one of our triumphs, and is very well known by Amec [American] tourists as a sauce, but no one knows how to make it. So we MUST keep this to ourselves until the book comes out." If Simca did reveal the sauce, she must write to the woman to insist she not give it to anyone else. "THIS IS IMPORTANT . . . as you may not realize how other people's ideas are stolen. . . . and any ideas we may have developed must be kept to our account until WE PUBLISH THEM."[30]

Tension between the two collaborators grew as they tried to finalize the manuscript. Both were on edge. When Julia suggested reorganizing the manu-script to group the recipes by sections, such as stews and fricassees, rather than having a meat section organized by primary ingredients, Simca was horrified.[31] She wrote Julia that her letter left her "pantelante et démoralisée" [panting and demoralized]. Simca wanted to keep the book "simple, popular, practical, with recipes rather unknown to the general public, well explicated, very clear." Thus she would not agree to put together all the fricassees and braises: each recipe must be complete. She urged Julia to stop experimenting and concentrate on chapters to complete the book in December so it could be ready for Christmas 1959.[32] Julia complied with Simca's first demand and returned to work on the book manuscript. However, she resisted the second and continued with the practical work of testing the recipes.

With some of the pages before her, Simca sent Julia a battery of changes in the name of precision. Julia asserted that she understood "the peculiarities of some aspects of the American mind," and insisted on certain retentions. She wrote that, as authors, they needed to appear as "'Authorities,' which we are, who know exactly what we are doing"[33]

Julia became exasperated at the way that Simca was jumping around in her comments. She asked her to be more orderly and follow the existing pages of the manuscript. "I'm going crazy ma chere fille, as I am in such a hurry." In one instance, Julia demonstrated her careful record-keeping and filing. She had received from Simca a negative criticism of a souffle; Julia responded that Simca needed to check her own recipes, for the souffle recipe in question was the one that Simca herself had supplied on February 27, 1956.[34]

By December 7, Julia was in a state. Knowing their manuscript was due at Houghton Mifflin at the end of January, she wrote Simca, "I am going to have to plunge ahead at all possible speed, and I am just going to do on the whole, ONLY the recipes we have both done toghether [sic] and agreed upon . . . which is certainly plenty. There will be many ommissions [sic], and neither of us will be quite satisfied with the book. But I have no other choice." By then Paul had received confirmation that his next posting was imminent, this time to Norway's capital Oslo. Julia let Simca know that she and Paul were facing "a hideous amount of work . . . to get ourselves ready for an absence of 6 to 8 years." This involved preparing their Washington house for renting, doing all their finances (including taxes), and packing up. "It is horrid to contemplate, and I hope I survive, but suppose I will. What a shame this move should come right now. However[,] it forces your old bottle-neck soeur to finish the book, no matter how!"[35]

Julia did not meet the January 31 deadline and struggled with the manuscript over the next months as she attended to her other responsibilities. In February both of them tried to work on the poultry and beef sections of their book, but it was a complicated time for the two. Julia, in her effort to become a more gracious diplomatic-service wife, planned and paid for three catered and served cocktail parties in their house. Simca returned to work with Louisette in the cooking school, all the while complaining of her teaching partner's inadequacies. Simca also suffered from what she again labeled "tension." This time she was advised by her physician to bring down her weight.[36]

Much cookbook time for Julia was lost in the following two months, as she juggled the many tasks required for the move to Norway. By late March, in addition to supervising repair work on the house, she was getting ready for the packers to box up what had to travel to Oslo. That included her batterie de cuisine and Paul's art work and supplies. The book manuscript ended up in three trunks, two to be sent to Oslo. So that she could work onboard ship, Julia planned to bring with her a third trunk of cookbook materials. Paul was out of commission as he required surgery and hospitalization to remove an infected tonsil; and once home, he suffered a painful convalescence. Everything else had to wait.[37] Julia repeatedly shared her anger with Simca. She wrote at the end of March, "This has been a <u>dreadful</u> move, as I've hated every moment of it." Two days later, she exclaimed, "Hideous."[38]

By contrast, during those same March weeks, Simca had the experience of a new pleasure—occupancy of a splendid house in the south of France. Many months earlier, Bramafam, a property in Provence near Grasse, came into Jean's hands. It had been the estate of his recently deceased sister,

Marcelle Challiol. Initially it had gone to Jean's remaining two sisters, both married with children; Jean was named as the property's manager, with full responsibility for its maintenance. In return, he was given usage of what Simca described as a large fine, older, comfortable house on grounds of four-and-a-half acres with olive trees and flowers.[39]

When Jean's sisters chose to refuse the house and its furnishings because they did not want the liability the bequest imposed, life-use ownership of Bramafam—and all its responsibilities—fell on Jean. Initially, Bramafam seemed to Simca like a burden, not a gift.[40]

In March 1959, Bramafam became a reality, and Simca's state of mind changed. Visiting there with Jean, she was delighted. She wrote to Julia of the flowers and the warmth and light that made March feel like June. She longed for Julia and Paul to be there, and invited them to join her and Jean at Bramafam for a Réveillon during the coming Christmas holiday season.[41] As Julia prepared to leave the United States, she could already imagine Bramafam as a bright light for her distant future. She wrote, "When we have finally moved to Cambridge, and come to France for several months each year, we will accept with pleasure all kinds of delicious sorties with you."[42]

In the present, however, the book was not ready. Julia informed de Santillana in early April, "We are off again to a foreign post—unfortunately too soon for me to have completed the manuscript for our cookbook." She was sending only what she had ready, pages that included just one-fourth of the meat section. She promised to send the remainder of the meat in the future, along with fish, cold buffet, and a revised version of soups, sauces, eggs, and poultry.[43]

Her editor at Houghton Mifflin was understanding and sent Julia words that seemed to bode well. After expressing some concern about length—that Julia had promised a book of 350 pages, but the segment in hand suggested it was to be longer—de Santillana wrote, "I have read every word with care and attention and recognize a masterly job of accuracy, precision, and detail. . . . Surely the choice of food, the so evidently tested and painstaking directions of process, the aroma of distinguished cooking add up to a labor of love and a cuisine of elegance."

While de Santillana stated that the press required the full manuscript for a publishing decision, one that would be made on the basis "of possible gain or loss. . . . beyond my own ken," Julia was to know that "when the total manuscript is here I will do everything I can to expedite matters."[44]

Julia and Paul reached Europe on April 29, 1959. After landing at Le Havre, they met Simca in Rouen for lunch and then spent two weeks in Paris. The two women had carefully planned in advance Julia's time there, with special meals at every turn.

Arriving in Oslo in mid-May, Julia and Paul first moved into a hotel. Transition to a foreign post again went by slow stages, delaying Julia's work on the manuscript. Family members came to visit, and Julia found she had new responsibilities related to Paul's position. It took two months to find a house to rent and at last begin to settle in.

With this move Paul's voice finally returns in letters to his brother Charles. It is often, however, a distressed voice. In mid-July, when he and Julia were in the midst of trying to set up their disordered work rooms, he wrote, "This past week-end Julie & I spent unpacking her vast batterie-de-cuisine & getting it established in our kitchen." Describing his discouragement, Paul looked ahead to going through all this again "when we move into the Cambridge house—or worse still: if we go to another post between Norway & Cambridge. Creeps up on a man after 3 Washington houses, 2 Marseille houses, a Paris house, a Bonn house, and now an Oslo house."[45] By contrast, Julia wrote more cheerfully that Paul had gotten his rooms in order, with the house providing "a photo library in the attic, and a tool wookery in the laundry, and a paintery in his room."[46]

Behind Paul's distress was not the house, but his work at the embassy. It was proving to be complicated, with many details and great amounts of paperwork. "So far he doesn't seem to like it at all," Julia wrote. She explained that there were just three Americans to deal with all the special summer concerns involving students, Fulbright recipients, and traveling professors, all "here clamoring. Well, I think he will survive."[47]

Paul's own description of an event that he was required to attend conveys something of what his work life felt like. Held at a former estate, it was a seminar for Scandinavian teachers of English at which four American professors spoke. Paul understood that the program offered goodwill, useful as the U.S. vied for allies against Russian influence; and he assumed he was there because he would be running it in the following year. He nonetheless resented this intrusion, coming unplanned, into his life. He wrote to Charles, "This is just one of a large number of events that seem to pop-up suddenly in my new life here which I have never even <u>heard</u> about until a few days before it pops."[48] He wanted both more structure and guidance.

He also was having a negative reaction to those around him. After describing the antics of the barn swallows at the house, Paul wrote that he was choosing not to give his brother details regarding his human interactions. He explained that it would take too much time because he would have to make clear all the factors—"human, monetary, political"—that were involved. He ended with a quip about what was lost by his choosing not to write about it all: the disappearance of "piles of rich human garbage . . . down Oslo's disposall [sic]."[49]

As time went on, Paul began to adjust. He came to write of his pleasure in the generous Oslo house and its natural setting. With wine delivery and Julia's market routine established, they began to issue invitations for dinner. He enjoyed having company over and consuming the wine and spirits that he was able to purchase tax-free. As Paul saw the end of Julia's work on the cookbook nearing, he wrote more cheerfully, "The patter of our life will likely-enough take a decided turn toward social things once the last of the Scripple has been sent off to HM."[50]

"Oslo [J. P. and E eat supper]," Schlesinger Library, Harvard Radcliffe Institute.

And, of course, there was life with Julia. On her birthday, August 15, Paul accompanied his gift of a miniature brass elephant to her with a note that it was to "always remind us of what we owe to Ceylon for providing the golden moment, the perfect environment, the necessary atmosphere, which revealed us to each other." He continued, "I am happy astonished and delighted that we met at all, that we had the good sense to marry each other, and that our life together is such a pleasure. Thank you for every concession, every restraint, every thoughfulness, every cooperative act, every darling endeavor, that you contribute to our mutual life." He hoped that the two of them would "enjoy thousands of happy returns of your birthday together—in Norge, in Paris, in Cambridge—even in Ceylon. But failing that: perhaps in Heaven."[51]

After settling in, Julia returned to her usual practice of corresponding with Simca about their book's many details. Finally, in early September, Julia sent the full manuscript of the book to Houghton Mifflin. In a letter to Simca, enclosing the rewritten introduction and her letter to the publisher, Julia wrote, "so now there is nothing to do on bookery but sit and wait. Queer feeling, I must say."[52]

On September 22, 1959, after reading Julia and Simca's magnum opus for four full days, Dorothy de Santillana sent Julia her fulsome praise. "I was intensely occupied every minute and remain truly bowled over at the intensity and detail with which you have analyzed, broken down, and reconstructed every process in full minutiae." She not only found the work unique, but also "startlingly accurate . . . inclusive." She called it a "work of the greatest integrity" and sent both Julia and Simca her "warmest personal congratulations."[53]

Enclosing a copy of de Santillana's letter, Julia wrote to Simca, "I would think, from the evidently genuine enthusiasm of her letter, that we were probably IN." Paul thought that they had reason to be "fairly confident" because de Santillana carried "quite a bit of weight in the firm." In closing Julia wrote, "So all we can do now is sit and wait," then added, "H O O R A Y!"[54]

Julia wrote directly to de Santillana of the pleasure that came from learning of her editorial reading. She then turned to clarify the true nature of the co-authorship of the cookbook. She explained that due to "family difficulties," Louisette had "not been able to participate very much," but she did have "useful connections in the USA" via the American Federation of Women's Clubs. The book was thus a collaboration of Simca and herself. It was "a joint operation in the truest sense of the word as neither of us would be able to operate in this venture without the other." She went on to elaborate, "All of the dessert chapter is Beck, including many special twists to traditional desserts which make them especially good to eat." Simca's other triumphs were "unusual sauces," all of them hers. "It is entirely thanks to Mme. Beck and her life-long interest in cooking that we have not only the usual classical collection of recipes, but many personal and out-of-the-ordinary ones which are deeply French and, as far as we know, most are hitherto unpublished."[55]

Paul's disquiet returned during this period. Although his letters hold much that is positive regarding his life—Julia, their Oslo house and garden, and visiting with old friends—about his job he could only complain. For example, in October 1959, anticipating the "HELL week" that was to begin on Monday, eight days later, he wrote, "the law of Nature, so often demonstrated here, which says that Very Important Persons <u>always</u> arrive on a week-end," and that meant that it fell to him to meet and socialize with them. In this case, he was anticipating not only his ex-boss from Bonn, but also a "noted Negro Educator" and the representative of a youth program in Cleveland. They were coming to choose an American high school student to have the honor of studying abroad in Norway. This hosting, added to his normal office work, made him feel like "l'Apprenti du Sorcier." Immediately following this effort, he had to travel to Trondheim, where, as chair of the Fulbright board, he was to interview fifteen candidates.[56]

More generally, Paul felt that the required duties of his job at the embassy were too much for him. Writing almost a month later, he complained about the hectic, unremitting pace of work. "My life in Norway seems almost like the aftermath of an earthquake . . . heaps of useful & useless objects to be weeded out & set to rights, & more bricks falling all the time." He was distressed that, during his months in Oslo, he hadn't painted or touched his violin and had read little. He felt forced to lead "The unbalanced life—one of the things I hate the most!"[57]

In early November Julia got Houghton Mifflin's decision. Dorothy de Santillana was an important editor at the press, but she was only that. Julia and Simca's manuscript went from her hands to the publishing house's business department. Its evaluation landed on the desk of Paul Brooks, the press's editor in chief, and the letter was from him. He began softly with a compliment: "Your manuscript is a work of culinary science as much as of culinary art," and all at the press "respect the work as an achievement." Brooks followed with an explanation that a publisher's basis for consideration "must be practical publishing." In this case, the proposed book carried a "very expensive" production cost. Thus, the market must be perceived as "a large buying public for a cookbook which will have to be high priced." Continuing, Brooks reminded Julia of her agreement in a March 1958 letter to provide in her words "a short simple book directed to the housewife chaffer [sic]." Facing the manuscript that Julia presented, Brooks wrote, "The present book could never be called this. It is a big, expensive cookbook of elaborate information and might well prove formidable to the American housewife. She might easily clip one of these recipes out of a magazine but be frightened by the book as a whole." After suggesting Doubleday as a more likely publisher because of its book clubs, Brooks's final words were "best wishes for its success elsewhere."[58]

Reeling from the shock, Julia sent copies of Brooks's letter to Simca and Avis with these words, "Black news on the cookbook front . . . the answer is NO, Neg, Non, Nein . . . too expensive to print, no prospects of a mass audience." Julia continued, "We must accept the fact that this may well be a book unacceptable by any publisher, as it requires work on the part of the reader. NOBODY has ever wanted to publish ANY of our recipes in any publication whatsoever thus far. So that may well indicate something. In fact it does indicate that we are not presenting things in a popular manner." Nonetheless, she added her unwillingness to compromise: "I am frankly not interested in the chauffeur den-mother type of cooking, as we have enough of it."[59]

Addressing each in turn, she wrote, "Simca, I am most upset for your sake, as you have been on this bloody thing for so many years and years. You just managed to hook up yourself with the wrong collaborator! Eh bien." And to Avis, she addressed this question: "Do you have any ideas of to whom we should submit the MS. Don't know anybody at Doubleday. . . .

Should not think Knopf would be interested in another cookbook of this ty e [sic] as they have just released the Donan [Donon] book."[60]

"Do not despair. We have only begun to fight," was Avis's answer. On learning of Houghton Mifflin's rejection, she immediately requested that Julia's manuscript be sent directly to William Koshland at Knopf, and she herself sent him de Santillana's evaluation. As Avis did this, she knew, as she wrote to Julia, she was "assuming authority I realize I have not got."[61]

Chapter Seven

Waiting

At this moment, a new member joined Julia's team. Without Paul, Simca, and Avis, the first three, there would not have been a manuscript. Without William Koshland, the fourth, there might still have been a book. But even if so, it is certain that the book would not have been the one that emerged in 1961 as *Mastering the Art of French Cooking*. William Koshland was exactly the right person at the right time.

WILLIAM A. KOSHLAND

Unlike Simca, Paul, and Avis, William Koshland has remained relatively unknown both in Julia's story and that of American publishing and cultural life in the twentieth century.[1] In truth, knowledge of him is hard to come by, likely because he wanted it that way. However, persistent searching and the aid of John Sinton, his younger cousin and my helpful friend, have revealed much of his background—one that allowed Koshland to respond quickly to Avis and to appreciate Julia and Simca's extraordinary accomplishment. Given his relative invisibility in accounts of Julia Child, Koshland receives here a biographical treatment that presents what I have learned.

"Bill Koshland," figure on right, courtesy John Sinton.

Bill Koshland, as he was known, uniquely combined literary and cultural interests with business experience. A man in his mid-fifties in 1959, he had been at Knopf in varying capacities since 1934. His origins and life experience had prepared him to understand the workings of a family firm, as Alfred A. Knopf, Inc. had remained in 1959, when Avis had Houghton Mifflin send him the manuscript.

He came from a prosperous family with a proud lineage in San Francisco. His grandfather was part of the significant group of Jews from Bavaria who, facing rising anti-Semitism, sought opportunity in the California gold rush. These immigrants did not come to pan gold but rather to supply the goods and services needed by those who did. By the second half of the nineteenth century, Bill Koshland's paternal grandfather, Simon Koshland, had established a leading wool business in San Francisco. Simon's many children married within the prosperous community of those from similar origins in the Bay Area. Their world included families with such well-known names as Haas and Levi Strauss. When Simon Koshland retired, his business continued with his sons, including Bill's father, Abraham Koshland, an 1890 graduate of Harvard. This son's role was to establish the East Coast branch of his father's wool-trading business in Boston. At least by the time Bill was ready to graduate Exeter Academy, he and his immediate family were living in a handsome town house on Beacon Street.

The wealth and confidence of Bill's parents can be seen in his 1922 travel journal of a summer trip with his family when he was fifteen. It is one of those extraordinary documents that catch certain key aspects of a boy that would contribute to his personal and professional strengths as a man. Staying in the finest hotels in London, Paris, Brussels, and Munich, Bill wrote each day of where he went, what he saw, how he reacted, and what he bought. He was an enthusiastic tourist—he wrote "wonderful" in his diary thirteen times. He had strong aesthetic interests. On seeing *Die Meistersinger* in Munich, he wrote that it was "the most wonderful treat of the whole trip: a perfect performance in every way."[2] Some of his museum-going seemed dutiful, but at other times the works of art delighted him. At moments he seemed pleased with himself, as when, after visiting a famous tourist site in

London, he reflected, "My knowledge of English History made the place far more appealing to me."[3]

Bill was a dutiful son. Before his father joined the family midway in the trip, Bill often accompanied his mother on her shopping excursions. He abided the many family members and friends that his parents encountered abroad. He also did his own shopping, with special interest in augmenting his stamp collection and a chess set. His delight about his father's arrival in early August and their subsequent walks together convey his warm feeling for him. His father's presence also set off a special round of shopping when the family returned to London, as Bill, his older brother Steven, and their father made repeated trips to Harrods for the measuring, fitting, and ultimate purchase of their bespoke suits and tuxedos.

At Exeter Academy, in the early 1920s, Bill received a traditional education in languages—Latin, Greek, and French—along with English, history, physics, and mathematics. On his Harvard application in 1924, he listed his sports—swimming, tennis, horseback riding, and golf—some of which suggested his wealthy background as well as helped make him seem to be an "all round" student. However, in listing his interests—music and book collecting—Bill showed his aesthetic tastes. Membership in the chess club at Exeter suggested a competitive streak. Upon his graduation from the academy, he spent the following summer in Europe.

In applying to Harvard, Bill wrote that he chose Harvard because "First, my father is an alumnus of the college and my brother is a student at present." His second reason, a not unusual statement for a Harvard applicant in his era, was "I believe that a Harvard degree carries a certain prestige that a degree from other colleges does not." At that point he planned to concentrate in French or Romance languages. And, finally, a word about himself: "In addition to the course I expect to major, the Music Department offers much of interest to me."[4] As a Harvard student, Bill achieved scholastic distinction and ultimately chose English for his concentration.

After graduating with his class in 1928, Bill spent a year in England at Emmanuel College, Cambridge, and on his return immediately went to work for the Boston investment banking firm Lee, Higginson & Company. Beginning in 1932, he moved to New York, transferring to Salomon Brothers & Hutzler. Two years later, in 1934, he followed his literary and cultural bent and "went to work for the house at Alfred A. Knopf." There he found his calling. In reporting to his class for their fifth-year class book, Koshland proudly gave his occupation as "Publishing" and his address as "c/o Alfred A Knopf, Inc, 730 Fifth Ave, New York, N.Y."[5] With the exception of the war years of 1942 through 1945, when he served in the U.S. Navy, he remained at Knopf for the rest of his working life.

Beyond his professional life, key elements of Koshland's adult life stand out. The first is his public life as a Jew. Although nothing in his adult life suggests that Bill Koshland was observant, he expressed this identity through important Jewish organizations. Once established in New York, he affiliated almost immediately with the American Jewish Committee.[6] With Hitler's rise to power and anti-Semitic policies enshrined in the Nuremberg Laws, Koshland became active in the American Jewish Joint Distribution Committee, serving as its associate treasurer.[7] The second is his long loyalty to the institutions that educated him, signified by his contributions during his lifetime. His paid death notice confirmed both aspects in its suggestion that "donations in his memory be made to Harvard University, Phillips Exeter Academy, & the UJA-Federation of Jewish Philanthropies."[8] The third is his honorable service during World War II as a naval air officer in Asia and the Pacific, meriting him the Distinguished Flying Cross.[9] The fourth is more private, never revealed in printed sources: his sense of humor and his personal life as a guarded gay man, conveyed in conversations with me by his younger cousin, who often visited him and the man he lived with during the early 1960s.[10] The fifth came to me first-hand, through reading letters written by him and from his correspondents—his personal warmth and capacity for friendship.

At the publishing house that Alfred and Blanche Knopf founded in 1915, Koshland's role developed over time. The company, unusual in its family structure well into the 1960s, became known for championing many important authors in the U.S., leading to both Pulitzer Prizes and Nobel awards. Sometime after World War II and Koshland's return to the firm from military service, Alfred Knopf "began to delegate some of his responsibilities to other Knopf employees. While still taking an active role as president, he gave his wife almost total control over the firm's European operations and allowed trusted associates such as William A. Koshland to oversee the administrative business of the firm."[11] Koshland, however, remained an allusive presence, likely intentionally, given the firm's family dynamics.

These he was well able to understand. To put it simply, Bill Koshland's father was a principal figure in a prosperous family business. Thus Bill had been bred to understand and navigate the complicated relationships at Alfred A. Knopf, a family publishing house whose owners were Alfred and his wife Blanche. Koshland knew how to get his way by keeping a low profile, managing the system quietly, and being a calming presence in the midst of conflicts.

It is likely that in 1960, the words used in his 1997 obituary were already understood in the New York publishing world—William Koshland at Knopf "worked behind the scenes to extend and strengthen the firm's relations with authors, booksellers and publishers at home and abroad." Ultimately he received responsibilities at Knopf that carried important titles: with Blanche Knopf's death in 1966, he succeeded her as president; and then, with Alfred Knopf's retirement in 1973, he became his successor as chairman, the firm's highest position.[12]

In 1978, in the Harvard fifty-year class book, Koshland wrote of his long career at the publishing house: "The rewards have been immeasurable whether in the relation with Alfred and Blanche Knopf themselves, or with others in the firm or colleagues in the world of books both in this country and abroad: publishers, agents, booksellers, book manufacturers, and above all—authors."[13]

In November 1959, when Avis had Houghton Mifflin send the cookbook manuscript to Bill Koshland, her friendship with him was well established.

Its written record peeks out in her letters to Julia. In July 1957, when Avis was working as a literary scout for Knopf, she met Bill for the first time. Writing to Julia, Avis described him as "short, Jewish, pop-eyed, and has quite a lisp—and very nice he is, too. Bachelor I guess, but pansy [one of the words in the 1950s for a male homosexual] I would doubt." All of this was accurate, except for her last statement. [14]

Over a year later, Avis added more details gathered during an evening spent with him: "Somewhat set up by a dinner date come Friday with dear Bill Koshland from Knopfs, who is coming up for the Yale game with his nephew. Haven't had dinner alone with a man in I don't know how long. He is a real pet—bachelor, rich, been with Knopf's for 25 years, and I am easy with him but do not find him in the least exciting. Still, grateful for small favors." [15]

Knowing of Koshland's interest in fine food, Avis sent him some of Julia's recipes. When prepared, according to his cousin, they were likely cooked at his home not by him but by his partner Max. [16] Thus Koshland was aware mainly of the delicious quality they offered, but likely also of their clear guidance to the cook. While it is unlikely that Avis was grooming him for the book's publication, given the Houghton Mifflin contract at the time, Avis certainly knew that he was well prepared to appreciate the cookbook long before the manuscript arrived on his desk.

Somewhat disingenuously, Avis wrote to Julia, "Bill has seen part of the MS when he was sitting around here." She thought that he himself was a cook. The most important element was her accurate testimony that "he swings great weight at Knopf where he has been anchor man for 25 years, and every time I have seen him (and he was here last weekend) he has asked" about its publication.

Taking a step back, Avis added that in sending the manuscript to him she had been presumptuous. "So if you want to take my head off, do, but let's try this before exploring further."

Conveying her confidence that the book would get published, Avis wrote, "I know it, I know it." She now disparaged Houghton Mifflin for having "no cookery minded people but Dorothy [de Santillana]. . . . I suppose their reaction was a foregone conclusion." She hadn't known this, however, when many years earlier she "steered the MS" there. Avis was aware that de Santillana deeply regretted the decision of the press. She had written to Avis, "I promise you I feel very badly to see the perfect flower of culinary love, and the solidly achieved work of so many years, go begging" and that she would do what she could to help.[17]

The manuscript arrived on Koshland's desk on November 17, 1959, and he immediately sent a brief encouraging note. He regretted, however, that he would be unable to read it for at least ten days, as he had been called to California to attend to his 81-year-old mother as she underwent surgery.[18] Avis reported to Julia that she had replied that he should "take his time, that we have been in this for eight years and another few months won't kill us." What she wanted was for Koshland "to live with the ms. for a while and cook from it."

What Avis didn't want was Julia to "get down in the mouth, depressed, defeated." She was convinced "the book will find an eager publisher somewhere. I do think Dorothy is right that the house has got to be really sold. . . . Keep in touch. I love you both dearly. The truth will prevail."[19]

Koshland revealed at the outset that he would share the manuscript with Judith Jones, a young editor at the press with a great interest in food and cooking. He also let Avis know that he had already attempted to prepare the ground with Alfred Knopf by letting him read her letter. In replying to it, Alfred had attached a note: "has she never heard of Donon" (*The Classic French Cuisine*, by Joseph Donon, published by Knopf in 1959). In reassuring Avis, Koshland told her that he then reminded Alfred that when the Donon manuscript was being discussed "even he questioned some of the things in that book." Continuing, Koshland added, "Well, let's wait till Judith and I have looked at it a bit." He then asked Avis, "How long can we dawdle? Please have a note for me here when I get back, a week from Monday, that is the 30th."

At the end of Koshland's letter came the important information that Avis had shared with him her correspondence from Houghton Mifflin regarding the book. "Fascinating, is all I can say," was his reply, followed with "I really can't wait to get my hands on the manuscript."[20]

In San Francisco, after his mother's successful surgery, Koshland dictated a letter to Avis thanking her "for letting us take our time with the book," he wrote that "Judith Jones is already experimenting at home and I shall start in, I trust, next week."[21]

Reviewing Julia and Simca's cookbook turned out to be a long process. Both Jones and Koshland took their time, Judith reading carefully, and both of them savoring the recipes at home. Given the dynamics of the family firm of Knopf, advocacy required diplomacy even at the editorial level. Blanche Knopf had championed another French cookbook; Judith Jones was still considered a "young" editor; and Bill Koshland was on the management side. With those issues in mind, Jones and Koshland enlisted Angus Cameron, a senior editor, to speak for the quality of Julia and Simca's work. Although a new hire at Knopf, Cameron was an old hand at publishing and one whose judgment Alfred Knopf trusted. Especially important in this instance, Cameron was known for championing, decades earlier at a different publishing house, Irma Rombauer's *Joy of Cooking*, the 1936 cookbook known for its high sales, lasting through the decades that followed.

After Avis sent the manuscript to Koshland, she remained the point of contact between the publishing house and Julia. During the long months in which the manuscript was being read by the editors—and cooked from—she kept Julia (and thus Simca) informed about where things stood.

At that point Avis was working at Harvard in temporary positions as she awaited the start of her permanent job beginning in January 1960, when she would become the secretary to the Master of Lowell House. In early December she wrote that she had gotten a "hasty note from Koshland. He had put the manuscript in the hands of Judith Jones, and she is experimenting with the recipes at home. She is a very good girl down at that office, an editor now, and knows quite a bit about food, and her husband more, according to Bill." Avis also reported that Koshland was hoping to read the manuscript.[22]

By the end of December, Koshland had done so. In a friendly call filled with lots of news, he reported to Avis that he was "impressed to death with it" and that Judith "took it home and started cooking out of it, with great success." Avis wrote to Julia that Koshland "took the second half of the MS home and started cooking out of that, with several smash hits." Avis added, "He and Judith are now switching halves." Avis let Julia know that Angus Cameron "is also taking a hand as he, too[,] cooks." Supported by the positive reactions of Jones and Cameron, Koshland moved the manuscript to a new level, turning it over to the financial side of the firm, headed by Sidney Jacobs, for a determination of production costs. Avis closed with, "As Bill said, three enthusiasts can swing a lot of weight."[23]

Beginning in January, after taking up her permanent position as secretary to Elliott Perkins, the longtime Master at Lowell House, Avis was now in the thick of things at Harvard and finding her duties to be varied, often complex, and also personal. Although the pace was frequently exhausting, Avis kept her focus on Knopf. In mid-February, after writing that she had promised Koshland she wouldn't convey to Julia any information until there was a formal decision at Knopf, Avis wrote, "Much as I love Bill[,] I love you considerably more and it kills me not to be able to write and tell all." She then revealed that she had received a call from Koshland about three weeks earlier, telling her that "he is mad about the book, so is Judith Jones, so is Angus Cameron, all of whom have been cooking out of it at length. . . . They say it is unique, nothing like it or ever will be again, a real break-through, perfect. It's really French and it works."

Koshland had gone to production, and they agreed that "they can do a beautiful book for $7.50, no cutting." Koshland estimated that they could sell fifteen to twenty thousand copies in the first year. He then let Avis know that once final figures were in from production, "they will ram it through the forward no matter what." Avis also added that Koshland wanted Paul's photographs to use as the basis for the book's illustrations, as it was unlikely that the press would use the existing drawings that Julia had earlier commissioned. Julia mailed the photographs to Avis soon after.

Avis had recently asked for the Childs' phone number in Oslo. She now wrote that this was because Koshland had promised her that, once the decision was made, he would give her "the pleasure of telling the ladies." With that, Avis admitted she was, at that moment "falling apart" for she was not able to sleep at night because of difficulties she was experiencing at work and waiting up late for Koshland to call.[24]

Simca's letters to Julia during the late autumn and early winter months of 1959–60 mention only that she was awaiting news from Knopf. It is likely that Julia did not convey to her what she knew, even when she and Paul were at Bramafam over the Christmas holidays. In the meantime, both Simca and Julia were keeping themselves occupied. In February, Julia apologized to Simca for being a poor correspondent, explaining, "It took a long time to get re-organized after our trip, and I seem to have gone into a mental collapse ever since that book got off back in November! Must pull myself together and start to work again." Work meant that she would try to work out one or two "cooking research problems per week" and also "Start a cooking class." She was seeking to be a better diplomatic wife, now giving an official dinner party every Thursday. She was also studying Norwegian for an hour each day. Her real pleasure came with winter's opportunity to ski. "What a beautiful life it is here, really."[25]

In mid-February Julia began to send Simca some positive words from Avis, all the while trying to dampen her partner's expectations. The two of them had been burned once before at this very point. When she got even more promising news, Julia wrote Simca that she had received "A letter from Avis. . . . sounds quite encouraging about our book at Knopf's but she says not to mention it to anybody (which would include Louisette), because as usual there is no final OK from the money men . . . always the villains in the drama."

Julia continued, "Koshland of Knopf called her up 3 weeks ago and said that he and his two editors were 'mad about the book and had all been cooking out of it at length. They say it is unique, nothing like it or ever will be again, really French and it works.'" After repeating reports from the business side, she reminded Simca that ultimately there needed to be "the OK from the Knopfs themselves."

Although clearly excited, Julia made the effort to downplay both Simca's and her own her expectations. "We have been to this point with de Santil-lana, so it means nothing at all. But at lease [sic] it is encouraging to find three people who think it is a great book!" Julia closed with the promise to telephone Simca if Knopf accepted the book; however, if the book was again rejected, she would write.[26]

In early March Avis wrote Julia that she was planning to take some time off in April and hoped to visit with Koshland in New York. She still hadn't heard from him and was "getting furious about it." In the meantime, the drawings and photographs that she had requested from Julia had "arrived safely." She wasn't yet able to send them to the press for that would let Koshland know she had conveyed to Julia his positive words about the manuscript.[27]

Eight days later, Avis let Julia know she had finally heard from Koshland that "the boys have been wrestling with the estimates." Quoting his letter, she wrote, "Now the cookbook: well I didn't get much out of Houghton [Mifflin, regarding its financial assessment] and so what is happening now is Sidney [M. Jacobs, the production manager at Knopf] and his minions are struggling with the estimates and such. We're going to talk plans and I imagine we ought to set up some sort of session with you when you are here, so save some time on Monday the 4th [of April]. I suppose afternoons are usually best for such things. The long silence means nothing more than that I've been so damned busy I haven't known whether I've been coming or going." As if to prove this, he closed: "Something now!"[28]

Avis decided it was time to confess to Koshland. In a short note to Julia, she informed her that she told Bill she had suggested to Julia "discreetly that there was interest at Knopf." This had then freed her to request of Julia that she "gather up photos and sketches and estimates and send along to me, just in case." With the air cleared, Avis packed up all the material Julia had sent and mailed it to the publishing house. "This has been a hair-line to walk, as I did want to observe Bill's request not to tell you anything . . . until things were set. But I am vastly relieved by his letter—it's been so damn long!—and I really do think things are going to work out."

Avis now planned to visit the Knopf office in New York in early April to attend the staff meeting to discuss the book. "Let us pray. I will write you faithfully what goes on at the conference. But it still may take time."[29]

During March 1960, Julia confirmed in her letters to Simca much of what would make their joint work unique. The process they had worked out over the many years of development was that Simca would send Julia a recipe, Julia would try it out, and the two would test it repeatedly; then Julia would research the recipe in the authoritative cookbooks in her library, adapt it to American measurements, and simplify it, if possible, but not at the cost of flavor. Then Julia would work toward putting all she had learned in a logical order. This became explicit as she faced some recipes for cookies. She wrote to Simca, "What is needed is to make some sense out of all this stuff." She didn't want to produce "a group of unrelated recipes, as there are plenty of those." Rather, "the whole structure must be torn apart, put into related groups, and each change of proportion in each group must be explained."[30] Julia had worked through this process many times in the past years, as suggested in her letters; now she reaffirmed it explicitly. Establishing what would later be called a "master recipe" that was then followed by "variations" came to be an important contribution of their cookbook.

Avis fulfilled her promise to attend the conference over the cookbook, and it gave her great hope. She wrote that "Bill is beginning to move, and when he does he will probably move fast."[31] She then relayed the gist of the April 4 "conference." In doing so, she opened a peephole into decision-making at Knopf.

The meeting was in the library of the publishing house. In addition to herself, there were four attending—William Koshland, Judith Jones, Angus Cameron, plus Sidney Jacobs on the financial side. The discussion was largely about the cost of production, involving such matters as the type of paper and the nature of illustrations. Avis herself seems mainly to have listened, but she did urge that there be numerous drawings, as they were "absolutely necessary in some places." In a note regarding Paul's photographs to serve as the basis of the new drawings, Avis penned on the side of her letter, "Hope all around that Paul would <u>not</u> charge for Photos wh. wd add to Cost."[32]

After the group adjourned, Avis read the written reports on the manuscript by Judith Jones and Angus Cameron in Koshland's office. With her newly acquired secretarial skills, Avis took notes in shorthand and transcribed them for Julia. These allowed Julia to know early on something of Judith's approach and her thoughts about the work.

Judith noted that she had spent two months trying out the recipes. In doing so, she found the cookbook "not only first rate but unique" in that its authors "emphasize technique." Working with the book was better than a course at Cordon Blue because "the authors' whole focus is on how to translate the tricks learned to the problems that confront you at home— different meat cuts, utensils, materials, etc." It enables the cook to rise "to that subtle perfection that makes French cooking an art."[33]

Her report on the book's quality was strongly seconded by Angus Cameron. Given that the publishing house had a concern with costs and profits, Cameron then added the important ingredients that the book "does for French cooking what Rombauer did for standard cooking." He was convinced of the book's broad market, stating that "a path will be beaten to the door of the book." The work had "solid sales appeal. . . . cooks will know this by word of mouth very soon." Cameron gave a diplomatic nod to the recently published French cookbook by Joseph Donon championed by Blanche Knopf. While the present manuscript under consideration "could stand alone as the only one needed," Cameron wrote, "we need not injure other French cookbooks by making that point exclusively."[34] Jones and Cameron made a formidable team. They were supported by a note from the production side of the house, reporting confidence regarding "20,000 sales the first year."[35]

Avis understood that Koshland was to "draw up a formal production proposal for the Knopfs," the press's ultimate deciders.[36] She called Judith Jones "a complete convert." Avis added that instead of seeking to shorten the book, Jones planned to ask for more recipes.[37]

Avis also conveyed something of the informal office dynamics at Knopf in 1960. During the meeting, Alfred Knopf walked into the library and was "dumfounded [sic] at seeing me." After Avis returned to Cambridge, she received a letter from him in which he wrote, "I really was very embarrassed to walk in on you the way I did the other morning, and even more embarrassed not to have had any chance to talk to you while you were here. The explanation is that I never knew you were coming or that you had arrived. Why Bill didn't inform me once the appointment with you had been made is the sort of thing I never attempt to understand or explain." Avis thought it likely that Alfred "probably had a tantrum with Bill . . . he frequently does."[38]

After the meeting Avis and Judith Jones had a long conversation. Avis wrote that Judith reported that "she goes home for lunch and blanches the vegs. the way she learned from you, then finishes the cooking at night." Avis then related the experiences she had enjoyed in New York City—successful shopping for clothes, leaving her "broke but happy"; museum going; and dining out "two nights, once with Bill."[39]

On her return home, she received from Koshland "a brief note . . . which says, 'I don't think you should write Julia until I say that I've got the initial on the important sheet of paper.' . . . All awaits on their [the Knopfs'] decision."[40]

Eight days later, Avis sent Julia a clipping with "blockbuster" news. Although the clipping is absent from the file, it clearly involved the acquisition of Alfred A. Knopf, Inc. by Random House, one allowing the Knopf branch to retain editorial independence. "Perhaps this is what has slowed up our particular deal, though I must say I had no smallest hint of anything like this when I was in NY, and wonder even now if Koshland and the others knew what was in the wind, but think they must have." Avis stated that both Alfred and Blanche were sixty-eight years old. (She did not mention the widely circulated news that Pat, their son and putative successor, had left the firm in 1959 to start his own publishing company.) Avis wrote, "I suppose something like this simply had to be done." Although Bill was about to be away on a vacation in Greece, Avis believed all would be well for the book. "I know the complete involvement is there, in Bill, Angus, Judith, and Sidney Jacobs, and cannot believe they would have got this far, and got themselves in so deep, without the very strongest belief that the deal would go through." She herself would simply have to "continue to wait," and she hoped that Julia could "continue to bear it."[41]

Julia resigned herself to the wait—but with her hope aroused and her gratitude to Avis constant. As she wrote on April 20, "Just think, if it weren't for you this book MS would be as dead as a codfish."[42] Avis believed she deserved this recognition. "Well you know I do think that except for me the book would be dead. . . . Because I think you and S. would just have given up, convinced the times weren't ripe for it. But I did, do, and will continue to do so, and if by any wild fluke Knopf turns this down, I will simply start pummeling another publisher. But the more time goes by, the more I am sure that Knopf will do it, only I do not say this aloud."[43]

As April wore on, Avis suggested to Julia that positive news might be coming. She made Julia aware that the Knopf editors wanted larger portions, given that Americans dined with fewer courses. They also wanted the addition of a recipe for cassoulet; and with that, Julia went to work immediately to produce it. As she did so, she wrote Simca that she had "looked up everybody just for fun, and have 17 sources including Mme. S. Beck."[44]

As April came to a close, Paul did not share Julia's seeming optimism. Instead, he was facing deep mental distress. In writing of his condition to his brother, Paul described himself as having a psychological disorder, using the term of an earlier era, "neurasthenia." He caught a cold, and with it came deep anxiety. "I've died so many deaths in this life I cannot believe that the real thing, when it comes, will be any worse." He didn't have fever, but rather a temperature below normal: "so, according to the rules I have laid

down for myself to help me battle my neurasthenia I <u>couldn't</u> go to bed."
While "Julie's skillful and imaginative cooking, plus <u>les</u> vins de France,"
provide "a wonderful solace . . . they impose a penance." So he chose not to
eat or drink too much. He then added, "I only wish emotional self-restraint
(in the realm of fear & frustration) were as feasible for me."[45] Along with
the many unwelcome aspects of his job in Oslo, perhaps Paul's increasing
distress had an additional source, the long period of waiting.

Chapter Eight

The House of Knopf

On May 9, 1960, Avis made the late-night call to Julia in Oslo to tell her that Knopf had accepted the book. In a letter written an hour after hanging up, Avis told Julia that she was "limp and stunned," feeling "deep, deep pleasure and great gratitude to the House of Knopf." She had just sent Judith Jones "a night letter," important in that it opened the way for Judith to write directly to Julia. Avis had no way of reaching Bill Koshland, however, who seemed to be on his cousin's yacht somewhere in the Greek islands. With the wish that they were "all together so that we could dance around the maypole, emitting loud cries of joy and relief," Avis promised she would write to Simca and then try to get some sleep.[1] But first, she sent a night telegram to Judith Jones.

YOU HAVE CORRECT ADDRESS FOR MRS PAUL CHILD SO WRITE HER
AT ONCE I HAVE JUST TELEPHONED HER MY PLEASURE AND READ

HER YOUR LETTER HAPPY DAY FOR US ALL PLEASE SEND BE [sic]
CARBON YOUR LETTER TO HER AND CARBONS FROM NOW ON AS I
MAY BE ABLE TO LEND A HAND MAILING YOU NEW WORKSHEETS AND
TITLE SUGGESTIONS MY OFFICE TELEPHONE UNIVERSITY 8-7600
EXTENSION 3383 FOR THE RECORD

AVIS DEVOTO.[2]

Avis clearly wanted to remain a player, but from May 9 on, Judith Jones
called all the shots.

JUDITH JONES

The very next day, May 10, 1960, Judith Jones wrote the all-important letter to
Julia that marked the beginning of their important professional and personal
relationship. Koshland had known exactly what he was doing when he shared
the manuscript with Jones. A respected editor at Knopf, at that time primarily
of fiction, she was known for her independent judgment and appreciation of
quality. She was also an avid cook. When Avis sent the recipes of Julia and
Simca to Bill Koshland, he shared many of them with Judith. Thus she was
prepared—one might even say "groomed"—for the manuscript.

Judith Jones was the ideal editor for Julia. Although the two had grown
up on opposite ends of the United States, both were daughters of privi-
lege, educated at private secondary schools for girls and women's colleges.
Judith (then Bailey), a New Yorker, attended the Brearley School and then
Bennington, where she majored in literature. In college she interned at
Doubleday, and after graduation in 1945 became an editorial assistant
at that publishing house. She moved to Paris, where, in 1948, she met Evan
Jones, the man who became her husband in 1951.

It was in Paris that Judith Jones first made her mark in the publishing
world. Working alone in the Doubleday office, she rescued for American
readers the work that became *Anne Frank: The Diary of a Young Girl,*

written by Frank while in hiding from the Nazis in Amsterdam during the Holocaust.[3] Many years later Judith related that one day, after her boss left for a long literary lunch, she faced the work of writing rejection letters for the pile of submissions to Doubleday. When she picked up the advance copy of the book's French edition, she recalled, "I was drawn to the face on the cover. . . . I started reading it—and I couldn't stop." Her enthusiasm persuaded her boss to allow her to "get the book off to Doubleday in New York, urging them to publish it."[4]

After Judith and Evan returned to New York, she joined Knopf in 1957, working primarily with Blanche on the literary side of the house. Judith Jones's love of food and cooking expertise were well known among her associates. Bill Koshland often shared recipes with her. Later, when Avis put Julia's manuscript into his hands, he chose Judith to vet it for the house. Judith's admiration for the work and her suggestions for additional recipes and larger portion sizes made her the natural choice to be the book's editor.

Julia Child and Judith Jones work in Julia's kitchen. *Nancy Palmieri, Associated Press.*

By May 10, the time of her letter to Julia, Judith had been deeply involved with the manuscript for months; but she had respected the editor's code of silence prior to the publisher's final decision. Writing to Julia in Oslo, Judith began by acknowledging her engagement with the work over the last months. It had been more than a manuscript to read and assess financially. It had been studied, and its recipes tried out in home kitchens. Convinced of its unique quality, Knopf would be pleased to publish it.

With this, Judith presented Knopf's financial offer, explaining that she was given the task because Bill Koshland, who normally was responsible for such assignments, was traveling abroad. In words that were clear and direct, she wrote that the press proposed a $1,500 advance, against royalties (equivalent to roughly $13,900 at this writing). For the first ten thousand copies, the authors would receive 17% of the wholesale price; for the next ten thousand, 20%; and beyond that, 23%. Subtracted from these figures, however, would be payment for new line drawings. When Judith discussed the pricing of the book she estimated it would sell at $10 a copy (over $90 at this writing). Finally, Judith pointed out the new responsibility Julia was to hold: rather than having the publishing house deal with the three listed as co-writers, the contract put Julia in the position as business manager, representing the other two in all dealings and holding the power to make individual arrangements with each of them.

After treating these business matters, Judith turned to write words of high praise. She followed Angus Cameron's assessment that the future book's importance for French cooking was comparable to that of Irma Rombauer's *The Joy of Cooking*: it was a basic book that offered instruction. With that, Judith repeated the caveat that helped to convince the press's owners to publish the cookbook: it was to be sold not in competition with other cookbooks but as one that enables the home chef to use the others with greater success.

Judith then added a few minor suggestions about the cookbook's content. For example, following experimentation with recipes, she judged that, given American appetites, the portions needed to be larger. And, rather than cutting, she proposed that Julia and her co-authors offer more recipes in specific instances. These matters, however, were ones to be dealt with only in the future, once the contract was signed.

With those official words stated, Judith closed with high praise for the manuscript. She expressed her admiration for its organization, clarity, and instructive nature. She gave autumn 1961 as the anticipated publication date. And finally, on a personal note, she added her hope that this letter would be the beginning of their fruitful working relationship.[5]

Julia responded with equal warmth. "We are absolutely delighted that the firm of Alfred A. Knopf has decided to accept our cookbook." After speaking with Simca, Julia wrote that the team felt it "an honor to be associated with such a distinguished house, and we shall do everything in our power to cooperate with you in the task of publishing a complicated book such as this is. I must say, also, that we are very much impressed with the fact that you and your associates have done some real cooking out of the MS— which means that we can have truly meaningful communication on the subject of food and the technical terms concerned with its production." She closed with thanks to Judith "most sincerely for your generous letter."[6]

To family, Julia expressed her unabashed joy. Informing Charlie and Freddie, she wrote, "Great news in this establishment is that our cookbook has finally been accepted, and by Knopf. See letter enclosed. Isn't that wonderful! And we think it is a wondeful [sic] firm to be connected with as they do such nifty printing, and they sound as though they would really push it." Julia then wrote of the person about whom Charlie had once expressed some qualms: "This is all thanks to that nice Avis DeVoto, who has pushed, and hammered and enthused. Heaven knows what would have happened to the MS were it not for her—probably nothing at all."

Julia followed with a splash of realism. Acceptance by Knopf meant that "real work begins. I guess there will be horrendous revisions in the MS; then all the various proof-readings, index, etc. etc. I expect to have a right busy year starting in as soon as the contract negociations [sic] are concluded."[7]

Julia immediately informed Simca, at home in Paris. She, in return, wrote of her joy and gratitude to Julia: "I have just spent a day so exhilarated, reading and re-reading your letter, that despite the late hour, I want to thank you this very evening, my darling. Judith Jones' letter with the first terms of payment gives me wings, and if they immediately brought me to you, I would use them on the spot. . . . Because it is to you, my dear darling, that all the congratulations go. Yes, you can be proud of this result, because it is a Victory, won with much patience, without ever being discouraged."[8]

A contract meant the three named authors were now partners in business, raising the issue of money and its distribution. The contract also stated that the trio were no longer equals, for its terms placed Julia at the head, giving her "the power to make separate arrangements" with Simca and Louisette. That caused both Julia and Simca to reconsider Louisette's share of the advance and royalties.

Given that she had dropped out of the work of the cookbook, both Julia and Simca wanted to reduce Louisette's take of the proceeds, which had been set at 18%. After consulting with Paul, Julia tried out a number of ideas and decided the issue required lawyers. She turned to Paul Sheeline, Paul's lawyer and nephew, and asked Simca to obtain legal representation as well.[9] In a second letter on that same date, Julia wrote, "Money is a nasty subject, but we can avoid much trouble later on if we straighten things out as much as possible before trouble can arise."[10]

Louisette's response was simply to ignore all communications on the subject.[11] It was not until late October when she was offered a reduced 10% that Louisette agreed, and the conflict was at last resolved.[12]

Julia had begun to assert herself in her relation with Simca as early as spring 1958, but her need for authority reached a new level in early May 1960. Even before Judith Jones's letter, Julia knew of her possible editor's desire that the book have a recipe for cassoulet, causing Julia and Simca to correspond back and forth about it. Simca insisted that a real cassoulet required preserved goose. Given the difficulty of acquiring that in the United States, however,

Julia searched for and found recipes with substitutes. Simca refused them all, insisted that "nothing is a Cassoulet which does not contain preserved goose." Exasperated, Julia wrote to Avis, "I honestly wonder how anything scientific comes out of *la Belle France*, as this is so typical. None of my sources (which include the most reputable) are even considered. . . . I think that her remarks must just come under the list of dogmatic instances."[13] Julia tried to bend Simca by writing a "more explanatory letter," containing a preserved-goose-free recipe plus ten additional references allowing the dish to be made without goose. It did no good. Julia wrote Avis that Simca "ignores all of them. That is really so French—you just don't pay attention to anything, no matter how reputable, if you have your own idea about things."[14]

For a little while Paul remained his usual conflicted self. In a very long letter to Charlie, he first admitted that he was thrilled: "Our <u>Greater News</u> is of course the triumph of—after almost ten years of ceaseless endeavor [sic]—Julie-Mc W-Child—Special: The World's greatest cook! so I will say no more, as I know she is writing you, but yr correspondent is in a glow of vicarious pleasure, pride and deeply-felt satisfaction." Then, he turned to his dark side, beginning with a report on the anticipated death of the mother of the American ambassador in Oslo. He wrote, "Death is a painful subject for me because scarcely a month goes by that I don't believe I am dying, & though so far it has proved to be wrong I still go through the cruel preliminaries, inevitable if one fears death as I do." At the moment, he was experiencing not the "stomach-cancer" scare of the previous week, but rather "complete fatigue, & particularly what seemed to be a slow, almost <u>desperate</u>, laboring of my heart & some difficulty breathing."

With that, he told the tale of a recent visit to his doctor, who was beginning to have "a faint spark of sympathetic cynicism in his eye." After examining Paul thoroughly, he asked, "Do you ever go to the horse-races?" When Paul questioned why, the doctor responded, "Well, if you ever feel like going in there with the horses and racing against them you can certainly do so."[15]

Paul, though honest about his anxieties, likely included his doctor's words as an ironic commentary on his state of mind. Perhaps he, too, with Julia's news, was ready to race with the horses.

On June 23, Julia announced to Charlie and Freddie, "The contract has finally arrived—this AM—and has been OK'd by our lawyer, P. Sheeline (who is in Paris). So we are definitely in."[16] With this final confirmation, Paul and Julia made a critical decision: Paul would leave the Foreign Service. They would return to the United States for Julia's book and whatever might then follow. The timing makes the grounds of Paul's resignation clear, for on the following Sunday, three days after receiving Knopf's contract for the book, Paul wrote his brother, "I must reveal to you one of those life-decisions which has been brewing in our minds for a long time, and which we have disclosed to nobody yet except Marshall Swan [the Public Affairs Officer at the Norwegian embassy]. I've decided to leave the Foreign Service when we reach Home-Leave-time next May." Alongside, in Julia's hand, was this entreaty: "Do not mention this decision to Anybody—including girls or anybody."[17] During the years that he was posted outside of France, Paul had become increasingly unhappy in his work life. With his decision to resign from the Foreign Service—at least through the end of 1966—Paul never again wrote of experiencing psychological distress.[18]

Avis had long been hoping for the opportunity to have Julia and Paul nearby. Soon after Knopf made the decision, she wrote to Julia, "My goodness I do wish you two would come back here and live in Cambridge. Feel, longingly, that with your remark about the escape clause in lease for Irving Street, that perhaps you might just do that, and not serve out your six years or what-thehellever. Haven't you been in Europe long enough? We need you here. About time Paul stopped being statesman type, and became artist type."[19] Avis understood Paul well.

One measure of Julia's growing distance from Simca was that, in contrast to immediately telling family and Avis about their decision, she failed to let Simca know until late in August. Julia then wrote, "Haven't told you yet, but we have definitely decided to leave the government next spring when this tour is up, and will settle in Cambridge. Paul just realized he was about to be 59, and with 20 years of active life left, he wants to do what he wants for a change. (We have not announced this publicly.)"[20] After learning this, Simca sent only a polite reply.

Judith Jones now took center stage as Julia's partner in the shape of the book. Julia was truly fortunate in having Judith as her editor, for she brought her many gifts into play in working with Julia's manuscript, helping to shape it in significant ways into the book it became. Along with her close reading and culinary knowledge came her clarity regarding prose. In addition there was her great and unfailing tact in dealing with the author. This is clear in Judith's initial response to a May missive from Julia with the full manuscript and additional illustrations. Apologizing that she was not sending the final contract due to Koshland's absence, Judith promised that the press would be in contact with Julia's lawyer to use the correct language of the law enabling Julia to act for Simca and Louisette. Sensitive to Julia's concerns, she also let Julia know that, once a new illustrator was chosen, she would send sample sketches because she understood fully that Julia wanted the illustations to enable the reader to visualize each process "clearly and exactly."

Judith then addressed the issue of ingredient quantities, one that, because it involved the entire manuscript, would take time to alter. With this, she gave a telling example of her hands-on approach to the book. She had cooked boeuf bourguignon following the directions with two-and-a-half pounds of beef. While the manuscript stated it would serve six to eight at the table, in fact all was consumed by five. And because beef was easily available in the U.S., she urged more beef recipes, as well as the cassoulet and hearty French dishes eaten by peasants.[21]

As the letters between the two proceeded in the early weeks, each could take the measure of the other, and Julia learned of Judith's careful attention to detail and her precision regarding both text and illustrations. One comment of Judith's does stand out. As she returned to the question of increasing quantities, in this instance regarding beef recipes, she stated it was a judgment of one of the male editors who had read the manuscript, then added that since men were engaging in cooking "we want to please them, too."[22]

Judith also let Julia know that she was using one of the editorial secretaries, a newcomer to cooking, to test a recipe. In this instance, the result led her to burn the onions; thus the cookbook directions needed to say to turn the flame down. The secretary also reported that too much juice evaporated when the dish went into the oven. That meant that the recipe needed to direct the reader to cover the casserole and check the oven temperature so that it wasn't too high. With her customary tact, Judith softened these suggestions by letting Julia know that "as to flavor and tenderness, the verdict was excellent" as judged by the young cook and her male guest.[23] Both Judith's reaching out to inexperienced cooks on her staff to try out the recipes and her thoughtfulness in conveying the results to Julia proved useful in the effort to make the resulting cookbook foolproof.

Julia had asked Judith if she would be sending the manuscript back to her. Giving a hint about her future work, Judith wrote that she would decide later on, for she would need, after the contract was signed, to take the time to go over the manuscript with care.[24]

As the days passed, Julia faced the problem of many authors that her editor seemed to move slowly. In frustration, Julia wrote at midsummer, "This is a wail from the far North. I am at a standstill waiting for your final word on manuscript corrections. Poised and ready to go, with insert pages all typed, I can't do anything more until I hear from you. I realize, of course, that ours is not the only fish in your sea of books—but the Aug. 15 deadline has me worried."[25]

With the writer in Oslo and the editor in New York, letters such as this one sometimes crossed. Likely before receiving Julia's wail, Judith had written that she had gone over the new recipes for cassoulet and beef carefully and was enclosing the carbons that she had marked in red with a few questions regarding style. Judith added the procedures Julia was to follow if she had changes to the text.

Continuing on a different note, Judith found the book now had sufficient number of recipes to represent true French cooking at its best, and it was organized effectively. Thus neither she nor Julia should make changes in the text, unless they found issues that emerged along the way.

Judith had requested more recipes for French "earthy dishes," and Julia had complied by adding several. Nonetheless, Julia pointed out that there were actually many scattered in the book. Judith thanked her for this and then explained the source of her request: recently she had visited a French charcuterie on Ninth Avenue in New York City. When she got home with the goods, she found few recipes in her collection of recent French cookbooks that called for the shop's ingredients, the food she remembered "eating with such pleasure in people's homes in France."[26]

Judith also confirmed Julia's suspicion that her editing of the manuscript was being delayed by her responsibility to work on other books with earlier publishing dates. When Julia replied, she made clear what was concerning her the most. "Just as I thought, you are swamped with all kinds of other work! Well, I shall just be patient; but we shall not make that Aug 15th deadline, and I hereby wish to point out this will not be due to the authors' dilatoriness."[27]

During this time of Julia's correspondence with Judith over the details of the cookbook, Simca was having difficulties that Julia suspected were due to rheumatism or arthritis. In writing to Avis, Julia told her that Simca "can hardly type her hands are so stiff." To deal with this, Simca was planning to "take a 'cure' at one of those French watering places in July."[28] The "cure" was now a regular feature of Simca's life. Nonetheless, wherever Simca happened to be, she continued her work on the book.

Simca was finding many errors, especially in the French titles of the recipes, and in a series of letters offered corrections. Julia's first reaction was to compliment Simca on her work and reassure her. "That is just fine that you have been able to go over the MS. All your suggestions look fine to me, and I shall just incorporate them. You are, after all the authority of French titles, so whatever you say goes." She then added a caution, writing that in order to be professional, "We have to get everything right at this point," not at the later stage of proofreading.[29]

The next day, however, after she had gone over Simca's suggested corrections, Julia took a step back, for she found that Simca was changing titles that the two had earlier agreed on. Julia now realized that she had to take charge and make certain executive decisions. She wrote to Simca that she had made too many small corrections on the text to send it back to her. It was "one trouble in not being together, but can't be helped."[30] Julia did enclose some new pages to be inserted in the manuscript, presumably the new recipes. Perhaps to appease Simca, Julia closed with these handwritten words, "Much love, mon adorable amie, from us both."[31] At this point, Julia was balancing firmness with heightened words of affection, saving expressions of her frustrations with Simca for Avis's eyes and, likely, for Paul's ears.

Avis's role shifted after Knopf made its decision. With that goal attained, she clearly wanted to participate in the process of turning the manuscript into a book. During the book's long development Avis had sent recipes for testing to Ben Fairbank, a friend who was an engineer and home cook. She later loaned him her copy of the entire manuscript. With its acceptance by Knopf, Fairbank returned it to her, and Avis noticed "on leafing through it that he has penciled in queries here and there." Avis was limited by her heavy work schedule until Harvard's commencement, but when it was over she wrote Julia that she planned to "go through the ms. and make note of same for you."[32] By late summer, when that manuscript was in Julia's hands, she mentioned to Judith that she could use Avis's copy of the manuscript to make the changes, although it was "a bit used as it has been cooked from."[33]

In the meantime, Avis tried to help Julia understand the workings at Knopf, but she was, to her regret, now cut out of the loop. Although she had asked to be copied on Judith's correspondence with Julia, this had not happened. Thus, in responding to Julia's frustration in mid-July, likely regarding Judith's slowness in getting the manuscript back to her, Avis wrote that she failed to "understand why Judith doesn't get you off the hook. . . . I don't know what has been going on, except Koshland told me over the telephone a week or so ago that they are all more enthusiastic than ever, and that the girls around the office are always borrowing a page or two, just for the night, to do something special." Avis also wrote that she didn't think Alfred Knopf had seen the manuscript, but she wasn't concerned, as, "we have plenty strength down there."[34]

Although she was cut out of the editing process at Knopf, Avis was fortunate in having Bill Koshland to keep her informed of what was happening at his end. He was her primary tie at Knopf, and he played a gentle hand, informing her of all good news. For example, when he conveyed to Julia that the British publisher Cassell was seeking to acquire a British edition of the cookbook, he wrote, "I have not had a chance to pass the word along to Avis yet, but will try to get her on the phone before the week is out. Although I think she is just about due to go off to Breadloaf. [sic]"[35]

In the meantime, Paul, newly invigorated by his decision to leave the Foreign Service, took on important work for Julia's book. For the earlier set of drawings made by the illustrator John L. Moore, in anticipation of the cookbook's publication by Houghton Mifflin, Paul had photographed Julia as she prepared many of the recipes. The powers that be at Knopf, however, were unsatisfied with these drawings and, after trying out several illustrators, ultimately chose Sidonie Coryn to create a new set. The book's illustrations had always been intended as serious contributions, not decoration. Some were chosen to capture the look of certain dishes in progress or completion, but many were meant to clarify difficult processes from the perspective of the cook. To capture Julia's hands at work, Paul had taken photographs from above, while standing on a ladder at Julia's back.

Knopf had the photographs Paul had prepared for Moore, but, even before choosing the future illustrator, Judith asked for additional ones. For example, because of the difficulties that Judith and other testers found with preparing the rolled omelette, there needed to be a line illustration that showed one hand grasping the pan handle and the other the plate or fork, as well as other drawings to represent visually the complicated motions required with both hands on the handle of the pan for shaking and rolling the eggs. Writing to Charlie, Paul stated, "I have been taking a series of pix of Julia's hands. Technical cooking processes (making an omelette, slicing carrots) to send to Knopf, to be used by whoever they decide on as illustrator for the book." Noting the change of illustrators, he reported, likely with pride in his new commission, that the publisher "will pick someone else who will work from photos by me."[36] All of Paul's work was uncompensated by Knopf and received no credit in print. In a gender role-reversal for his era, he was the supporting spouse.

Judith got back to Julia in mid-August, a month after their last communication. She belatedly reassured Julia that she was in the clear regarding the contractual August 15 deadline, as she had met its requirements months before by sending the requested additional recipes. Judith offered her full apology for the length of time it had taken her to work through the manuscript. As Julia had guessed correctly, her cookbook had competed with many other projects on Judith's desk, but more importantly, Judith went slowly because she found that to deal with the text in the careful manner required she could only work with a limited number of pages at any one sitting. Finally came words that linked editor and author. In reading the manuscript, Judith found "the temptation to stop and cook something is ever present." She then reassured Julia that she should not worry about the publication schedule, as the press had planned for plenty of time. Judith then went beyond both apology and reassurance to compliment Julia as being "marvelously quick and responsive." To that, she added her own feelings: "you can't imagine what a pleasure it is to work with such a diligent author."[37] As an editor, Judith Jones had a special way of bonding with her authors.

She sent editorial notes only on the first section of the manuscript, in the expectation that Julia could begin working on its issues while she edited the next section. Noting that many of her suggestions involved only minor editorial changes, Judith turned again to offer praise: "The instructions are so beautifully clear that it is seldom I find any minor slip or confusion."

During the long wait Julia had sent a list of issues regarding the format of the book, including the use of two columns on the page to make it "easy to follow when one is cooking" and having running heads, "so when one is thumbing through the book one knows where one is." When Julia explained the importance of "French accents in titles," she gave this example: "Who knows what a PATE might be; could be 'pâté' [head], or 'pâté' [forcemeat or paste]. Also, the accents make things look more French." On the original letter, Judith marked each of Julia's directions with an affirmative response.[38]

Later, in the mid-August editorial report, Judith explained how these elements would be translated on the pages of the book and promised she would work on these issues with the book's designer. She praised Paul's new photos, taken to guide the book's illustrations, writing that his images give "such a clear and immediate picture of each operation." Understanding how important the look of the cookbook was to Julia as author and Paul as her photographer and helper, Judith offered Julia reassuring words that gave her commitment that the final book should "look marvelously elegant and appetizing." And she added an issue important to Julia, the promise that Julia would have the final right of approval for all the drawings.[39]

In early August, Bill Koshland checked in to give Julia the news that Cassell & Co., an esteemed British publisher, without having seen the manuscript, "have on the basis of our enthusiasm agreed to make a formal contract with us for a British edition of your book." The offer included the normal British "standard for all cookbooks." With the title still undecided, Cassell asked for the freedom to change it and also, with the approval of Knopf, to adjust the text for the British audience.[40]

In learning this, Julia replied in a letter to Koshland, copied to both Simca and Louisette, that the offer from Cassell was "most welcome news. As agent for the three of us co-authors, I formally accept." However this came with one condition: "the text must definitely be changed wherever necessary to fit the English terminology and products. If this is not done, many of the recipes will be meaningless to British cooks." Julia continued, "As all three of us have close British Contacts, we have been hoping for a British edition somehow, so couldn't be more pleased."[41] Bill conveyed all

Julia's requirements to the British publisher and, with his usual tact, wrote to Julia, "Your position is sound and I know they will be as careful as can be." He then added some new information, that the idea of a French edition was in the wind. It needed, however, to wait until Knopf could give evidence of a book either through galleys or with the book itself. He would be consulting with Knopf's Paris agent when she visited New York in October, to "see where we go from there." Koshland then added that he was going to check to see if all the packages Julia had sent to Judith had arrived; and in a postscript, he wrote that they had. Though the primary manager at Knopf, Bill Koshland seems to have found no detail beneath him.[42]

Judith's editing of the first section of her manuscript was a nineteen-page document titled "NOTES ON PART I OF FRENCH COOKBOOK." In preparing it, she likely followed the publishing house's practice. She first addressed technical matters and then turned to general issues involving style. She went beyond simply making corrections to giving their rationale, enabling her author to understand why a change was needed. For example, Judith cautioned against the use of the impersonal "one" and urged that Julia change it to the more familiar "you." In Judith's judgment, "one" was both "mannered" and sounds as though it were a translation from the French "on." She gave Julia an added reason for the suggested change that likely hit home: "you attract the reader more by addressing him or her directly."[43]

In working through the manuscript, Judith focused on language, raising issues large and small. Recognizing this cookbook's innovation was its teaching of French culinary methods, she suggested an important word change: The initial recipe offering instruction for a cooking procedure needed in all cases to be renamed "the master recipe." Judith preferred that term because it suggested that it is not only important "but the one that establishes a standard."

As editor, Judith offered directions for making the text more precise. She insisted on page references regarding procedures previously discussed, suggested format changes, and offered language to ensure that the author remain tactful and respectful to readers. But Judith Jones also brought to this book her own advanced culinary knowledge, her love of French food, and her experience as a dedicated home cook in the United States. She retained, as well, her own clear memory of the directions needed by someone just learning to make her way around a kitchen. She used this personal knowledge and experience to call for meaningful changes and additions to the text.

In various ways, she sought to ensure the future book's careful consideration in dealing with inexperienced readers. For example, she twice suggested that Julia adopt the word "novice" as a polite way of referring to them. In many cases it seemed like Judith was putting herself in the position of "novice," imagining herself as a cook working with a recipe for the first time. For example, in dealing with a sauce recipe, she wrote in regard to the pan being used, Julia needed to add "then empty and dry it quickly."[44] At another point, when encountering tomatoes in a list of ingredients, Judith wrote that Julia needed to state that the tomatoes were to be "skinned or peeled."[45]

The novices on Judith's staff at Knopf aided her suggestions: their ignorance of the meaning of herb bouquet led Judith to suggest instead its ingredients—laurel, parsley, and thyme. Judith explained, "cooks are forgetful and I think we should give them this small help here."[46]

Judith's knowledge of cooking tools came into play. Copper pots were coming into American use, and that required attention to their potential toxicity. If the lining intended to keep poison from the copper from leaching into food was faulty, Judith wrote, how could one know the danger point? Was it "when the copper begins to show through?"[47] Later in the report Judith requested Julia discuss plastic bowls as good substitutes for copper ones, as the latter could be expensive and difficult to find. Judith brought Avis into the discussion as she remembered learning from her that Julia had reported that she "had found the American plastic bowl almost as efficient as the French copper one."[48]

In one of her most interesting comments, Judith wrote a "confession" regarding Julia's rolled omelette recipe. She had spent much of a Sunday morning "trying to perfect your technique. I even practiced with dried beans outside on the terrace, and managed to use up a whole box of them before I could turn them over in a single group." Turning to eggs, she failed completely, as her two-egg omelette came out looking like a "fritter." She wondered if Julia should even offer this omelette method for she did not want the book to "scare beginners." It should instead "lead the reader by the hand, showing them that even the most difficult is not impossible." She would ask Bill Koshland, whom she regarded as a good home cook, to give the recipe a try. If he had the same experience with its difficulty, she would suggest Julia add an easier method.[49]

Judith then gave her own method of making an omelette. Although Julia might judge it "a poor tough thing," Judith liked it because its result was "deliciously soft and tender," as well as "certainly easier for the novice."[50] The end result became two omelette recipes in the cookbook, both the relatively easy one to make and the more complicated rolled one. The latter got special care, with four drawings demonstrating its difficult maneuvers.

An issue that would clearly require much work to resolve involved the different measurements used in French and American recipes. Julia and Simca had decided to translate French weight measures into American cups. Judith realized that while this worked in many cases, in dealing with fish, the amounts needed to be in pounds and ounces. Moreover when the ingredient was potatoes, neither would work, because Americans counted potatoes by their quantity.[51]

Judith took care with the illustrations. In one case, she felt there needed to be an additional drawing to go with the recipe for "molded French Pancakes," as she found the "directions a bit hard to visualize."[52] She also pointed out that the photo illustrating a particular recipe showed an oval dessert spoon, not the round soup spoon described in the text. No detail was too small to attract Judith's notice and, if need be, to correct.

As Judith finished the fish chapter, she realized it was lacking a full discussion of mussels. While there was a recipe for moules marinières, the manuscript presented it only as a garnish. Judith wrote, "a fish chapter without a mussels recipe in a French cookbook seems inadequate."[53] This led Julia and Simca to return to their records to find mussels recipes and develop them for the book; by August 24, Julia put that mutual effort in the mail.

The poultry section of the book raised a number of important issues. Significant were the different standards of doneness in the U.S. and France. After testing, Judith found the method in the manuscript left the chicken "by American standards . . . slightly underdone." Julia needed to warn readers of this, as their thermometers would not go as high as they normally did in roasting. After going over Julia's chicken directions in detail and requesting slight changes, Judith returned to the doneness issue to ask the question, "Is 'ten to twenty minutes roasting' really enough?"[54]

Desiring to keep the future book French, Judith rejected Julia's deletion of a sentence about the French not washing their chicken. Asking for it to be restored, she revealed her interest in conveying its connections to life in France. "Frankly, I like this kind of note because the whole book is so full of the way French do things and I think this kind of detail adds a special flavor."[55]

As Judith ended her report, she returned to some larger matters, including giving instruction early in the book on clarifying butter, degreasing, and preparing stock in advance from poultry scraps. She closed with the previously expressed need to alter the ingredient amounts or number of portions, because as written, the dishes will not "satisfy American appetites."[56]

At moments, Judith's own likes and dislikes peer out of her "Notes." Sausages had been one of Judith's announced interests, and when she turned to recipes that included them, she both commented on the different kinds and asked Julia to specify which one was to be used.[57] Judith held a clear distaste for commercial potato chips. Thus when she saw the term mentioned as a food accompaniment, she feared readers might think of "the American packaged kind, heaven forbid." At that point, Julia needed to give a cross reference to the recipe for homemade ones.[58]

The single instance when Judith criticized Julia in a direct way was on noting Julia's negative reference to competing recipes for the "average coq au vin." Seeing this as an "advertisement for your own book," Judith asked Julia to delete it. She informed Julia that Knopf would play this part when its staff created the book's promotional material. The press was working on ways to demonstrate that the instruction in Julia's book was necessary "to use effectively the other cookbooks readers may have already on their shelves."[59] Judith also attempted to temper Julia's exuberance by requesting that she avoid throughout the word "happy," perhaps using "delicious" for a substitute.[60]

One element in Judith's report led to extended conflict with Simca. Judith asked Julia to specify, when mentioned in the text, some of the good orange liqueurs available in American stores.[61] Julia's compliance caused Simca to fight against this insertion. Members of her family were still in the Benedictine business, the liqueur created by her grandfather, and they would be angry at seeing brand names of competing liqueurs in her book. Ultimately, Simca saw the names excised.[62]

Upon receiving Judith's "Notes," Julia must have taken a deep breath before setting to work on its many suggestions. One thing is clear from the markings on her copy—Julia recognized the knowledge and skill that Judith brought to her reading of the manuscript. As a polite editor, Judith had framed all her corrections as suggestions. This led Julia to put check marks in the left margin as reminders that she had made the changes Judith sought or had in other ways resolved the issue. Only twice did Julia not make a check, but on both occasions this was because the changes she made were in a manner somewhat different from her editor's suggestions.[63]

By this time, Julia and Simca had worked together for many years, but since 1958 Julia had grown more independent of her cookbook partner's judgment. Evidence of this is even clearer after Julia received Judith's reading of the first half of the manuscript. Julia had kept records documenting the cookbook's development and could track the countless decisions they had made. Simca, so important in the creation and testing of the recipes, had only her memory and her authority as the "authentic" Frenchwoman. As they dealt with decisions that were seemingly minor—but important because

Julia was facing Judith's suggestions—Julia saw greater need to assert her authority.

In late August, Julia gave Simca only a summary of the changes to their manuscript, stating that "Most of the corrections are matters of English style and grammar, and don't concern you." One exception concerned the recipe for omelettes. Julia wrote that Judith has "so far be[en] unable to make an omelette following the MS directions. Actually, that technique needs to be demonstrated. She suggests that we also include another method."

Judith had also written that "people will be disappointed if they don't find a master moule [mussels] recipe." Julia let Simca know that she thought they could add a section of three pages based on Simca's "two pages from your magnificent fish chapter of 1953—and what a lot of work you put into that!" With that, Julia suggested five recipes, asking Simca only to approve names or suggest new ones. Possibly realizing that she might insult Simca by moving ahead without her, Julia penned an afterthought on the side: "Any more or less suggestions?" Nevertheless, once again, Julia took command: "I will work up the moules, and the omelettes, and send them along to you as soon as possible."[64] Three days later, Julia sent her editor both groups of recipes.

In a follow-up report almost a week later, Julia let Simca know that she was coming to the end of Judith's suggestions and would soon send Simca the new pages. With this, Julia commented, "Have done a bit of re-writing, as usual. It would be quite easy to start re-writing the whole book, of course! But shall refrain." All of this was happening at a complicated time, as Julia's father—with whom she and Paul had profound political disagreements—was about to arrive in Oslo with Julia's stepmother to visit the Childs.[65] About this interruption in her work, however, Julia had nothing to say.

Judith Jones sent Julia her "NOTES ON FINAL PORTION OF FRENCH COOKBOOK" on the last day of August. They were not as extensive as the first, she wrote, because Julia had seemed to accept "most of the general style matters." With a clear understanding of Julia's "whole design of the book," she urged Julia to think of "the proper format" to make visually clear on the page "that sub-recipes . . . were dependent on the master recipe." For example, it was important to persuade readers not to "rush into a chocolate soufflé . . . without studying your whole section on the making of soufflés."

Delighted with the news that Julia would be resettling in Cambridge, Judith wrote that it meant "we can do so much more with you here, in terms of publicity." And with her usual grace, she added, "by that time I think you and I should have the pleasure of sitting down to a meal together."[66]

Judith's fifteen pages of notes on the final section again revealed her knowledge of cuisine, her experienced hand with cookbook directions, and her attention to the style and clarity of the text. As with the earlier "NOTES," this second one is filled with specific instructions going page by page, adding words here, cleaning up language there. Occasionally Judith caught a missing step or a vague direction. She suggested adding two elements that involved the whole manuscript, an asterisk at the point in which the dish could be prepared ahead of time and putting in the timing involved for such processes as marinating ingredients.[67]

Again, as Julia read these notes, she made comments meant for her eyes only. Late in the notes, one response stands out. Judith had registered surprise at finding no eggs in a rémoulade sauce and then wrote that she trusted Julia with these words: "I am sure you are right but I was just checking because it seemed unusual to me. As a matter of fact, in this whole book I don't think you have missed a single ingredient, and that is astonishing." Reading this, Julia wrote in the margin these words: "She ain't seen the misses!"[68]

Keeping to her decision to limit Simca's involvement in these revisions, in mid-September, Julia reported to her simply that she had been working hard after receiving Judith's letter "commenting on the rest of the MS." Julia explained that this involved "mostly questions of style, messy grammar, things she [Judith] didn't think were quite clear. How lucky we are to have someone like her to go over the book! She sounds like such a nice person." In addition, Judith had stated that they needed "a recipe on sautéed potatoes, as they are mentioned as garnitures in many veg. suggestions for main course dishes." Julia then wrote that she was enclosing her worksheet on "the various recipes I have, including yours" for sautéed potatoes, and that she planned to "work up a formal recipe tomorrow."[69]

In October, Julia and Paul traveled to Simca's retreat, Bramafam. Reporting to Avis, Julia wrote, "The vacation was good. The S. of France with Simca was heavenly; and our 10 days in Paris were just right."[70] Julia was continuing efforts to keep her collaboration with Simca alive. Understanding the importance of publicizing their work and gaining a reputation in the food world, she had written to Simca, "Think we must go right ahead collecting and experimenting on new recipes, for our future collaboration on articles, etc. for US magazines. If we can ever get ourselves a reputation in the US, and manage to crack that difficult coterie of magazine writers who try so hard to keep new people out, we can have a very good thing for ourselves."[71] It was Simca, however, who was about to "crack" that world. She received an offer to write for *Cuisine et Vins*, an important French culinary magazine.

Julia was delighted, but first it was necessary to check with Judith Jones to see if Simca could use recipes from their forthcoming cookbook, and she wrote her right away. In replying to Julia's letter, Judith relayed that she had given it to Bill Koshland. She explained that there were issues regarding copyright that needed to "be judged by our expert," and promised that Koshland would quickly be in touch with her.[72]

Bill immediately sent Julia a long response, carefully explaining the copyright issues involved, the gist being the possibility that taking recipes from the future cookbook could throw "the entire work into the public domain." Then, in his tactful and thoughtful way, he wrote, "Needless to say, we do not want to stand in the way of the TROIS GOURMANDES and the editor of <u>Cuisine et Vins de France</u>. Why don't you, from your vast store of recipes not included in our book go ahead with them and instead of saying or having them say in the magazine that the menu is from the author's book, something could be said to the effect that the menu is 'similar to' recipes to be included in the authors' forthcoming book on French cooking etc. How does this strike you?" Summing up, he added, "To repeat then, by all means, tie yourselves up with the French magazine but use material that is <u>not</u> to be in the book."

Julia hoped Simca's contributions to *Cuisine et Vins* would establish her as a French culinary authority, imagining this as useful promotion for their book. Her understanding in this case clashed with that of Koshland. His eye was on the promotion of the book itself. As he informed Julia, he gave her a business lesson from a publisher's perspective. Knopf was planning to promote the cookbook with important American magazines, such as *Vogue*, *Harper's Bazaar*, and *House & Garden*, but were reserving this for a time "much nearer to publication when the impact is, by common consent, regarded as more effective." He ended his letter with a friendly, personal close: "I haven't seen nor spoken to Avis in ages, but as I plan to be in Cambridge over Thanksgiving I know we will have a reunion."[73]

With Koshland's clear directions, Julia began to work with Simca, using material not in their book manuscript, to compose a monthly menu with recipes for *Cuisine et Vins*. In early December she wrote to Charlie and Freddie, "Simca has gotten in with a good French magazine, Cuisine et Vins de France, and we are going to do one menu for them per month starting January. None of the recipes can come from our book, so it means a pile of cooking to be sure all is foolproof and fine." Julia also wrote that she was very busy, for in addition to this work, she was giving two cooking classes each week: "I have literally hardly been out of the kitchen or off the machine for weeks, and I love it."[74]

The magazine job brought Simca some income for each issue. Additionally, it offered her a diversion and gave Julia a chance to praise her for establishing herself as an important culinary authority in France. When the first issue came out in early February of the following year, Julia was ecstatic. She wrote to tell Avis that Simca was sending her a subscription, "and there you will see the first recipe by LES TROIS GOURMANDES published

ANYWHERE IN THE WORLD. Hooray! I confess I can hardly keep my eyes off it. . . . they have printed it up just fine, with a center spread.[75]

Lingering during much of this period was the question of the cookbook's title. Julia and Paul got into the spirit of the chase. In an undated missive decorated with the "Ecole Des 3 Gourmands" stamp of Paul's design, they offered this challenge to an unknown body of friends and family members: "WANT TO WIN A FOIE GRAS ? ? ?

"Do Y*O*U want to win a great big 'Fois Gras en Boc Clouté de Truffes'? . . . All you have to do is to think up a nifty title for the greatest French cookbook in the world today. Just invent a short, irresistible, informative, unforgettable, catchy book title implying that this is the book on French cooking for Americans, the only book, the book to supercede [sic] all books, the basic French cookbook." Takers should "submit as many titles as you wish, and send them all to Paul Child." Taking charge, Paul used his stamp to give his address in Norway along with his name.[76]

As this contest suggested, the title seemed to require many hands on deck. At Knopf, titles fell in Judith's domain, although many others at the firm needed to approve the one chosen. In mid-July, writing to Julia, Judith expressed her hope that Julia had title ideas, as she was finding herself unable to find the right words. In an unusual expression of self-deprecation, Judith wrote that all titles that had come to her mind seemed "heavy handed."[77] Coincidentally, Judith was about to receive Julia's letter containing a list of possibilities, many likely coming from Paul's unknown "contestants." Julia underlined three of them for emphasis, and two of the three were "The Art of French Cooking" and "The Master French Cookbook."[78]

As late as October 26, when Julia reported to Simca that the manuscript was now in the hands of the copy editor, she added that the work still had no title.[79] In mid-November came word from Bill Koshland that the search at Knopf was still in earnest. "It has been rather fun testing one another out on them and I know we will in the end come up with something that will satisfy all concerned and be what is known in the trade as a 'selling' title."[80]

Actually, that fun had just come to an end. On that same November day Judith wrote that such a title had been found. She let Julia know that she had not been neglecting her, as she had been focusing on the title, a project that engaged everyone in the office. She had explored the ones Julia had sent and also asked those in her office to come up with their own suggestions. Among Julia's suggestions, the group focused on mastery and master but avoided "the master of." Inspiration had hit and they had a solution:

"MASTERING THE ART OF FRENCH COOKING."

Although Judith sought to learn the reaction of Julia and her two co-authors, she announced peremptorily that everyone at Knopf not only approved but also felt they had finally found "exactly the right title." She explained: "'Mastering' becomes an active verb now." At the same time, the title nudged the prospective customer to think that it was necessary to purchase this book prior to buying any of the others. With this came a postscript asking Julia to give the choice serious thought so that the title could be set.[81]

Of course Julia obeyed, and likely even cheered, for her underlined suggestions offered in July may well have provided the trigger—"The Art of French Cooking" and "The Master French Cookbook." Written confirmation of Julia's acceptance came in her letter to Bill Koshland, where she described "MASTERING THE ART OF FRENCH COOKING" as "a fine title, and we hope you have really decided upon it."[82] No one at either Knopf or in the households of the authors ever regretted that decision.

Moving from manuscript to book, especially a lengthy and intricately detailed cookbook, can take both time and much tedious work. In Judith's case this was enhanced by her deep interest in the work and in what it could teach her. In early January 1961, she wrote to Julia that for Christmas she received a new omelette pan with slanting sides, and "now that I have broken it in sufficiently I am going to have another go at both of the omelette recipes." She promised to let Julia know the results.[83]

By January 1961, Julia felt close enough to Judith to write about what she perceived as a failure. She had performed terribly at an interview for a women's weekly in Oslo in talking about herself and French cooking. "I should have prepared a selection of points to bring up in the conversation. . . . They want a good story, and they won't get one interviewing a naïve bumpkin who politely answers a lot of dumb questions. I should give the works, subtly, but tellingly—drama, etc. Invent a personality, in other words, or at least invent something." Julia went on to add, "I think it is very lucky for me to be having a few experiences like this here [in Norway], where it is not a matter of life and death; and I just hope some one else wants an interview so I can practice out a new technique. This kind of thing is not my line at all, but I think that if I can remember that I am purely a book, or part of a book to be more precise, and that it is not they but book/me who is leading the interview, I may then be less naïve."[84]

In the months that followed, letters and packets of manuscript and drawings in various stages of development moved back and forth between New York and Oslo. Although always concerned about the book's publication schedule and delays, Judith often ended her careful instructions with complimentary words, such as those in mid-February 1961: "you are such an extra-ordinarily efficient worker that you will help us to make up for the lost time."[85]

Judith was the one at Knopf who was not only delegated to move the work along, but also was charged with conveying certain financial arrangements. She wrote that by contract, Julia was responsible for paying the illustrator Knopf had hired, Sidonie Coryn, her flat fee of $1,000 [close to $9,000 at the time of this writing] for the drawings, deductible from future royalties. Judith attempted to soften the blow by letting Julia know that Knopf had hired Warren Chappell, "one of the finest designers," for the book, and he will "do handsome decorative illustrations for the title pages as well as his usual fine typographic handling," and that the funds for this were "part of the publisher's investment."[86]

Paul's enthusiasm for Chappell's work likely helped, but in accepting these terms Julia first put forward the instructive purpose of the drawings, to give "the point of view of the cook, as she will see things," before mentioning money. She then stated that as the fee was "a good, fat price . . . I shall have no hesitation in being very finicky indeed." She closed with words of happiness about being published by Knopf: "you do pay careful attention to design—and that is a rare thing in modern, competetive [sic] publishing."[87]

Even as Judith worried about getting behind schedule, she took great care in seeing that the manuscript was free of errors. When a second copy editor took over from the first, Judith had her go over the work of the first one to check for inconsistencies. One example of the lengths the new copy editor took was that she checked the accuracy of information in the manuscript regarding pressure cookers by calling Bloomingdale's, a New York store that had them in stock. When she inquired about the pounds of pressure of the pressure cookers in the store, she learned that their maximum was fifteen pounds, not the twenty in Julia's text. Julia then made the correction.[88]

The copy editor found problems of language and consistency, understandable in a book written with a co-writer for over eight years. In early March, reviewing the vegetable chapter, Julia wrote to Judith that she wondered "how I could have written such a mish-mash." In offering thanks to the copy editor for pointing out errors she hadn't seen, Julia wrote that their invisibility was because she had "become so used to the mumble of my own words."[89]

In early March, Judith wrote that the first part of the manuscript was now at the printer after the copy editor had finished her work on it. This first round of printing would produce galleys that would be sent to Julia to read and correct.[90] During this time Julia was continuing to send new pages on vegetables to be copy edited. Calling the manuscript a "rabbit warren," she admitted that the complications of publishing the cookbook were beginning to hit her: "Cook books are horrible things to print, aren't they?"[91]

As Julia worked steadily over the manuscript, returning to it in its various stages to catch mistakes, she found her work made much more difficult by

Simca's continuing demands for substantive changes to the recipes. Julia repeatedly reminded her that she had earlier agreed on the text, and it was now too late in the publishing process to change her mind. In mid-March, she had informed Judith that she wanted to send Simca the "extra MS copy," if Judith didn't need it. Julia wanted Simca to "give a final check to all the French titles." In addition, she asked if Judith "could send Mme. Beck a few pages of the galley, just so she would get an idea of the splendor that is to be?"[92] Julia was to regret both these requests.

As the galleys were ready to send, Judith sent Julia a stern warning, likely a version of what she normally sent to authors at this point. She wanted Julia to realize that she was "the one fully responsible for this job." First-time authors often wrongly think that the publisher also corrects proofs, and Judith wanted to be clear with Julia that this was false assumption.[93] Julia's initial reaction to actually receiving her work in print, however, was ecstatic. She wrote to Judith that the first set of galleys arrived, "and they look wonderful. It is hard to believe, even seeing with me own eyes, that we are really in production. A world-shaking event!"[94]

A serious complication arose, however, after Judith sent Simca not just a few pages of galleys, but forty-four. This opened the door to a new set of problems for Julia that threatened serious conflict with her co-author. Julia explained to Simca that she had requested galleys for her not to make corrections, but rather because "you had worked so hard for so many years, you deserved to see something at last in print regardless of expense." Ignoring this assertion, Simca sent Julia a very long list of corrections on the galleys she received.[95]

Julia reminded Simca that the time for revisions had long passed, and that she had warned her regarding this when they were in each other's company at Bramafam in October. To keep herself from being shocked by what she was reading, Simca needed to go over their correspondence to refresh her memory of what she had approved in writing.

Julia then turned to describe their long-established mutual understanding regarding their joint work. She wrote that her own job had been "to translate your recipes into English, after trying them out, send them back to you for comment and suggestions, changing them as we . . . mutually agreed, and then send[ing] you the final form, which you also were to (and did) personally OK." This final agreement by Simca was essential, "otherwise it would not be a joint book. If you now do not agree with what you formerly said, it is just—malheureusement—too bad." Then, announcing that this would be the last time, Julia went over each of Simca's comments, in the hope of putting her "mind somewhat at rest."

She closed with these words: "I think it is a tragedy that we cannot be together for all this final work; however, it seems to me that we have done pretty well together through our years of separation. But I just want to be sure that you don't feel anything is being put over on you, and this is not your book!" Reminding Simca of her importance in generating the recipes for the book, Julia wrote, "It is GOUT [taste] SIMCA, and there is no doubt about it. The only thing is that you have forgotten what your GOUT used to be!" In the hope of getting support, Julia headed the letter: "Please let Jean read this, SVP [s'il vous plaît]."[96]

With Paul away from home, Julia needed to vent to someone, and that proved to be Avis. Julia seemed to be shouting as she wrote, "I am just going WOOOOBIS with our dear old friend, Simca, and I have to talk to somebody or I'll burst even more." She described Simca's letter as stating "in effect—change everything. How did you ever put this in? This is not correct, etc. etc. The big boob has had all of this stuff for years, she has OK'd everything, again and again and again, and again and again. I took the whole MS down to her last October, and she presumably went over everything." In her list of examples, Julia wrote, "WHY ADD A SLICE OF BREAD TO THE PISTOU SOUP, she says. This was HER SUGGESTION, god dammit. . . . I am not going to make one correction on the stuff she has changed her mind on, not one. I will correct any downright errors, certainly, but not until I have consulted proper French sources, which luckily I have."

After this explosion, Julia reassured Avis, "There shall not be a break between us, as I am far too fond of the old goat; but it will take some delicate manoeuvering [sic] to try and make her realize some of the truths of publishing, and of the truths (if such they be) that she herself has written and/or approved."[97]

Within days, Julia received four letters from Simca that eased her mind. Feeling their relationship was restored, Julia wrote, "I am glad we now understand each other about the galley proofs. . . . I could not bear to have anything come in the way of our close friendship—as you are our soeur—but better than a blood-born soeur, because you are of our own choosing." Soothed by Simca's letter, Julia wrote, "I can breath [sic] and sleep easier."[98]

Some years afterward, Avis visited the two women in France and watched while they cooked together. She wrote to herself these words, reflecting on Julia and Simca's long relationship: "Simca is a creative genius. . . . She is also inaccurate, illogical, hard to pin down, and stubborn as a mule. . . . Julia is deeply logical, orderly, accurate, painstaking, patient, determined to get all this knowledge clearly on paper. And she can be just as stubborn as Simca is, and will plug away trying to convince Simca until suddenly Simca changes her position, and from then on she [Simca] will talk as if it were her own idea all along. I have seen her do this on a number of occasions. Like the great cassoulet argument, mostly conducted by mail." Unwittingly, Avis also gave an apt description of the two authors' conflict over the galley pages.[99]

Toward the end of April, Julia and Paul decided to leave Norway sooner than planned and booked passage by ocean liner across the Atlantic on May 27, with a June 5 arrival in New York. Julia wrote to Judith, "The book actually is more important than anything. Then we shall be home, and entirely at your command."[100] In the exchange of letters that followed, the two planned to have lunch on the day after the ship's landing, June 6. Confirming this, Julia wrote, "It will be great fun to meet you at long last!"[101]

As letters flew back and forth from New York to Oslo, a great respect had developed between author and editor. And because both women were who they were, Judith and Julia added to their respect something more—friendship. Although always maintaining her position as editor, Judith had now come to be—in Julia's mind at least—a member of her team.

Chapter Nine

The Launch

On June 5, 1961, when Julia and Paul arrived in New York, Julia had taken the last big step toward the publication of *Mastering the Art of French Cooking*. On board the ship, she had spent her time creating the book's index. Once she met Judith Jones the next day, it would be out of her hands, and Julia could begin to think seriously about the book's promotion.

But first came the beginning of Julia and Paul's new life in New England. As they awaited their household possessions coming from their Washington house, Avis took them in, and they went with her to Maine. Avis had the opportunity, during this time, to read proofs with Julia. After Avis went to the Bread Loaf Writers Conference in Vermont, the Childs initially stayed in her house; but once Avis wrangled an invitation for Paul to take the conference's photographs, he and Julia joined her at Bread Loaf. Finally, in mid-August, the movers arrived from Washington with the Childs' household goods. This came with a bill for $500, but because the Childs had neither ready cash nor an American bank account, Avis had to cover the cost with a loan from her bank.[1] Julia and Paul moved into 103 Irving Street on September 6.

Prior to that date, Julia was able to write two publicity pieces for Judith. In summer 1960, early in the process of preparing the book for publication, Julia had sent Judith her response to Knopf's author's questionnaire, meant to aid the campaign to publicize the book. Judith focused her efforts on print media, and after receiving Julia's response and those of Simca and Louisette, she wrote to Julia, "I think we shall be able to weave a wonderful story about les trois gourmandes and their activities and how this book came into being. . . . I think that we can work up an excellent brochure about you to be used for advance publicity." This notice would also include the advertising words she had earlier described, "showing in graphic terms just why this French cookbook is so superior to all others."[2]

Julia had somewhat different ideas. For the writer of a first published book, she had an unusually good understanding of publicity, shaped in part by her earlier advertising experience, Paul's work as a cultural attaché, and her own business sense. Responding to the questionnaire, she filled out pages and pages of names of people who might potentially help in promoting the book. And she definitely wanted what is today called a book tour.

That was not, however, what was in the collective mind of her publisher. Undaunted, Julia, likely with Paul's help, developed a plan. Once the book was in print, Simca would come to the U.S., and the two, assisted by Paul, would launch the book by traveling across the country. In selected cities, the two authors would give demonstrations and thereby stimulate their book's sales.

In early September, in writing to Judith that Simca was coming to the U.S. close to the book's mid-October publication date, Julia inquired about publicity and made this request: "Will it be possible to give us some idea of what your plans would be for her in New York and/or elsewhere?"[3] When Judith replied a week later, she wrote of potential New York appearances.

Missing, however, was an important element for Julia: Judith was silent regarding plans for "elsewhere."[4]

On learning that Simca definitely intended to be in the U.S. for four to six weeks, Julia responded with her excitement both about the book and her delight in their future efforts to promote it. "I never thought I would see the day, and the fact that you can arrange to be here for that great event is too good to be true." Here she wrote of the importance of Simca's presence for their tour: "it's got to have the French woman, or it will not have an authentic flavor." Grooming Simca for the events ahead, Julia coached, "Practice speaking American with a great French accent, but speaking it so that it can be clearly understood, a great advantage!" Julia had offered to pay at least part of Simca's transportation to the U.S. but wanted to be clear that once she arrived, they needed to economize. She asked Simca if she might stay with a friend in New York or at an inexpensive hotel. Julia claimed that she and Paul had put themselves "now on a pretty strict budget, as Paul has no more salary, and neither of us is producing anything yet."[5]

Two days later, Julia wrote again to Simca, this time stating that she had sent Judith a letter "in hopes to get some kind of response from that office about plans. We are quite in the dark, but I thought that if I proposed, something might come out of them."[6] In that letter Julia informed Judith that once Simca arrived, Julia, Paul, and Simca would "be at the command of Alfred A. Knopf, Inc." But for this, "we should like from your offie [sic] a schedule of dates in the New York area." Simca was planning to be in the U.S. for only a few weeks, "and her time should be used is [sic] the most profftable [sic] way."

Julia gave Judith their planned itinerary. After a week in New York, they would travel first to Detroit and then to California, with a focus on San Francisco and the greater Los Angeles area, especially Pasadena. The last of their five-week "tour" would land them in Boston. Julia hoped that in these places they could give cooking demonstrations for large numbers, adding, "They are usually done through gas or electric companies, or through society benefit groups. Dione Lucas is in continuous demand for such affairs, for example."

With this spelled out, Julia then explicitly asked for support in advance planning. As she and Simca were amateurs, they needed "the professional help of the Knopf office in promoting these appearances," help that "would be beneficial to all concerned." With that stated, Julia inquired: "What may we count on from your end?"[7]

This question did get a response, though likely not the one Julia had hoped for. It led to a phone call with Judith, who let Julia know that future planning would be a wait-and-see. As Julia explained to Simca, Judith let her know that although the press expected copies of the book in the following week, "they feel more time is needed, so that the book may be seen by various people, and therefore have decided not to schedule any events for us in New York until the 10 days or 2 weeks beginning Oct. 23rd. J[udith]. Jones says it is really not possible to know exactly what we shall be doing in NY because, naturally, it all depends on how the book is received. I have said we will plan to be there from Oct. 23 (Monday) through Nov. 2nd or 3rd, and will be available for anything she wishes." Thus, Simca should delay coming until October 22.

More distressing than tentative planning for New York events was what Julia learned in regard to arrangements beyond New York City. Knopf had nothing in mind, and it appeared that the press would offer no significant help. Julia conveyed this to Simca: "I discussed the possibility of Detroit and California with her, and she said there was really not much their office could do to arrange anything—that we would have to do that ourselves."

With this, Julia asked Simca a direct question: "Do you think that Lucille Tyree would want you for another demonstration or two? If so, P. and I could come also. I shall try to drum up something for us in San Francisco and in the Los Angeles area."[8]

At this point, after Simca expressed her desire to include Washington, D.C. on their itinerary, she let Julia know some of her limitations. Perhaps in response to Julia's effort to get her to practice speaking in English, Simca wrote that she feared that Julia would find her without her former "hauteur." In the three years since her time in the U.S., she had aged, and her "surdité," her deafness, had increased.[9] Julia had long known about Simca's health issues—her problems with sleep, weight, and rheumatism, and her resort to many stays in spa towns in southern France where she took "cures." Yet, to hear of her aging and deafness—at age fifty-seven—was perhaps a shock. Given what followed, Simca's fears about her own performance on their promotional trip proved unnecessary.

With the book itself soon to be a palpable reality, Judith let Julia know that she and Simca would each be sent four complimentary copies (with two more coming to Simca to give to Louisette). They also could purchase additional books at the authors' discount rate of $6 (for the $10 book).[10]

When *Mastering the Art of French Cooking* arrived at 103 Irving Street on September 29, 1961, Julia was ecstatic. With Judith now on her annual vacation and incommunicado, Julia wrote to Bill Koshland of her deep pleasure: "Mastering the Art of French Cooking has arrived and we are overwhelmed. It is a perfectly beautiful book in every respect, and we could not be more pleased. The jacket is handsome and distinguished, the printing is a joy as is the layout, and the illustrations are perfect. It also lies flat on the table, and the cover is waterproof. Who would dream of anything more satisfying to clasp to one's bosom? On looks alone it ought to do wonders."[11]

Bill responded, "I can't begin to tell you how happy I was to receive your letter about the book, copies of which I have circulated far and wide in the office so that all involved may beam properly with reflected pride." He had called Avis "last Friday after I had seen the first copy here in the office. It is really hard to believe that all this has finally come to pass and I think we're all just as pleased as you." Apologetic that he had not met Julia face-to-face during her time in New York in June, he hoped to see her when he was next in Cambridge.[12]

Bill Koshland, however, wasn't the person at Knopf delegated to deal with Julia's plans for the book tour; rather it was Knopf's publicity manager, Harding Lemay. On October 3, Julia wrote him regarding the San Francisco leg of their "tour." She had anticipated that her sister Dorothy, living in the area, would set up engagements for them, only to be disappointed. Turning to Lemay, Julia wrote that she had just learned that a cousin of Simca's husband was the "Consul Gen of the French CG [Consulate General] in San Francisco." She was hoping that someone in the press's publicity office had a connection with him. "We might be able to do something there as SF is very French conscious."[13] There is no record that Julia received an answer.

Nonetheless, Julia trudged on. On October 15, right before coming to New York, she wrote to Lemay that she needed "plenty of copies" of the book to be sent to Detroit, San Francisco, Los Angeles, and Pasadena. "We plan to do numerous groups of cooking lessons, and it would be useful to have 8 copies or more of the book available at each lesson." She had in mind that she would buy books at her author's 40% discount that she would then sell at the special price of $8.95, using the difference to help defray some of the costs of travel. She admitted that she was then having difficulty getting the San Francisco and Los Angeles/Pasadena segments of the trip organized, "as no one has seen the book yet." It was her hope to generate newspaper publicity in California. She would discuss this with Lemay on October 23, when she planned to meet with him in New York.[14]

Whatever disappointments Julia faced in planning the book tour, she quickly learned what Knopf could do—and did brilliantly. The publishing house was focused on print media in New York City, especially on earned publicity via the city's influential newspaper, the *New York Times*. And here, Judith knew the steps to take.

In August, describing how she was working for Julia, Judith told how she had arranged a lunch with Craig Claiborne, the paper's influential food editor and critic, "in order to try to persuade him to do something on the book and we had a lovely chatty time, so pleasant that he decided my husband and I would make a good piece during the slack summer season." She reminded Julia that she had earlier sent her Craig Claiborne's resulting article in the *New York Times* about the meal she and her husband had prepared for him outside on their balcony, illustrated with a photo of her and Evan. "We cooked that spit-roasted lamb for him in 93° heat at noon!" Given that successful ploy, Judith expressed her confidence that "he is going to return the favor." She added, "As a matter of fact, he was very interested in the book and does want to do a story on you and Simone Beck, if she comes over, in your Cambridge kitchen."[15]

Judith's cultivation had wonderful results. On October 18, 1961, Craig Claiborne published a rave review of *Mastering the Art of French Cooking* in the *New York Times*, calling it "the most comprehensive, laudable and monumental work on the subject." He wrote of its clear writing and directions and praised its recipes as "glorious," with each one written "as if it were a masterpiece and most of them are."

For the newspaper's wide and influential readership, this review launched a hitherto unknown Julia Child into the influential New York cooking world. It led to an introduction to Dione Lucas and James Beard, and through Beard, to the city's coterie of food writers.

With a strong belief in the power of print, Knopf's primary financial investment in publicity for *Mastering* was the 200 books sent to food editors across the country. This was an approach that Avis bought into fully. Although she had failed to inject herself in the book's editing process, as publication approached, her ideas and efforts meshed with those at Knopf: sending books to influential people. In late July 1961, writing to Judith, Avis began with kind words: "Everything I see and hear about the progress of the great cookbook enchants me, and I do hope you know how much the Childs like you, and enjoy working with you. And, if you have got half the sense I credit you with, I know you admire them too—a really wonderful partnership. Well, it has all turned out beautifully and I couldn't be happier about it."

Then came Avis's pitch. "I have yipped about this cookbook for so many years that I have whetted a good many appetites for it, and now I want to sow a number of complimentary copies where they will do the most good." With this came a list of those she proposed to be sent the book. Avis described them as friends, "interested in the subject, and all very apt to talk about the book." (Today they would be called "influencers.") Avis proposed to write to each, "well here it finally is, and please use it and talk about it and leave it around on the table where people will see it." She asked for the press to give her the date it would be sending the copies to those on her list, "so that I can write the letters."

Avis's list included the names of those and/or their wives currently serving in President Kennedy's administration: Mrs. McGeorge Bundy, Mr. and Mrs. George Ball, Ambassador and Mrs. Kenneth Galbraith. Adding to these dignitaries, she gave the name of a Harvard Law School professor, whose wife "gets around a great deal and loves to cook"; an editor of the *Rocky Mountain Herald* in Denver, who was "good for a quote"; and Nancy Hale, a writer she had earlier scouted for Knopf—"dying to get at this book and who is always good for a nice juicy jacket quote." Hale had given her the name of a prominent professor at the University of Chicago, "the most influential gourmet type in Chicago." She would write each person once she got "a green light on this little project."

Avis also wanted to be included in the New York launch. After asking about the release date, she wrote, "Is there going to be any kind of publicity party? If there is, that's one I must get down to New York for, difficult as it will be to arrange" (because of her job). She herself planned on giving her own kind of "publicity party" in Cambridge—three "whacking big cocktail parties" in the fall "To Meet Paul and Julia Child." For this she gave her own ask: "I very much hope I can have a copy of the book to display on those occasions."

Avis closed with a reminder of her important role in the book's development. "You can't say I'm not getting behind this book—but I rather regard it as partly my book since it probably would not have been published except for me. Well, it's been quite a merry-go-round ride, and worth every minute of frustration and anxiety."[16]

Judith Jones responded warmly, "What a delight to get your good letter and to know that you're going to be putting heart and soul into the promotional end of the cookbook, as you already have in the making of it and in getting it to me." Judith praised her list as "excellent" and shared her letter with Bill Koshland. She then sent her and Bill's promise "that you will get the complimentary copies you need to plant where you feel they will do the most good."[17]

Avis next let Judith know of her efforts to promote the book in Boston. After insisting that the press send a copy of the book to Marjorie Mills, a columnist at the *Boston Herald* who wrote on women's concerns "and swings one hell of a lot of weight," Avis added, "I would like to write her a letter," noting that she planned to stress the Cambridge residence of the Childs. Avis also needed firm dates when Julia would be free for her own large cocktail parties of seventy to eighty guests because she needed to get on the barman's calendar. Avis added a note of his distinction in Cambridge, one that Judith Jones was unlikely to understand: Avis had hired "Archie [the steward] of the Signet Soc[iety]," a club for Harvard undergraduates involved in literature and the arts. Avis went on to convey her personal news. She was about to give up her column in the *Boston Globe* reviewing mysteries: "I have had two raises at Harvard and I don't need the Globe money any more."[18]

After apologizing for her delay in writing due to an indisposition, Judith wrote Avis that she was free to plan her parties on October 18 or on any weekend. She also gave Avis news of the plans at Knopf for additional publicity for the book. "We are going to try to interest as many newspapers as possible in stories on the three ladies and, as Julia may have told you, we are preparing some feature pieces stressing different angles of their story. And, of course, we have that marvelous batch of photographs which Paul took." She added something that must have warmed Avis's heart: "Incidentally, I detected you in a number of them, absorbing all that culinary knowledge."[19]

At Avis's cocktail parties would not only be Julia and Paul but also Simca. On October 9, Simca received her copy of the book, delivered to her while she was outside of Paris visiting her mother. Simca was ecstatic, in words that need only a bit of translation: "C'est magnifique, cela se présente bien [it looks good], c'est clair, joliment relié [nicely bound], élégant, chic et solide."[20]

In mid-October Julia had good news to relay to Simca about New York events. Harding LeMay "has just telephoned that they have arranged to have us interviewed for the MARTHA DEAN[E] radio show, which is evidently heard all over the East coast, on Tues. Oct. 25th. I have never heard of this myself, but it is supposed to be the cat's whiskers." They would meet LeMay soon after they arrived, "and he will give us our schedule." After stating that their evenings would be free, Julia added, "we do not have to stick to gethether [sic] every minutes [sic]!" As Julia closed, she burst out on the page, "My! Quelle Emotion!"[21]

On October 22, Julia and Paul traveled to New York to meet Simca. The three would be in the city for a full week.[22] While Simca stayed in a hotel, Julia and Paul were housed in the Upper West Side apartment of Charlie's daughter Rachel and her husband, Anthony Prud'homme. Julia appreciated the homestay, for it not only gave her Rachel's good company, it also allowed her to cook and invite Simca for dinner.

After Craig Claiborne's review, Julia and Simca found themselves no longer nobodies, and their New York week was filled with important meetings. In addition there were social pleasures and entertainments that Julia listed in her appointment book. On the day following Simca's arrival, both authors spent the morning with those at Knopf involved in marketing their book, and they met with a representative from the television program *Today*. Judith Jones joined them for lunch. Later that day, Paul and Julia went to a movie and in the evening hosted Simca at Rachel's home. On October 24, Julia visited with Simca, and then the two went to the Cosmo Club to meet with two representatives from *Vogue* magazine. On the following day, they met in the late morning with a person from *House & Garden,* and that evening Julia and Paul attended a ballet performance with Rachel and her husband.

Two important events had been arranged for October 25. In the morning, Julia and Simca were to be interviewed on the *Martha Deane* radio show.

Reading the interview today, recently reprinted in full, one can only marvel at the skill that both Julia and Simca had acquired by the time of the book's launch.[23] Julia clearly was a quick study who had learned from the unfortunate interview in Oslo earlier in the year that she needed to present herself not as herself, but as the "book/me who is leading the interview."[24]

The second important event that day was a lunch meeting with Jose Wilson, the food editor of *House & Garden,* to discuss a future article for the magazine. Earlier in the month, when Julia learned of this appointment, she had written to Simca, "This is G R E A T. It means that if they like this article, and want more WE ARE IN. H O O R A Y!"[25]

October 26 was an especially important day. At an early 5 A.M. hour, Julia and Simca arrived at the NBC studio to rehearse for and appear on the popular television show *Today,* then hosted by John Chancellor. Their segment included Simca's demonstration on the proper way to make an omelette, a feat that both women would repeat many times in the coming weeks. Next was a visit with Dione Lucas at her New York restaurant, the Egg Basket. Ever since an early letter from Avis in 1952 told Julia about Lucas, Julia had been aware of the British-born cookbook writer who had pioneered cooking on television early on and had continued until 1960 with several programs, her most recent being the *Dione Lucas's Gourmet Club.* Later, in the afternoon, Simca and Julia met with Judith.

The culmination of all these introductions and meetings came near the end of Julia and Simca's time in New York. On the afternoon and evening of October 31, they returned to the Egg Basket and met first with Lucas and then with James Beard. It was likely then that Lucas made the generous offer to give a dinner at her restaurant for the authors when they returned to New York, and Beard agreed to provide an invitation list of important persons in the city's food world.

Julia and Paul returned to Cambridge with Simca on November 2, staying there for a few days to gird their loins for the trip ahead, have appointments at a hair salon, and celebrate the book at the first of Avis's cocktail parties. Avis had, by that time, reduced these events to two, with the second party coming on their return in December.

The "book tour" began on November 5, when Julia, Paul, and Simca boarded a train and headed west to Detroit. (Paul's fear of flying meant he and Julia traveled by train, and in this case Simca joined them.) On the train Julia carried a typed itinerary (copied to Judith), to which she added additions in ink along the way.[26]

Detroit was the initial destination because of Lucille Tyree's importance to their enterprise. A wealthy and prominent woman residing in Grosse Pointe, she was the person who made the original suggestion to Louisette of the French cookbook for Americans. In 1952, she became one of the early students of L'École des Trois Gourmandes, and during Simca's time in the U.S. in 1958, hosted Simca for a long visit.

Tyree planned a significant program for the two authors. As written in the itinerary and in Julia's appointment book, it appears largely social, except for the day of their arrival when the authors were to give a brief talk at a luncheon in their honor. There was also an evening cocktail party for the press, followed by dining with their host's guests, who included the society columnist for *The Detroit News*. On the next days, there were many luncheons and dinners as well as a large reception for them at the hospitality center of the Michigan Consolidated Gas Company.

Appointment books and itineraries can be deceiving, however. Writing to Judith on the train taking them from Michigan to California, Julia told a very different story. "Thanks to Mme. Beck and her good friends in Grosse Pte, and her previous cooking visit, I think everything went off very well. We did two taped radio broadcasts, got several write-ups, did a demonstration in a model kitchen, etc." Julia reported a bookshop sale of 125 copies, adding, "I hope we shall run into more little gold mines like this." The *Detroit News* had called their cookbook, "the greatest book to come out of France." The article asserted, "Now you really may cook at home in French, even if you feel you're an amateur."

Next came important news. "Mme. Beck has also lunched with Julius Wile, who has been giving wine lessons to Craig Claiborne, and who knows Dione Lucas quite well. He has offered to give the wines for the Lucas dinner, and also to put a few needles in her about getting the invitations out as soon as possible." Julia asked Judith to send him the book "as he is being so helpful." Wile, an important importer of wine and spirits and a man deeply interested in gastronomy, also planned to help promote the book in Los Angeles. Julia gave Judith the address on Park Avenue of his New York store, Julius Wile Sons & Company.[27]

When Paul later wrote to Avis a narration of the book tour, he filled it with rich detail.[28] "Detroit was a kind of mixed bag." He contrasted the city—depressed, yet prideful, filled with labor conflict—with the wealthy suburb of "Grosse Point showing off its houses, cars and furs." He found the suburb's residents to be "sheep-like, apparently," copying each other in everything. That, however, turned to the two authors' benefit and lead to remarkable sales of the book. In one case, a bookstore sold its entire lot of 125 copies, and a department store the 50 copies that Julia and Simca signed.

"Our two troopers also made two radio tapes, gave a cooking demonstration at a gas company's chic show rooms for a seated (and excited) audience of women, were the principals in a reception for the press (wine & food), were dined at THE club in town, with about 25 other guests, and were rushed off their feet socially in between."

In writing to Avis, Paul gave Simca great praise, and at this point elevated her to "wonderful dame." He related that on arriving in Detroit, she learned of the death of two of her oldest and closest friends in an automobile accident. Although she was greatly distressed, "she carried on with magnificent sang froid her job of the gay and expert French woman. I could see then the tough core that allowed her to join the Resistance when the Germans controlled France."[29]

The next stop for the three travelers was California's San Francisco Bay Area. Arriving there on November 11, they stayed in Sausalito in the home of Dorothy ("Dort") and Ivan Cousins, Julia's sister and brother-in-law.[30] Dort was hospitable, but she had been unable to help them arrange any demonstrations or book presentations in San Francisco. Earlier in planning, Julia had explained this to Judith. Dort had told her on the phone that "she has never done anything like this before, knows none of the people in the business, but is trying earnestly. We shall at least have a good time seeing the city and the country, but I don't think the stay in SF—at this point—is going to do much for the book." Asking again for help, Julia requested directly that Jim Russell, who represented Knopf in California, meet with them "and help us out with something, or advise us, or etc."[31]

This time Judith moved quickly: "I had another talk with Dick Krinsley about your San Francisco activities and he assures me that Jim Russell will be the man to take care of you there. Bill Koshland has already written Mr. Russell a note just to give him an extra push, and I gather he is a real live wire and will certainly take you around himself and introduce you to the book stores."[32]

Judith, with her efforts on print media, now reported that "through an intermediary," she had successfully approached Jane Benet, the food editor of the *San Francisco Chronicle*, and sent her a clipping. She also gave other good news regarding a piece to appear in late November. The intermediary in question was likely Charlotte Jackson, the widow of the *Chronicle*'s literary editor, to whom Judith had sent a copy of *Mastering*.

Offering a sense of the dynamics at the Knopf office, after the letter was typed, Judith added this handwritten note: "Bill K. has already had an answer from [Jim] Russell and he says things are really buzzing out in San Francisco in your behalf!"[33]

The working days of the book tour in San Francisco got underway on Monday, November 13. Notations in handwriting on the typed itinerary suggest arrangements made after Julia had prepared it, perhaps even after she arrived in California. In any case, Jim Russell clearly came through.

Julia and Simca first had their morning hair appointments at Elizabeth Arden's salon. In the afternoon they met with Jean Woods of the *San Francisco Examiner,* where Paul reported to Avis that they were "interviewed and photographed." Following this, they worked with representatives of the City of Paris, the famed San Francisco department store, to plan the important Thursday demonstrations and book event.[34]

Tuesday brought them to KNBC, where Paul wrote Avis that they were on a "radio broadcast by Evangeline Baker." This was followed by a luncheon date at Trader Vic's, arranged by the wealthy and prominent Mrs. Madeline Haas Russell. Her guests were newspaper women, described by Paul as "three reporters there to take pix and notes." After that, according to Paul, they drove to Burlingame for an important dinner, and then on Wednesday visited with Miss Branson, the headmistress of Julia's secondary boarding school.

Thursday was Julia and Simca's most dramatic event in San Francisco, a cooking demonstration at the department store City of Paris given to a packed crowd of eager book buyers. Julia described it to Judith: "They set up a stove on the 5th floor, and we made omelettes, quiches, and madeleines again and again and again, and everyone ate and ate." Working from 11 A.M. to 5 P.M., Paul estimated that four to five hundred "greedy but interested women" attended. Julia didn't know how many books or madeleine molds sold, but she could see "that tours like this are extremely valuable." She offered a message for Knopf: a book tour's success required connections such as those of Bill Koshland and Jim Russell. She followed by adding that in San Francisco, "it seemed to us that we met cousins of Bill Koshland or old family friends at every turn."[35] Here, the close familial connections between Bill Koshland and Madeline Haas Russell likely played some part.

Paul was particularly delighted regarding the number of books sold in San Francisco. He wrote to Avis, "People—whether Mrs. Van Snoot or Mrs. Simplicima—seem to like the book enough to buy it, and the buying wave has swept through the city like the river through the Augean stables, leaving dozens of frustrated women behind frantically waving ten dollar bills at hapless clerks in book stores."

After the demonstration, the two authors' next appointment was a broadcast interview on tape. Then the three were off to Madeline Russell's home for what Paul described as a "snooty-but-well-arranged reception, with a mix of social and editorial and food and French consular folk."[36]

On the following day, they met with Jim Russell and ventured to the East Bay, first to Oakland for a visit to the local newspaper and then to Berkeley for a small tea for Julia and Paul given by Charlotte Jackson, important for her connection to the *San Francisco Chronicle*. After the event, Mrs. Jackson wrote to Koshland of her enjoyment: "Mrs. Child is utterly charming and she and my daughter discovered that they were both Smith girls." This contact proved successful in publicizing the book. "After a bit of pushing on my part the Chronicle assigned our club editor to do the job and of course Madeline Russell having lived in France with the Fischbacher family was a natural tie-in with the whole thing." (As a young woman, she rented a room in Paris from André Fischbacher. However, despite the name, he was no known relation to Jean.)[37]

Paul gave Avis a somewhat different account of that day. The three travelers first went to Oakland to meet the food editor of the local paper, then returned to San Francisco for a "horrid lunch at the Palace Hotel, from whence to KCBS to be tape-interviewed by a guy; then rush to Berkeley for tea with Charlotte Jackson . . . back to SF for cocktails with a University mob chez Chickering—old pals of Julia's—after which with Jane McBaine to dine at Jack's Restaurant, and then to call on her 82 year old mother, full of fire and beans."[38]

Paul fully understood the reason for all this activity—that Julia and Simca's presence was generating important purchases of their book.

He conveyed to Avis that he had learned that *Mastering* had almost no buyers in Portland and Seattle. By contrast, the outstanding sales in San Francisco were "the result of the hard work by J and S, and consequent publicity. Our authors are in there pitching every minute."[39]

Soon, it was off by car to Southern California, where they would all stay in Pasadena in the home of Julia's childhood.

Judith had written letters about plans for the return to New York that Julia had failed to answer, but Judith gave it a positive spin: "being busy is a very good sign indeed." After writing how she was continuing to try to lure Craig Claiborne to meet personally with Simca and Julia, she offered this bit of Knopf's office life: "Bill Koshland pops in practically every day to hear the latest from you, and sales continue to boom."[40]

In Pasadena on Wednesday, November 22, Julia paused to write a long, informative letter to Judith telling her about what had already transpired in San Francisco and in the early days of being in the Los Angeles/Pasadena area. The letter's most important element, however, involved the future—the possible dinner hosted by Dione Lucas at the Egg Basket. Judith had let her know that the critical time for sending out invitations was passing, but that she felt it would be inappropriate for her to contact Lucas. In the meantime Julia had become discouraged and fearful that the dinner would never happen, as she had heard nothing from Lucas.

In Los Angeles, Julia's itinerary listed only one event, an early-evening reception at the Bel Air Hotel, put on by Julius Wile and the Bollinger company, held on November 21, the day of their arrival. This seemingly insignificant occasion proved to be all-important for the Egg Basket dinner. The presence of Julia and Simca at the reception strengthened the relationship of the two with Julius Wile. With matters for the dinner at the Egg Basket up in the air, Simca phoned Wile, who had returned to New York.

Following that call, Wile immediately went to see Dione Lucas. He then wired Julia and Simca to "telephone her today." Julia confessed that at that point she was doubtful that the dinner would ever happen, but Simca—whom Julia assessed as "much more worldly"—saw things differently. To her Lucas was merely "a badly organized woman" who had simply not "gotten started on things." Simca believed "Lucas's offer" was "genuine," and that Lucas and she had "too many friends in common in France for Lucas to back out."

Toward the end of the long letter to Judith, Julia reported on the phone call to Lucas. She let Judith know that Simca, "who is a whiz at this sort of thing," did all the talking, first asking if Lucas had gotten the cookbook. The response was a strong yes, followed by Lucas's compliments on the book and agreement to their guestlist. They were, however, to be responsible for sending out the invitations.[41]

Paul offered Avis a much more colorful rendering of that call. It happened to be placed at Disneyland, because a McWilliams family friend had "provided Cadillac and uniformed chauffeur" for an excursion to Anaheim's fantasy world. The call to Dione Lucas was set for that day, "at a specific hour arranged by telegram. The two things came together, so with a bank-roll of 25¢ pieces we got into a Motel booth at Disneyland & the call went through OK, and final details on the dinner were arranged. D.L. generously said she'd now read THE Book and thinks it's magnificent, the recipes were remarkably explicit, and she's so enthusiastic she wants to have the dinner based only on recipes from the book!"[42]

The following day, as Julia was composing her letter to Judith, with its more discreet rendering, Paul was already at work, writing the invitations in his "beautiful script." Julia ended with the hope that the Knopf crew of Judith and her husband, Harding LeMay and his wife, and Bill Koshland would plan to attend the Egg Basket dinner.[43]

Following the November 23 Thanksgiving break, Julia and Simca enjoyed a rich social life of many private events consisting of teas, cocktail parties, and dinners given by Julia's Pasadena friends. After Phila,

Julia's stepmother, gave a reception, their work began. On Sunday afternoon, November 26, Julia and Simca appeared on *Cavalcade of Books*, a Los Angeles television show.

They gave a class for eight on Tuesday and a private demonstration for about twenty on Wednesday. Thursday was their largest event. The two authors gave cooking demonstrations twice for an audience of somewhere between three and four hundred as a benefit for the Rosemary Cottage for Delinquent Girls, sponsored by the Community Chest and held at the San Marino Women's Club.

"Julia Child and Simca Beck with the host of Cavalcade of Books," Schlesinger Library,
Harvard Radcliffe Institute.

These events generated publicity in the local papers. As Julia wrote to Judith on Wednesday, November 29, "Pasadena is proving extremely busy. We have so far had excellent coverage in the Pasadena Star News, but won't have a formal piece in the LA Times until Friday." That was to be their travel day, with Chicago as their next destination. Simca would go by air, while Julia and Paul took the train, something she was looking forward to "so we can relax a bit."[44]

On the train, Paul again wrote to Avis, and in this letter he offered his experience of the San Marino event that began with a reflection of his recent life abroad.

"My life continues to put me into unpredictable situations. For example: In May, 1961, when I was the American Government's Cultural Attaché in Oslo, whose crystal globe would have been clear enough to disclose the true image of me in November, squating [sic] on the floor behind scenery-flats in a theater in San Merino [Marino], California, trying to wash a heap of egg and chocolate covered bowls in a bucket of cold water? Out front, before an audience of 350 Club women, were Julie and Simca, demonstrating how to make Soufflé de Turbot . . . Quiche au Roquefort and Reine de Saba Cake. Our Girls put on 2 superb shows that day, one in the late morning & one in the early P.M., with almost no time between for the Cultural Attaché to wash the dishes, while they were signing books, being interviewed, and making polite noises at the Clubwomen. The demonstration could have been disastrous because the muddle-headed dame who was chairman of the lecture committee simply forgot to provide the towels, the garbage cans, the tables, the water, the soap etc[.] we had listed, but we got there an hour ahead, and due to my years as an exhibition expert I'm an experienced scrounger & Makeshift-artist, and we were ready on the dot."[45]

Julia relished the public attention they had received in Southern California. On the train, she typed to Judith, "Thought you would enjoy some of our newspaper publicity from the Pasadena/LA area. This is mosly [sic] of the local-girl-makes-good variety." The big Thursday benefit demonstration for the Community Chest "turned out fine, mostly thanks to the cooperation of the S. Cal Gas Co, who set up a fine array of stoves." Although it was a charity event, they had benefitted by the sale of "over 100 of our books."[46]

In writing to Avis, Paul stepped back to offer his general reflections about Southern California. His tone was harsh. Although he mainly spoke for himself, in one statement he included Julia. "The area was distressing to us both because we have the feeling that unrestrained and unaware commercialism are ruining Nature all over." Shifting now to his own opinion, he told Avis that he experienced in the region a general lack of understanding of public events, what was happening in science and art. Its inhabitants were "so busy w/ material consumption & social whirling," that they neglected reading and reflection. He contrasted the bragging he had heard of the rapid growth in population in L.A.—"1000/day"—with Louis Mumford's words in *The City in History*: "It is art, culture, and political purpose—not numbers—that define a city."[47]

Chicago was the travelers' next destination, and their days there were filled with many appointments set in advance. On Monday morning, December 4, Julia and Simca met two women at the headquarters of the *Chicago Tribune*. There they gave a private demonstration in the newspaper's test kitchen, were interviewed for an article, and were photographed together as Simca beat eggs with a wire whisk.

After a side trip to a downtown bookstore, Simca and Julia took themselves to suburban Winnetka for a book reception. Personally responsible for the refreshments, the two authors brought appetizers that they had prepared the day before. In the evening they attended a private dinner given by Peggy Harvey of the *Chicago Tribune*. She had invited a radio interviewer, as Julia noted in her itinerary, who had "interviewed cooking types such as J. Beard."[48]

After Chicago, came Washington, D.C. Despite the Childs' many earlier connections in that city, Washington proved to be a disappointing stop. It offered only social events, not the newspaper or radio interviews that the two authors had hoped to garner. Nonetheless a lovely prospect lay ahead, Avis's long planned second cocktail party on the day Julia, Paul, and Simca returned to Cambridge.

Avis had sent Judith an invitation to this December 9 event. Writing that she could only be there "in spirit," Judith told Avis that the party came at "a very busy time—particularly with the sales conference following on its tail the very next Monday." Judith then told Avis that she had gotten letters "from the Child-Beck expedition and they seem to be going great guns. Wait till you see what Craig Claiborne has to say in his roundup of cookbooks for the Christmas issue in this Sunday's _Times_ Book Section. And it's sandwiched right in between our steepest competition. Yes, it has certainly been worth every minute of it." Judith concluded by inviting Avis to the "Egg Basket event on the 15th. . . . It certainly would be fun to have you there."[49]

The New York dinner at the Egg Basket, hosted by Dione Lucas, was scheduled for December 15, just before Simca's departure. As Julia later recounted, it turned out that not only did Julia and Simca have to invite the guests and provide the menu, "we had to cook most of the food." James Beard had kindly supplied the names of those to be invited, and it included "everyone we have ever heard of in the cooking business." Avis did not attend this New York event, but Julia, thinking of the leading figures in New York's culinary establishment, remembered that "everybody came." With no way to recognize them, Julia reported that Beard, who "was just darling to us . . . introduced us to our guests."[50] It was a breakout moment. Warmed by Craig Claiborne's reviews and the cordiality of James Beard and Dione Lucas, the New York cooking world now opened up to embrace Julia Child. As Julia expressed it to Simca in a letter to her after her return to Paris, this meant "we are now accepted by the big food people . . . we are now quelqu'un [somebody]—HOORAY."[51]

Julia's letter also gave Simca high praise for making the book tour successful. "You were perfectly wonderful throughout, gay, tres francais, parfaitement Simca, and a wonder."[52] And in return, Simca's following two letters paid tribute to both Julia and Paul. She thanked them for their assistance, aid, constant affection, and moral support throughout the entire tour.[53] Both Simca and Julia returned to their homes satisfied that their book tour had given _Mastering the Art of French Cooking_ the launch it deserved.

Chapter Ten

The French Chef

The book tour ended, but for Julia the work was far from over. Thus far, her efforts had yielded good publicity, but at significant financial cost to her. She had paid the expenses both for herself and for Simca (to be reimbursed out of Simca's hoped-for future royalties). *Mastering the Art of French Cooking* may have been a labor of love, but, with the exception of the advance, it was thus far an uncompensated one. In mid-January 1962, she wrote Simca of her delight when a check for $150 came from *House & Garden*: "Our first $$$$ in 12 years!"[1] At that point she could only hope and keep her eyes open for opportunities.

Mastering was out there with good reviews and early publicity, but as winter came, it needed a boost. Avis certainly thought so. In mid-February, Avis let Simca know she had written to Bill Koshland that "what we all want is SALES, and I for one do not care how they are got, and . . . if Knopf would hire a glorious nude to parade through Times Square wearing a sandwich-board advertising the book, that it would be all right with me."[2]

A chance for increasing sales of the book came on February 25, 1962. In the middle of Paul's long letter to Charlie written the day before, Paul wrote, "Tomorrow Julie will go on television (an Egg-Head T.V. Educational Station, in Boston) to talk about cooking, and to demonstrate one or two processes. Could be interesting. We hope there'll be a solid plug about the Book in it somewhere! because this is a book-review program."[3]

Paul's casual words about the TV interview hid the fact that Julia worked hard for this television appearance. She was aided by a friend from their Paris days, Beatrice Braude, who was now in Boston working for educational television's WGBH as a production assistant for Henry Morgenthau's *Prospects of Mankind with Eleanor Roosevelt*. During World War II, Braude had been in the OSS and, like Paul, came to Paris and worked at the USIA.[4] Writing about her months later, Julia wrote that the Childs had known her "for years, both professionally and socially." Julia valued many of Braude's attributes, among them "her real nose for promotion."[5] At this point promotion seemed a very good idea, as Julia and Simca had only recently earned enough through royalties to cover the costs of their "book tour."

Because Julia served as "agent" for the three co-authors, she received the total semi-annual royalty check from Knopf for the book. She then divided it according to their final agreement. After subtracting Louisette's 10%, Simca and Julia were thus each entitled to 45%. Julia was scrupulous, apportioning each royalty payment to the penny. In March 1962, she and Simca each took in $2,610.43 (equal to $22,895.46 at the time of this writing).[6] Royalty money was important to both women. Not only did it represent payment for the unpaid years of work on *Mastering*, it also brought significant income into their households. After Paul left government service in 1961, he not only had no salary, he brought in no income because he retired before the number of working years that would have given him a pension. In spring 1962, Simca's husband Jean, age fifty-five, lost his job and was never able to get another. Although Julia and Simca each had family money, both women understood that although they might spend the dividends, they should not invade the principal for daily expenses. Simca's situation cannot be fully known, but Julia and Paul did have enough to manage. They were, however, living then on a strict budget.

For Paul, despite the economic sacrifice, retirement from government service proved to be a lasting relief. He quickly found that their move to 103 Irving Street in Cambridge gave him the life he had long desired. It put him on home ground in a commodious house in an elite Cambridge neighborhood. It gave him Julia's kitchen to organize and provided many walls and surfaces for his artistic creations; its grounds offered outdoor spaces to plan and develop. Turning the house into their home brought Paul great satisfaction. One can see this in the comment he wrote to Charlie after he had completed making a wine-storage area in their cellar, in early March 1962: "All done, and neat's a pin."[7]

By autumn Julia learned that book royalties could be a shaky foundation to rely on for significant financial support of their household. In autumn 1962, her next 45% yielded a disappointing $1,366.67.[8] This money went quickly, as she and Paul bought an adding machine, a rowing machine for exercise, two sturdy bags (one for Paul's camera equipment and the other to carry Julia's omelette pans), essential clothing such as winter coats, and a luxurious item for Julia, "a chic suit."[9] Along with her clear business sense, Julia was always careful about expenses, and in 1962 she was clearly eager to grow the book's sales to provide more disposable income.

The TV program *I've Been Reading* was hosted by Albert Duhamel, a long-established professor of English at Boston College. On each half-hour show, Duhamel discussed a book with an author. Julia, still fresh from the launch, saw this as an opportunity to give one of her well-practiced omelette demonstrations, and brought ingredients and cooking equipment with her to the studio. At WGBH in 1962, all programs were taped, to be aired at a future time. Paul reported to Charlie that the taping had gone "extremely well for two reasons: the 1st was because instead of the usual 5 minute spot it lasted half an hour. The 2nd was because the man who interviewed Julie was calm, clear & professional. Also he loves food, likes to cook & had read the book. The time-allowance made it possible for Julie to demonstrate cutting & chopping, 'turning' a mushroom-cap, beating egg-whites, and making an omelette—apart from sitting & being interviewed."

Unusual for Paul, he added here a negative criticism: "Julie got so interested in how to do things that she forgot to put in a plug for the book. She should have said, 'Of course all this is described in greater detail on page 56 of Mastering the Art. . . . Etc,' but she didn't . . . There was a large blow-up of the book's dust-jacket back projected on a screen behind her all the time, but that's not quite the same."[10]

Paul's judgment was not that of WGBH. After the show aired on February 11, the TV station saw the interview as a hit. WGBH received praise from twenty-seven viewers, an unusually large number for Boston-area educational television in 1962.

As far as television went, Julia knew little about the medium, for although she had appeared on several television shows during the launch, she and Paul did not currently own a TV set. That was soon remedied. With her March royalty check from Knopf, Julia wrote Freddie that—along with home-improvement purchases and a dictionary—she and Paul had "bought a TV."[11]

Julia's ignorance regarding the specific demands of television did not mean she was unprepared for her appearance on *I've Been Reading*. By 1962 she had gained the important experience of instructing others in how to cook for a full decade. Teaching began in early 1952 with the advent of L'École des Trois Gourmandes, her cooking school in Paris with Simca and Louisette. Although the move to Marseilles meant Julia could no longer be a regular member of the teaching team, she was able to continue when she visited Paris. Over time, Julia gave numerous private lessons in French cooking. More dramatically, on the launch of *Mastering the Art of French Cooking*, she gave many public demonstrations with Simca. One senses that Julia liked to perform. Although there was no live television audience at WGBH, in the studio she was not alone. Beyond the camera, there were a fair number of people who were involved in its production and who, along with Paul, watched from the sidelines as the show was taped. Her appearance on *I've*

Been Reading before that audience and the potential viewers on television clearly provoked her desire to repeat that experience.

Thus following her interview and omelette demonstration on *I've Been Reading,* Julia composed over the next two and a half months a document to present to WGBH. Written in the form of a long memo, it was a proposal for an unnamed television cooking show. Julia's understanding of what she wanted it to be had to come from her own imagination as she had no model in mind. Dione Lucas ended her show in 1960. There were women's television programs, some for a local audience, that included cooking, but Julia, without a television set, would not have seen them when she was abroad or back in the U.S.

Julia's vision was her own, but evidence from the proposal makes it clear that she did not write it alone, for it was not the work of a novice, but rather a thoroughly professional piece of work. Its development was clearly aided by a person fully conversant with the medium, specifically someone on the inside of WGBH who knew all the elements needed to address such a proposal to the station.[12]

Who was that person? Julia's helper was likely Margaret ("Miffy") Goodhart, and perhaps also Beatrice Braude. Though a young producer at WGBH, Goodhart was well placed to do this, as she was married to Charles Goodhart, a cousin of the TV station's executive producer, Henry Morgenthau III. A reference to the proposal's origin comes in a mid-March letter Paul wrote to Charlie: "And this noon, for lunch chez nous, comes a Miss Goodhart, of a Boston Television Station, who will lay the groundwork for putting Julie on one of their programs in the near future."[13] Later, of course, Julia and Paul invited both Miffy and Charles Goodhart to dinner and asked Avis to join them for drinks.[14]

At an unknown later date, when Paul had in his possession his letters to Charlie and was reviewing them, he wrote in the margin a note regarding that luncheon visit of Miffy Goodhart: "The TV life begins and we are still unknowing how it will coerce our future."[15] "Coerce" is a strong word, likely expressing how Paul came to remember those television years.

Written in the form of a memo to WGBH, dated April 26, 1962, Julia began with words that were clearly hers: "I think we could make an interesting, adult series of half-hour TV programs on French cooking addressed to an intelligent, reasonably sophisticated audience which likes good food and cooking. 'How to make cooking make sense' is an approach which has always interested me, and I would like to expound on it publicly. As I conceive of cooking and as my French colleagues and I have tried to illustrate it in our book, the whole business boils down to a series of themes and variations in which one learned the basic techniques, then varies the ingredients." After giving several examples, Julia declared that by "mastering the fundamentals you are beginning to divorce yourself from slavish dependence on recipes and are on the way to becoming a real cook." French methods had universal value in their precision and were applicable to cooking generally, whatever the national origin of the recipe. "Thus the emphasis of each program would be on the hows and whys, as illustrated by one fundamental, mouth-watering recipe."[16]

The proposal continued in the first person. "As I conceive of the programs, they would be informal, easy, conversational, yet timed to the minute." Julia then offered the time sequence of the half-hour show.

When the proposal turned to practical matters, with paragraphs on "financial support," "basic equipment needed," and "TV technique," the hand of the unknown advisor is evident. For example, regarding the actual taping of the show, the proposal stated, "Cooking processes must be very clearly and closely shown. Would reflect mirrors over work surfaces be useful? Could camera shoot over the cook's shoulder so that everything is view[ed] as from the cook's view? (Camera work on recent TV heart surgery program, "Breakthrough" was especially good from detail point of view.)"

With treatment of the next issue—How would a recipe requiring lengthy preparation be handled in a half-hour show?—Julia was in her own element. Under "PREPARED FOOD INGREDIENTS," Julia wrote, "I would therefore bring to the studio any pre-cooking necessary, so a dish would be on hand in various stages as necessary" and, with this, offered several examples.

The list of "SUBJECTS FOR 20 half-hour programs" was wide-ranging, from specific dishes, such as "Coq au Vin" and processes, to the more general "how to stew." Next came "DETAILED OUTLINE OF ONE HALF-HOUR PROGRAM," with columns that designated "Minute Log," "Minutes Used," and an unlabeled third offering the specific process being accomplished. Such detail clearly required the work of a knowledgeable television professional.

During the first half of 1962, Julia's personal life intervened with her plans. At the year's outset, Julia had faced surgery. Then, as the TV proposal was being developed, she took an unplanned trip to Pasadena. She had learned that her father was desperately ill, suffering from lymphatic leukemia. Writing to Freddie, she related that she was going there because she felt the need to be supportive of Phila, her stepmother. She also reminded her sister-in-law that although he had been "a terribly generous father financially," she had not been close to him.[17]

During the time she was away, Paul took an important step in helping Julia get the house in order. Writing to Charlie, he told of what was to become the iconic element of Julia's kitchen: "Tomorrow I'm going to start designing how Julie's copper batterie-de-Cuisine shall be hung on the blue peg-board wall planned for it."[18]

A constant theme for Simca and Julia during these months was their frustration that Knopf was not doing enough to promote the book. Simca faced continual disappointment that bookstores in Paris were not stocking *Mastering the Art of French Cooking*. Julia had her own issues to address. In New York, toward the end of April, she had a long lunch with Bill Koshland, during which he carefully explained to Julia the intricacies of publishing. Relaying them to Simca, Julia wrote, "It appears that publishing is far more complicated than we realize." Essentially Knopf had underestimated the number of printed copies. Although the first printing was for 10,000, they actually had put into print only a fraction of that. "They print in batches of 2, 3, or 5 thousand. Everything is estimated beforehand in sales meetings,, [sic] budgeted out, and each sales representative agrees to be responsible for a certain number of copies." Koshland gave her the current number of books sold, about 12,500, and the mailings that they had sent out to publicize the book. With that, she wrote, "I don't frankly think there is anything at all we can do about Knopf, as we can't bully them. Every author is in the same boat. But Jim Beard says that it is amazing how authors who do demonstrations and public appearances manage to keep their books selling. He has been going over a list of cookbooks from another publisher and finds people like D. Lucas just sell and sell. So, if this TV cooking program which I might do next year here comes off, that will help us a great deal." Julia ended with her hope for future sales and these pacifying words, "So we really can't complain, and we have a perfectly beautiful book."[19]

Julia's 1962 appointment book entry for Friday, May 11, gives the important meeting Julia was vying for: "11 A.M.-Mr. Larson [sic] WGBH," i.e., Robert Larsen, the station's program manager.[20] Everything suggests that Larsen was ready to talk with Julia about her proposal. As Julia reported to Simca on the following day, "They are definitely interested in a series of half-hour cooking programs, conducted by me! And they want to start right in this summer. They will tape one pilot program on July 19th, and three others in the following weeks. And, if they go well, they will want one a week for I don't know how long."

Julia found it a positive that WGBH was not a commercial station, for it would allow her to have "a reasonably sophisticated audience." They were offering her a wage somewhere between $50 and $100 for each program. She wouldn't be allowed to "do any actual advertising of the book, though I can mention it about once every three programs!" She had learned something of the amount of work involved, and thus decided she was not going to make any plans to teach "until this business, if it goes, gets into full gear."[21]

A handwritten note on May 24, 1962, was the prelude to the next step, the naming of the show. Although unsigned, because of its informality, familiarity with Julia's life story, and its playful use of Paul's nickname for

Julia, it was likely from Beatrice Braude. Addressing "Joooolie," the author reported that she had a call from Robert Larsen. "He's now working on a written prospectus, or proposal, which is to raise money for the cooking-series. He called for background information on you, and how you got started, where you'd been, where taught, with whom studied. This I gave him, subject to correction & further checks or changes by you." The writer also wrote that Larsen needed from the two of them "a good short title for the series," one that was appealing, not more than three words, including one French one, and able to "tell the whole story to the potential backer."[22]

Julia herself was thinking through the content of the forthcoming trial programs that were to begin on July 19 and go into mid-August. She let Simca know, "I've told them I want to use the idea in our book that cooking is a series of themes and variations, and if you can do one process, it relates to many others. Thought I would do Coq au Vin for the first, and relate it to braisage [braising] in general, and Boeuf Bourg. This would also, of course, show how to sauté mushrooms, braise onions, etc[.], as well as how to final-flavor a sauce." She was clear that, in working on the later programs, she needed "to have each program so that it sounds interesting."

Simca had let Julia know that she had again been in touch with Kosh-land regarding sales and royalty payments. Julia then described Knopf's mysterious system of sending an account each May and September, but waiting four months to send the check, adding "I don't know why!" After Julia prodded Simca to "Keep after him, and let me know what happens, please," she expressed what was on both their minds, "We've just got to get the sales going on that old book."[23]

When Paul and Julia went to WGBH, they learned what was in store for the future. Paul wrote Charlie, "They are going to put on (1st time it's been done on a non-commercial basis) a series of half-hour programs featuring that famous woman Julie McW Child Special." He saw himself as a part of the show. "I shall probably act in locus stoogensis, as the hands that come from the side to take away the dirty dishes. (FAME at last!)" He suggested that the show was to be pitched to an informed audience, as he put it,

"People You Might Know," not the "least-common-denominator" type. If the programs were to catch on with WGBH's "viewing public," they would likely "be interesting to do." He hoped that Charlie might be able to see them on his Channel 13, as there might be an arrangement for the two stations to exchange "taped TV shows." Such was educational television in 1962.[24]

When John McWilliam's death came on May 20, Julia immediately traveled to Pasadena to be with Phila and attend the funeral. On returning home, she wrote Simca that Paul was now gardening and enjoying physical labor out of doors: "I am just so grateful to our fortunate circumstances which allowed him to resign from the government, which he never enjoyed, and live as we are now."[25] He had in fact worked for months to make the house meet his artistic standards, and, as spring came, was developing an aesthetic area for dining out of doors. In leaving government service, a great weight had been lifted from Paul's shoulders: he was no longer living what he had earlier called his "unbalanced life."[26]

During the time Julia was in California, Paul was drawn in directly to help find a title for Julia's possible cooking show. Someone from WGBH called him and clearly spoke the exact words of the May 24 memo sent to Julia. Paul found the requirement of a French word in the three-word title to be the difficult part, for, as he explained in a letter to Charlie, "the only French cookery words most people know are gourmet and cuisine." He was working on possibilities, however, "I don't think Table d'Hote is too bad. I've got [the title words] down about 30 so far."[27]

When July came, Julia began to prepare for the three trial programs. These were videotaped in two days in mid-July, with airings to come at a later date. In her 1962 appointment book are listings for July 18 and 23. "WGBH #1" and "WGBH #2 & #3."[28] As would become her established practice, the first taping was preceded the day before by "hair," meaning time at a beauty salon, likely Elizabeth Arden. Because a disastrous fire had destroyed WGBH's building in October 1961, its programs were now taped in a variety of different settings in the Boston area. In this case, Julia's early shows took place in the demonstration kitchen of the Cambridge Gas Company.

Late in July, Julia wrote Simca a "REPORT ON TV SHOWS." Before the airing of the first one on omelettes, she and Paul invited six guests for dinner, including Ben Fairbanks and his wife. "You can imagine my anxiety when 8:30 came around and we turned on the infernal machine." Although Julia judged her performance "OK," she felt that, if given the chance to "do any more—they must all be much slower, all movements must be slow, talk must be slow, not too much must be done and all must be done as though the movements were under water. Eh bien. Lot's to learn. The cooking part went OK, but it was the performance of me, as talker, and mover, that was not professional."[29]

A week later, she invited eight of the WGBH staff and Avis for dinner before the 8:30 airing of the coq au vin show. "I rather dread seeing it, as it will be just as fast in pace as the last. I just hope some sponsor will think that there is some hope in me as a performer, and that I can do better. The whole technique is so different from anything else, particularly in that one must be so slow and deliberate in movements, and speak slowly and distinctly, etc."[30]

Paul waited until these two trial shows aired before reporting to his brother that "Julie's 3 telecasts were taped. Two of them made on the same day—to save $—the third we have not seen. . . . The first one to be shown was—from our standpoint—not altogether successful." Once again Paul turned critic, letting Charlie know that this was due to "Julie's lack of experience as a television demonstrator: There was too much crowded into the 28 minutes allowed[,] therefore she was under pressure & moved too fast in some sequences. Also there was a sense of breathlessness due to her habit of gasping when she is self-conscious—as a kind of pause, or punctuation, between phrases—Also her habit of closing her eyes from time to time." By contrast, "There was absolutely nothing wrong with her technique of omelette-making, of course. The demonstration was very good and quite dramatic, as phone-calls & fan-letters prove, but there's room for improvement. Happily the second telecast went <u>extremely</u> well." It featured coq au vin, and, with more rehearsal time, "the many complications of the new medium were pretty well overcome. Things like not talking to an audience (too loud), looking at camera A. while demonstrating to camera B." Paul also noted the fine gustatory results, as afterwards the staff "descended on the coq au vin like vultures, gobbling up every last morsel."[31]

At one point in this long letter Paul confirmed his deep engagement with Julia's work. Writing in sympathy with his twin brother's tooth abscess, Paul recalled his own such problem during "our book-promotion trip to the West." What stands out here is the "our." He was united with Julia in what was now their family business.

At the same time, once he was fully settled in at 103 Irving Street, Paul's own life took on new dimensions, and he began to enjoy the cultural and social experiences he valued. In May, Paul was pleased at the request of the Boston Art Festival that he serve as the "MC [of] two of the art shows, which means making some kind of commentary on the works as the cameras move around" the tents of the Boston Public Gardens. He wrote his brother that he believed his "years as a Diplomat will not be wasted," when he had to comment on paintings that offended his taste.[32] (Here Paul was likely referring to the modernist abstractions he anticipated viewing.) In late spring he enjoyed festive events with their many guests, including some out-of-town student chefs and his niece Erica and her husband Anthony Prud'homme.

In this congenial context, Paul felt he could develop ways to become the photographer and poet he wanted to be. This became fully apparent in their first long summer in Cambridge, when Avis brought Paul and Julia fully into the world of Bread Loaf, the well-established writers' workshop, located eleven miles from Middlebury, Vermont. (Bread Loaf took its name from a nearby mountain.) As Julia wrote Judith in 1962, "The Breadloaf Writer's Conf. starts August 15th, with Avis as House Mother and Barkeep, Paul as official photographer, and me as assistant deputy typist. . . . Great fun."[33]

While at Bread Loaf, Paul wrote Charlie about his memorable moment at the conference when he went to "Robert Frost's cabin to photograph him." Julia accompanied him as "a long-experienced talker-to-people-being photographed-by-Paul." All went well during the six indoor and six out-door shots, for Frost "was having a cooperative day. . . . Sometimes his old bastardry comes to the fore & he turns into a rhinoceros of mean stubbornness." Frost shared with the Childs his worries about transla-tion of his work, "given his use of simple words." Paul found him both deaf and egocentric, describing his talk as a "monologue at people." Now eighty-eight years old, Frost seemed to want "to spill out this wisdom-cup while he can." Paul preferred that he should "shut up & write: Better that God should have struck him dumb, not deaf, but the ways of the Lord are devious at best."[34]

In the months that followed, Julia and Paul's social life would continue to grow. In early fall 1962, Paul described to Charlie plans for the evening: "Jim Beard coming for dinner, w Bob & Mary Kennedy, Ben & Ginny Fair-bank, & Avis w/, of course, special food by our own Chef." In addition, there would be their houseguest, "a Greek dame . . . a lively & worldly librarian of the Chambre des Deputés in Athens." She was staying with them because the Childs, not fully putting aside their life in the Foreign Service, had joined a local group that hosted visiting foreigners "for the Department."[35]

The Childs' life, however, was soon to change. During the summer, Julia viewed the trial WGBH programs. In early August, she wrote a thank-you letter to David Davis at WGBH: "I love doing the shows, and thoroughly enjoyed working with Russ and Ruth Lockwood." From the experience she had learned "how complicated the medium is, requiring much more from the performer than just cooking." She understood that she had to learn "particularly about pace, smoothness, and talk." Russ Morash, the director, had told her "all these things, but I had to see them to digest them." Regarding Russ, she added, "he knows what he wants and inspires utter confidence."

Julia then turned to the new person who had now entered her life. "It was also a tremendous help to have Ruth's good advice in working up the scripts and dry runs, to say nothing of all her help during the actual rehearsals and performances. If we continue, I do hope we can keep the same team." Julia noted in handwriting on her typed carbon that she had sent a copy to Ruth Lockwood.[36]

RUTH LOCKWOOD

Julia's letter gives the first introduction in writing of the sixth person who joined Julia's team, Ruth Lockwood. She may have been hovering for a while in the background, given that she knew Beatrice Braude and had worked with her on the Eleanor Roosevelt series. Beatrice may have even suggested to Ruth that she watch the taping of Julia's "interview" on Duhamel's show. What is on the record is that Ruth Lockwood stepped up to the plate to work with Julia on the trial programs.

Ruth Lockwood shares with William Koshland her relative invisibility in the story of Julia Child's rise to eminence. As it was with Bill's background, Ruth's initially proved to be difficult to discover. Once again, I was fortunate in my friendships. In this case it was Ruth's daughter, Susan Lewinnek, who provided important sources of information on her late mother. Also, my professional ties to Smith College aided my research and understanding.

Ruth Lockwood was born Ruth Jeanne Edinberg in 1911. As a child, Ruth and her immediate family lived in the Boston area in the large home of her wealthy grandfather, Jacob Goldberg. Another prosperous relative supported Ruth's college education, as well as that of her brothers. Ruth went to Smith, entering the class of 1933.

In 1931, after she was accepted by Smith's junior year abroad program for Italy, then a fascist country ruled by Mussolini, Ruth was introduced by her Jewish parents to an eligible bachelor, Arthur H. Lockwood. He was a successful businessman and a distant relation, Ruth's senior by over a decade. As a young lawyer from New York, he had come to Boston in 1922 to join the Olympia Theater Company. Three years later he founded Lockwood and Gordon Enterprises with Louis H. Gordon. The company proved to be successful, with movie theaters throughout New England.[37] In a very short time after his meeting with Ruth, Arthur proposed, and on August 2, 1931, the two married.

Ruth's marriage and the birth of children interrupted her higher education but did not end it. In mid-life, she went back to school, first to Emerson College, where she took significant course work in television and drama. After receiving her B.A. from Emerson, Ruth entered the master's degree program at Boston University, completed a thesis in 1958, and received an M.A. in TV production.[38] By the early 1960s, Ruth Lockwood was at WGBH, working as a volunteer. She appeared in the public record when she worked on *Prospects of Mankind with Eleanor Roosevelt*, as assistant researcher under the program's producer, Beatrice Braude.

"Portrait of Ruth Lockwood (as a young woman)." Copyright © Susan Lewinnek.

Following many months of focus on the television project, Julia received important news from Knopf. On August 10, Bill Koshland had called to tell her that the Book of the Month Club was taking *Mastering the Art of French Cooking*. She wrote to Bill, "What really great news," and let him know that she had immediately telephoned Avis, who was "beside herself with excitement." Julia added that she next wrote to Simca, "telling her what the BOM is and what it might mean"—although at that time Julia herself hardly understood its potential.[39]

As Julia communicated with her team over this development, we are reminded of Avis's importance in her life. They now lived in the same town, with personal visits and the telephone taking the place of letters. Thus while their deep friendship and Avis's support for Julia continued unabated, the written record is limited to the times when one of them was away from home.

Fortunately, Bill Koshland and Julia normally communicated by letters, and these reveal Julia's unceasing efforts to promote *Mastering the Art of French Cooking*. In October 1962, as she waited to hear from WGBH about her future, Julia gave lectures and demonstrations in the Boston area for nonprofit organizations. As these events got underway, she worked out arrangements with Bill to sell copies of *Mastering* to her audiences. She wanted bookstores to provide the books at a discount to the group hosting her, allowing some of the profit to "go to the benefit organization." Working through the appropriate channel at the press, Koshland set this up.[40]

Julia also reported to Koshland that she would be coming to New York for a week in late October. "That nice James Beard has asked me to teach 3 lessons [at $50 per lesson] at his cooking school, the 23rd and 24th, so that is our glorious excuse. . . . I have suggested that he have The Book on sale at the classes, naturally."[41] Bill wrote back enthusiastically that he hoped to see her and Paul. In addition, he asked, "Just what time of day are your lessons to be taking place at Jim Beard's school? Perhaps I could sneak off and attend one of them. I assume one is allowed to be a one-time attendant and pay the necessary price. Yes?"[42] Koshland then took care of business by contacting Dick Krinsley. A later memo to him confirmed "for the sake of the record that you agreed you would do your damndest to get twenty copies of MASTERING THE ART OF FRENCH COOKING to the James Beard Cooking School . . . for availability when Julia Child gives demonstration lessons at Beard's request on Tuesday and Wednesday of next week."[43]

When Paul wrote to Charlie with the news that WGBH "now says they will positively go ahead w/ plans for a 26-unit series of telecasts of Julie's cooking show, begining [sic] shortly after the New Year," he let his brother know how busy Julia's life would become. He also conveyed his imagined distance from this new venture: "I have decided to keep out of this new series and persue [sic] my own life, though the temptation is great to lend a hand as I did w/ the first 3. But I believe Julie is now pretty well established in that new world & won't really need anything more from me than psychological support." Little did he realize how the "cooking show" was to change his life as well as Julia's.[44]

His concern at the time was the many calls on Julia. In mid-November, when he was writing this letter, Julia was in New York to give a lecture/demonstration at the Women's City Club. Paul put it this way: "Our Wifelet appears to be a better mousetrap, and I am beginning to make husbandly noises about her not running herself ragged." He admitted that it was difficult for a person to resist the money and respect, as well as taking pleasure in the work itself. He even admitted, "I get a touch of it with photography"; but in contrast, "Old Joolie is riding that success-wave like a hawk on an up-draft."[45]

Bill Koshland had long maintained his ties to the Boston area through regular visits, often around the important Harvard home football game against Yale or Princeton in late autumn. Avis had enjoyed these visits, and now Julia and Paul did as well. When the Childs hosted Thanksgiving at 103 Irving Street, he was invited, along with Avis, her current escort, and her son Mark and his girlfriend. In informing Charlie of this, Paul added that Koshland was "a very nice chap."[46]

After coming to her Irving Street home with wine for an evening, Bill wrote to Julia, "The rest of my stay in Cambridge I did nothing but rave about your kitchen, the dinner, the company, the evening and all else. It was a perfect evening in every respect. I'm so glad the wine turned out so well." He then turned to business to weigh in on the pros and cons of sponsorship for the future television show. It might bring "a bit more publicity and brouhaha, but maybe less for you." Knowing that something was about to appear in the *Boston Globe*, Koshland asked for a copy to possibly use for "a little release." Finally, he wrote something that was always important to a publishing house: "I'm delighted too that you are going to do your best to get full credit for authors and so forth and so on."[47]

Anything that brought Julia to New York and into the cooking world seemed especially important to Koshland. When he learned that she had been asked by Albert Stöckli, the famed chef at the Four Seasons, to help prepare pastry for a grand banquet at the restaurant of the invitation-only wine club, the Confrérie des Chevaliers du Tastevin, Bill was impressed. He commented that this was "really quite something. . . . What a wonderful opportunity and I too agree that it should be good for business."[48]

Julia, in a full and candid report to Simca, described her time at the Four Seasons as "a strange experience." First there was a trial run in mid-November when she worked all day into the late evening to create the right pastry base for a dish. The workroom at the Four Seasons was "a real hell hole. Very hot, no place to work, very little equipment of the type I needed. Luckily I had brought my rouleau, pastry brush, measure cups, etc." On the following day she returned in the morning and "got everything rolled out and ready for Albert [the pastry chef], and . . . we assembled things, baked them in time for the luncheon at 1:15 or so." When James Beard arrived, they watched Albert work, something she enjoyed. What she likely may have enjoyed even more was sending her bill that included all expenses. "Jim said to charge $150. for consultation! (I'm getting extremely mercenary.)"

Following that, she gave classes at Beard's cooking school, where she was paid "$50. per lesson. Bill Koshland nicely sent down 20 books (which I paid for) and we sold 19!" Those who already had the book bought them for Christmas gifts.[49]

After a return trip to the restaurant at the end of the month and more extensive preparations, the dinner itself came in early December. Julia returned, this time charging $75 per day plus all expenses over a long weekend.[50] In a letter that followed the event, she sent Simca the menu that included the list of the 260 Tastevin members who attended. Julia wrote, "you will note that Alfred Louis XIV Knopf was there!" While the dinner itself was a "theatrical presentation," Julia reported that she and James Beard could only watch from an office. Hidden from view, she and Jim drank wine and ate bits of the food snitched from the returned platters. After all the guests had gone, "W*H*O*O*P*E*E! Out came the champagne, all the wines, and everybody toasted everybody, sang, hugged everybody, and a great time was had by all until the wine ran out."[51]

On the days of the dinner preparations, Paul joined Julia in the kitchen of the Four Seasons. He photographed the work in the kitchen, attempting to seize "the moment juste of actions or facial expressions." However, he was careful to protect a new feature of his life in Cambridge. Reporting to Charlie, he wrote that he had gone with Julia to New York to work with her as her "commis," assisting her by following her commands—to break eggs, butter pastry molds, measure flour, set the oven to the correct temperature, etc. He worked with her on preparations until midnight.[52] However, despite his love of great food and fine wines, he chose not to stay for the great dinner to follow. Instead, he left New York to return to Cambridge to attend his own dinner, in this case one held at the Harvard Faculty Club by the New England Poetry Club. Paul explained to Charlie that he had done so because he was "a prospective member." He had canceled the previous one and thus felt he had to attend because "I couldn't do it twice in a row without psychological dammage [sic] to myself as a new member of Cambridge society."

After listing in detail the courses and the many great wines for the elaborate dinner at the Four Seasons, Paul wrote, "So, it wasn't easy to switch" and return to the Poetry Club dinner and its "different rhythms, plans & people. But I believe it was probably worth while for the long run—just as Julie's firmly-established relationships at the Four Seasons are useful for her new life in USA."[53]

In late November, Julia had asked Bill to let her know the last six months' sales figures for *Mastering*. These he didn't yet have, but he did know that the total sales since publication had reached 16,110, and that orders at the Book of the Month Club were now roughly 6,400 and likely to rise to at least 12,000. All was not business, however. He and Julia had been planning a special meal at Le Pavillon for when the Childs were next in New York. Since reserving a good table required a prestigious name on the reservation, Bill wrote, "I think maybe I can manage to get Alfred to use his name."[54] Clearly both understood, though at different levels, Alfred Knopf's importance in New York City.

The three early shows of *The French Chef* served as Julia's audition, and over the next months she waited to learn if she had gotten the part. In late November 1962, word finally came. Julia received a call from WGBH that the station "would definitely go ahead with the half hour TV programs, starting in January." She immediately wrote to Simca with the good news: "They are coming to do a color photo of me in the kitchen, which will be on the front page of the Boston Globe TV Sunday magazine—so I guess it is serious. Now, if we don't get some good publicity for the book out of this, and sell a great many copies so we can spend a great deal more money, I shall be mad!"[55]

On December 18, she wrote Simca that she was awaiting "WGBH types" coming over in the afternoon to talk over the television programs. "They had originally intended to use the 3 programs we did this summer, but have now decided to do all new ones. 26. We shall do at least 2 a day, and perhaps 4 in two days—I don't know how that would work!

But Paul has bought a rowing machine, so I am gathering strength. Anyway, if we can get them all taped by April 1st, that will be wonderful."[56]

The show still lacked a name. A title under consideration in mid-December, "Looking at Cooking," caused Julia to write a strong letter of protest to Robert Larsen. This proposed title and its variations were to her mind, "cheesy, little womanish, cute, amateurish." She wanted what she had been informally calling the show since at least September: "THE FRENCH CHEF." Julia argued that the word *chef* was as applicable to a woman as it was to a man, "is short, to the point, dignified, glamorous, and appeals to men as well as women."[57] With that, Larsen relented, writing in a memo to Russ Morash, "After having racked our collective brains for weeks to find a good alternative title for the French Chef we have decided that a good alternative title does not seem to be available. And since both Julia and Paul Child are extremely fond of the original title I have capitulated. Let us call it: THE FRENCH CHEF now and forever!"[58] Ruth Lockwood's initials were on the list of those copied on the memo, signifying that she would continue working with Julia on the show.

Once production was underway, Julia wrote Simca about Ruth: "There is a very nice girl, Ruth Lockwood, who is about my age, and is the asistant [sic] director. She and I work together all the time, and she rehearses with me. Is also very interested in cooking, and never moves without THE BOOK. She is just fine, and devoted to the series. How lucky! All is done on a shoestring, and there is no one to clean up but Ruth and me, and that dear Paul who comes for the afternoon taping and then remains to wash the dishes." Ruth worked out a system of using flash cards, each giving the task and the time allotted. Julia gave an example: "BROWNING CHICKEN, 5 min" was held up for her to see by one of the crew. After that "the chap also has little cards saying 5, or 4, or 1 or ½ to show how many minutes there are left."[59]

"The French chef; souffles and chick-fric (Ruth adjusts Julia's hair at cook top),"
Schlesinger Library, Harvard Radcliffe Institute.

As the months went on, Julia kept Koshland in the loop. She and Paul had gone to California to spend the Christmas holidays with her sister, Dort. As 1963 began, Bill wrote, "How good it was hearing your voice in California and then to have a note from you to greet me upon my return to the office this morning." Continuing, he revealed what Julia had related on her call, "I'm delighted with the details as to the TV cooking program and your fierce schedule of making the tapes. What channel is it in Boston? What station?" Koshland then said something that clearly pleased Julia: "Do give me much more by way of details so I can pass word along to the salespeople."[60]

A little over a week later, he had good news to report. "Don't look now, but the phone rang today and my friend Allan Ullman at the Book-of-the-Month Club called to say (are you sitting down?) that the total orders received thus far from the mail order campaign are somewhat in excess of

35,000 copies. I haven't recovered yet! At the moment they are some 18,000 behind in unfilled orders and the end is not yet in sight. Three cheers for all of us, and a happy New Year to you.+ Paul & Avis."[61]

Julia was thrilled: "Can it be true? After you have digested and confirmed it a bit more, tell me again." She added, "Avis says she's not surprised!" In his letter confirming the 35,000 copies, Bill wrote, "Well, it just couldn't have happened to a group of nicer people is all I can say." Julia had asked for a subscription to the club's mailing list. She added a request by Avis, always on the alert for ways to publicize *Mastering*, that Bill push Book of the Month Club to give more publicity by mentioning the book in their monthly magazine.[62] Julia's request was easy to arrange; but Koshland was not able to honor the one by Avis. He wrote that there was nothing in the contract with BOM that justified it, adding, "There's a mystique about these things. . . . I think we can leave that to the experts!"[63]

As Julia prepared for the tapings of *The French Chef* to begin on January 23, her hope, clearly expressed to Bill Koshland, was that the show would become a major marketing tool for *Mastering*. With Book of the Month Club distributing it for their members, future sales were promising, but Julia was eager for Knopf to sell more books in bookstores, as the proceeds from BOM were a meager $.50 per copy.[64] Promoting this, Julia gave Bill the schedule of the show and followed with, "If any bookstores wanted to put THE BOOK in the window saying 'This week's recipe FROM THE FRENCH CHEF, "Beef Bourguignon".' [sic] That would not be a bad idea, would it? (We'd send schedule and page numbers for the weekly change.)" She was also eager to promote the show in New York. Currently the plan was for Channel 13 to show it midafternoon on Wednesdays. Julia clearly did not want *The French Chef* to be regarded as a program fit only for women who did not work outside the home. She had pushed WGBH to schedule it in the evening for the southern New England audience, and now New York needed prodding. She suggested that if "2 dozen people wrote in and said WE WANT THE FRENCH CHEF, or that great French cooking program what's-its-name, shown in the evening so we can see it—perhaps they might."[65]

On January 26, 1963, Paul announced to Charlie, "Life is speeded up." With this, he wrote of Ruth, gave her a title, and conveyed the nature of her work. He gave Julia's program for rehearsals first at home. They were "with either Ruth Lockwood (Production Assistant for THE FRENCH CHEF) or me, holding the stop-watch." Following this, "there are practice sessions, w/ just Julie & Ruth" at the studio's kitchen in the electric building, "followed by dry-runs w/ the Producer and the lighting and the camera crews, during which certain parts are rehearsed several times, often changed as better action is invented."

As Paul continued, he labeled the taping as "a blitz-type operation." Fortunately, he and Julia could rely on their earlier experiences: "We have had to lead scheduled & disciplined lives for a long time in my Foreign Service life, so this is new only in respect to Julie's proffesion [sic] dominating it rather than mine." This was not for him a time of soul searching, for he had no desire to crawl out "from under the layers of illusion which separate me from THE FACTS. I rather enjoy it down under here at the moment & I don't propose to let in any more light & air than I can deal with." Little did he likely know how deeply he would become involved in the making of each episode.

One pleasant connection linked Paul to his own past. He told Charlie that the prepared food at the end of the show was displayed for the camera on a well-set table with "the handsome" accessories furnished "courtesy of Design Research . . . A fresh table-setting for each of the 26 shows." Above these words, he wrote, "Thompson [the store's owner] turns out to be a former student of mine at Avon!"[66]

Once the tapings for the first full season began, Paul was fully engaged in Julia's work. And fortunately for a historian, he left a rich record. In early February, after twelve tapings, he wrote to Charlie, "These evenings when other folk are at the movies, or the symphony, or lectures, find Julie & me in our kitchen—me w/ stop-watch in hand, and Julie at the stove—timing the various sections of the next two shows. Over and over and over, with critical comments, and with suggestions for new language or new demonstration methods. This all counts strongly in the final filming. The engineers & cameramen say they have never seen a show so thoroughly prepared before."

Paul described the diagram he had devised that the crew had found "particularly impressive." It showed the stoves, shelves, and sink, "listing on them every single piece of equipment, and every bit of food, spice, flavors, liquids, spoons, dishes, oven-temperatures and so on." Before the filming, Ruth Lockwood and Julia wrote specific labels for each program.

It was a good method, but it wasn't foolproof. Offering a dramatic example, Paul wrote, "In the very mid-stream, w/ cameras turning, lights lit, every second being ticked off the other day, lo and behold! Julie reaches for the butter, supposed to be on Shelf #2, lefthand side, glass dish—only to find in the dish a piece of paper saying 'BUTTER.' It had been moved to the refrigerator because it had gotten too soft during the rehearsal." Paul praised Julia's improvisational skills, her "real pro's imperturbability when the chips are down."[67] Julia described to Simca what she had actually done. Looking at the camera, she said, "Merde alors, forgot the butter, always forget something." She went to the refrigerator on the set, pulled out the butter carton to find it had only a tiny amount. When a moment came when the camera was off her, she "was able to mouth an anguished 'BUTTER' to the floor manager, who snuck into the frig, with trembling fingers peeled paper of[f] a piece of butter, and snuck it into the work table, with no camera spotting him."[68] To Charlie, Paul put it this way, quoting what was likely said on the set, "we lose 10 years w/ every show."[69]

The initial program was to air on February 11, 1963. Paul told Charlie that he and Julia were going to view it at Ruth Lockwood's home and would be joined there by others from WGBH.[70] With this, Paul revealed that Ruth shared with Julia a warm spirit of hospitality.

During this time, Julia and Simca kept Bill Koshland informed regarding the availability of their book in bookstores, and he was paying close attention. In memos to Dick Krinsley, responsible for sales at Knopf, Koshland tried to get results. Prodded by the efforts of Louisette and Simca to publicize the book abroad, Koshland had given approval to the

French edition of the *Herald Tribune* to publish two recipes from the book each week. This effort, however, was proving fruitless because there were no copies of *Mastering the Art of French Cooking* in the major bookstores in Paris with English-language books.

When a letter came to Knopf from a woman in France, frustrated that she could not find *Mastering* anywhere in Paris, Koshland wrote an angry memo to Krinsley, one that took an unusually strong tone: "Here we go again! I've sent you a rash of memos over the past months having to do with MASTERING THE ART OF FRENCH COOKING and the interest of the [French] authors in promoting their magnum opus." With this he listed his several efforts, beginning with a memo on June 16. For the October 12 entry, he wrote, "and yet here again never have I had any word from you as to your continuing to see that the leading accounts in Paris are stocked."

Attaching a copy of the letter from the woman in France unable to buy the book, Koshland continued, "The lady may be a crank, she may be dishonest, she may be sincere. But I do think on a $10 book such as this that has proven itself over and over again, we are absolutely nuts if we don't <u>force</u> the sale abroad," by which he meant getting it on the shelves of such stores in Paris as Brentano's. Although Koshland had reassured the woman of his efforts, he nonetheless had "a hunch that nothing has ever been done to push this abroad, where I think we'd really get some sales."[71] Over time Koshland learned that there was a limit to even his reach, that neither he nor Krinsley had the power to compel foreign bookstores to stock a title.

Opportunity for book sales in the U.S. proved to be an altogether different matter. In this same memo, Koshland alerted Krinsley, "There'll be more to come to you shortly because Julia Child, who is [in] Cambridge, is in the next week or two getting down to taping a 26-week TV program based on herself, the book and so on which will be broadcast in Boston local and possibly extended through Channel 13 here. Details to come in due course."[72] Although Koshland could hardly foresee the future, he tried to prepare for its possibilities.

And in her jaunty way, Julia knew how to prepare him. Two days later, she wrote to him, "We are now deep in final plans for the great TV cooking series. We start taping on January 23, and shall do between 2 and 4 a week through the end of March." She enclosed a summary of the series and informed him that her show would air each Thursday evening from early February to the beginning of August; and it would reach an audience covering much of southern New England—from the Cape in Massachusetts to Pittsfield in the west and on to Keene, New Hampshire. At that time regional distribution was facilitated by the Eastern Educational Network (EEN), covering New England states and western New York.[73] Julia added, "We are hoping other stations in the National Educational TV will take up the shows, particularly Channel 13 in NY, but imagine they will want to see the first few tapes before they make up their minds." With that, she wished Bill a "most happy and wonderful 1963, in which Childs and Koshland shall meet frequently to gorge on wonderful kweezeen."[74]

In early February Bill Koshland, then in London, got more news from Julia of *The French Chef.* Beginning with "The TV programs are marching along," she related that WGBH had now taped eleven episodes (of twenty-six), and the first one was about to be aired that evening, February 11. Without naming her, Julia began with Ruth Lockwood's contribution. "I've got a most able girl who is assistant director and rehearses with me until we're black in the face—we find a show is only as good as its rehearsal." Julia then gave her sense of her own role. Preparation aside, "All the material . . . has to be pretty ad-lib, as one never quite knows what's going to happen on the stove. The least one can say is that the shows will have a definite informality and spontaneity! We'll soon know whether they are going over, I guess." She then wrote Bill regarding what was important to him: "They are giving audio credit to the book, and I see that it is prominently displayed in the book shelf over the frigo."[75]

Her next letter came to Bill in Paris. Simca had written of his visit, and Julia wrote him that both Simca and Jean "just loved seeing you, and both just loved you." She then told him of the TV work. "Two showings of the French Chef have appeared so far, Boeuf Bourguignon, and Onion Soup. I thought the Beef was OK, but thought the Onion Soup was pretty amateurish, breathless, confused. However people seem to like the shows— something new in amateurism, I guess, and the station has received 200 cards and letters which they think remarkable."[76] Writing two weeks later with seven more tapings to go, she confessed, "I'm wearing down a bit, but still teniring le coup [holding on]. It sure is a lot of work though—7 days a week, what with scripts, preparations, rehearsals." Four of the shows had been aired at this point, and WGBH had received more than 600 positive cards and letters from viewers. Turning to the important issue for Bill: "It appears that book sales are . . . encouraging, but I've had no time to inves-tigate and probably shall never do so."[77] Julia's prediction of her behavoir proved to be inaccurate, as her wait to investigate sales of *Mastering* lasted less than a month. In early April, in a letter to Simca about an upcoming trip to New York, Julia wrote that when she and Paul dined with Koshland at Le Pavillon, "I hope he may be able to have some figures on whether or not the TV programs are helping the sales of the book in the Boston area."[78]

The French Chef became even more important to Julia when she faced a shrinking biannual royalty payment. In early March she sent Simca (and kept for herself) a check that was "A puny thing after what we're used to": $727.50. Although she hoped for a surprise in the April 31 statement, Julia thought that the two of them might "have to resign ourselves to the fact that our sales may just dwindle off in a year or two." In the meantime, she was "Madly busy with TV. Four shows this coming week." The response to the three shows that had aired was very good. WGBH had received over 500 letters, "which they think is amazing."[79]

After the completion of the final tapings for the first season, eight over several days, Paul gave Charlie a sense of Julia's growing skill, listed the many workers on the set, and jocularly conveyed his own contribution. He delighted in comparing tapings to the "successful rocket-launchings" of the era. He wrote, "It's a combined-Opp, of course: Julia, Ruth Lockwood;

Russ Morash (Director), Stan (floor manager), plus a crew of 13 . . . (not to mention Pearl Diver, Parsley-Chopper, Chart maker, Driver, Packer, Prune-stuffer cum Handy-Man: that's me)."[80]

Julia now had two loyal unpaid assistants at her side, Paul and Ruth. Ruth began to handle much of the correspondence, following Julia's directive, meant to confirm her image that "We are old-shoe, kindly, easy going, but basically efficient."[81] And both extended their service beyond WGBH. As Julia got caught up in assisting the TV station in fundraising, Ruth partnered with her in planning and giving cooking demonstrations for women's groups. In May 1963, Paul listed events in three places, Weston, Boston, and Newburyport. Paul explained to Charlie, "These help to raise $ for WGBH's operating fund, and also keep Julie's name before the public which is good for book sales." Paul noted that 350 women had attended in Weston, and that, in Boston, she had signed and sold 33 copies of the book.[82]

It is difficult to know cause and effect, as many factors contributed over time to the immense sales of *Mastering the Art of French Cooking*. First were the positive reviews, in the *New York Times* and elsewhere. Then there was the launch of Julia's book tour with Simca. Nonetheless, what proved to be unusual about *Mastering* was its widening appeal over time, after its initial burst had slowed. Without a doubt, the Book of the Month Club played an important part. But clearly *The French Chef* and Julia Child's continuing television presence and growing audience aided *Mastering*'s climb in sales. It kept the book alive and selling year after year. At the time of this writing, a representative of The Julia Child Foundation for Gastronomy and the Culinary Arts offered information that over three million copies of the book have been printed.[83]

Unquestionably, by spring 1963, Julia understood the impact of the show, and continued to track book sales. Bill Koshland encouraged her engagement with sales figures in his letters, such as in mid-March 1963, when he wrote, "This represents payment by the Book-of-the-Month Club for another 30,000 (count 'em!) of MASTERING THE ART OF FRENCH COOKING. Are we in business? As a matter of fact, at the National Book

Awards I ran into Allan Ullman who has been the drum beater down there through whom I have been working all these months, and he tells me it's the best selling dividend they've ever had. . . . I'll let you be the bringer of news to Simca and Mme. Bertholle (and Avis, too, of course)."[84] (Confession: I joined the Book of the Month Club to get that dividend.)

Julia replied with a written shout: "W*O*W! Followed your directions to the letter, and am still sitting! How grand for us all, and may they keep right on selling that old dividend. I've just sent off checks to Louisette and Simca, and put my share in the savings bank. My."[85]

As Julia continued, she wrote of finishing up the TV tapings in the week ahead. "Thank heaven. The house is a mess, the socks are not darned, the silver is tarnished, the bills are unpaid, etc. But it's been fun. The Harvard Coop says they've been selling books like mad (figures? 2 or 25 per day???) since shows began. It would be interesting to see what the sales figures have been in this TV area since Feb. 12, would it not."[86] Julia was clearly eager to learn relation of *The French Chef* to the rising sales of *Mastering*.

And Paul was attentive as well, as seen by his jottings on the letter Koshland had written in reply. In the margin of Bill's report that Knopf had sent a mailing to 107 stores in the area reached by WGBH, "south to Providence, north to Portsmouth, New Hampshire, east and west to the border of Massachusetts," Paul penned these words: "Julie: Doesn't he know about Albany-Schenectady and New Hampshire?" Paul also fumed about some misinformation on the two posters Knopf had prepared for the Coop and Jordan Marsh that Bill mentioned: "ALSO: The TV show will continue through 1st week in Aug, so why [did the poster] say 'It is slated to run at least until May 6th? Phooey.'"[87] As Julia shared her Koshland correspondence with Paul, he was attentive to Knopf's missteps.

Yet, as careful as Paul was to protect Julia's interests, with the taping at WGBH finished for the season, Paul could now focus once again on his own creative work. He began in earnest and, by early March, produced a painting of Venice. He was proud enough of this that he photographed the work in color and sent it to his artist twin brother, writing that he felt he was on the verge of an artistic breakthrough.[88]

Beginning in April 1963, Julia added another work obligation—one she was happy to accept—a weekly column to appear in the *Boston Globe*. She received help from Koshland and James Beard on contract negotiations with the paper. Over the phone, Beard told her that she would be lucky to get $50 for each column. (Julia actually received $30 per piece.) He also suggested that the contract state that it was to be renegotiated if the column were syndicated.[89] To Julia's delight, as the days drew near to its first appearance, the *Globe* publicized the column in an editorial. Writing, however, initially proved difficult. She wrote to Bill, "I am now cogitating for my first column for the Globe and suffering horribly."[90]

Gradually, through the back door of WGBH, Julia was coming to accept a degree of commercialism. In May, Julia reported to Bill that the station was having "money troubles," and Robert Larsen was hoping to raise money from local businesses. For this reason he wanted to learn if Knopf was seeing "an increase in demand for our books since . . . the French Chef went on the air." He also had been "scouting around the stores to see what effect the shows are having on the buying public." Julia related one of his forays, checking out the Boston department store Jordan Marsh. There he found no copies of *Mastering the Art of French Cooking*. He nudged Julia to see that Knopf urge their distributor to force "100 books down their throats," then check up on them "every couple of weeks." In writing to Bill, Julia relayed Larsen's humorous comment that in strolling around Jordan Marsh, a salesman told him that he had found the many recent requests for wire whisks to be such "a nuisance" that he kept them "hidden in a drawer."[91]

Already signed up by the *Globe* for a year, when asked by SS Pierce to do a lead article for their Fall-Winter catalog, Julia jumped at the chance. It paid $250 and promised "credit to The French Chef, and to The Book, on the title page in rather large print." With her sense of humor intact, she quipped to Bill, "and we are now living on doctored-up canned goods. Just as well you aren't here!"[92] Two weeks later, she wrote Bill a request in the form of a question: "I do wonder if sales will show any advance because of the TV?"[93]

As Julia took on more and more tasks, however, Paul came to feel its costs. In late July, he complained to his brother that "Julie's niceness, and a basic lack of worldliness (in the sense of self-protection) have let her in for too much slugging work which has allowed her to become too fatigued for common sense and has inhibited our capacity for social life and the cultivation of friends, of new acquaintances, of movies, music, theater, picnics. . . . or damn near anything but continous wood-peckering on that old typewriter."[94]

Julia's relationship to Judith Jones remained cordial, but—if their letters are any indication—their ties were more professional than personal. The difference between the approaches of the two members of Julia's team at Knopf may have been their personalities. While Bill Koshland appears on paper to be a very warm human being, Judith appears always considerate and attentive but cooler. Perhaps more important, however, may have been their differing professional roles at Knopf. While Bill was gaining more responsibility in the firm, Judith remained a member of the editorial staff, working with other authors who also needed attention. And in relation to Julia, in contrast to Bill, who sent royalties, Judith had a need to keep some distance as she regularly had to convey to Julia the bad news of debts owed. With each new print run, Julia found more mistakes in the text and sent Judith a new list of corrections. After seeing them into execution, Judith was required to charge the authors for the costs of correcting mistakes that they had let slip into the book. Finally, Judith was discussing with Julia a second volume, familiarly referred to as "Mastering II." Judith, as its future editor, may have felt that her role required her to maintain a certain reserve. A possible signal of this distance came in August 1963, before Julia and Paul traveled by ship to Europe. Bill Koshland invited them to visit him in Southampton before they sailed. Judith expressed only that she hoped to see Julia when she was in New York.[95] As it turned out, Julia and Paul actually stayed in the city, where they joined both Bill and Judith for lunch at a grand restaurant.

Of course, Julia's relations with Bill had a business side as well. Following this lunch, she wrote a long letter to answer all his questions and to raise her own concerns. She offered all the places where *The French Chef* would be airing in the fall, with the question lurking in the background: Does the TV show increase sales? For example, "What we would like to know is whether the sales for these two areas [New York and San Francisco, new on the list] show any significant kind of an increase because of the TV program." Was the big jump of sales in New England "due to summer visitors in the WGBH territory?" She also inquired about whether newspapers in New York and San Francisco might list the weekly recipe and take her column? Here she promised that when she and Paul were abroad, Ruth Lockwood would send samples of the column and answer any questions Bill might have.[96] To all this, Bill responded warmly and positively, although he cautioned the unlikelihood of New York taking up the columns, as there were "such entrenched figures in the food field on the various newspapers."[97]

A few days later, Bill wrote himself a memo that conveys the way that he blended professional and personal attention: "I've just had a conversation with Julia Child who is in New York on her way abroad for some time. This was all with reference to the increased sales resulting from the success of the TV show in Boston. I must try and check with Krinsley when he is back from vacation to see what if anything he can give by way of figures to show so that in turn the San Francisco station which is going to start the show in October will have some inkling of what's coming, to say nothing of the New York one when it's released. This will take a bit of doing, but maybe we can get help."[98]

In late summer 1963 Julia and Paul began a long period away from Cambridge, traveling to Norway, France, and England. It would be their first return to Norway, and on board the ship Paul typed a long letter to Charlie, reflecting on his memories of their New York arrival in June 1961 from

Norway on that very same boat. Then he had felt both a yearning to return immediately to Norway "and not have to face up to a totally new life for the umpteenth time. . . . But somehow it didn't work: Julie has become a TV Star, we have striven mightily together on our big old house, and a different set of plants have now taken root in a different garden." In contrast to his earlier complaints about Julia's workload, these words suggest his acceptance of the changes that had come so quickly and intensely into his life with Julia.[99]

When the Childs had come onboard, they found on entering their cabin "both flowers and champagne from Ruth and Arthur Lockwood."[100] This reveals Ruth Lockwood's similarity to Julia in understanding what gave another person pleasure. What followed were many letters between Ruth and Julia that traversed the Atlantic Ocean. They were filled with business matters such as the future schedule for the series, the knotty business of unauthorized uses of the name French Chef, the rejection of gifts from businesses, and an upcoming set of cooking demonstrations in March 1965 in San Francisco; but they also included many statements of affection. On one occasion, in the middle of writing a letter to Julia, Ruth received one from her. Ruth responded, "I missed you before your letter came, but I miss you all the more after reading it because it brought you near for just a moment and then you were gone again."[101]

Ruth's next letter to Julia brought a long, tactful request, at the same time hedged with concern. Could the annual Christmas party of the WGBH staff be held in Julia and Paul's home? Ruth set out a series of reasons for this request, along with her concerns about the large number of those attending who might cause "wear and tear" to the house. Using her own nickname for Julia, "Jule," Ruth assured her that no one at WGBH knew she was suggesting this, and she begged Julia to think about the party and "<u>please</u> be very frank." During these months, Ruth was also checking to see that all was in order at 103 Irving Street. In a postscript, she wrote of recently going by 103 Irving: "Everything, including the grounds, Paul, looked fine. Will check periodically."[102]

Julia's reply was a newsy letter from Oslo, telling not only of what she and Paul were experiencing in this, their first return to Norway, but also about her misstep, packing far too much for such a trip. She even included news from Avis regarding DeVoto family matters. Julia then listed the professional chores she had accomplished, including columns for the *Globe* and her goal for the coming months, preparation of scripts for future episodes of *The French Chef.* When she turned to respond to Ruth's report in a previous letter, Julia wrote, "We are both very much impresses [sic] with the efficiency of our AP [Associate Producer]! Makes great sense, every move she has made." Regarding the elaborate plans for demonstrations forthcoming at San Francisco's Museum of Art, she complimented Ruth: "SF should have all the material it needs with what you have sent—just the way the show ought to run on the road." Finally, as a postscript, Julia wrote, "We both think a Christmas party at our house would be dandy—plenty of room for 150 people, and we can have everything catered—and it probably doesn't have to be terribly fancy, either." Julia's letter was encased within her salutation, "Dearest Ruthie," and signed off: "Much love," followed by her pictorial signature, an inked heart with arrow and her initial, "J."[103]

Julia Child's "signature," Schlesinger Library.

In late September vacationing with her husband at a fishing camp in Maine, Ruth wrote "a quickie because Arthur is waiting impatiently for me to join him on the lake. He is sure that hundreds of salmon are ready just for us." With that came the all-important news that *The French Chef* would soon be viewed in New York in both evenings and afternoons. Ruth promised that if there were reviews, she would send them. She enclosed a "self-explanatory" copy of her letter to William Koshland. She followed this with "Wish you were here with us but next spring will have to do." Ruth closed with, "Love, handclasps, hugs . . . all of it from Arthur to you both . . . From me my special love."[104]

Once back home in Boston, Ruth had to contend with a knotty legal issue that emerged when a manufacturer put on the market a "French Chef skillet." Could he be stopped? This raised a related question, could Julia—and thus WGBH—accept goods, such as pots and pans, to be used on the show? These matters came at a time when "payola" was making the news, and thus they required a long, complicated letter from a Washington, D.C., law firm setting down restrictions.

Then came something more personal for Ruth. The *Smith Alumnae Quarterly* was planning an article on Julia and her. Learning of this before her vacation, she had phoned the writer, Dick Fish, and reached his assistant, making it clear that she "wanted to be left out of the story." The assistant told her that her request would be honored. On her return from Maine, however, she found a letter, waiting at the house, from Dick saying, "that they very much wanted me in because I was a Smithie, etc., etc., and ended by begging me to reconsider." She wrote that she had not changed her mind: "this should be an all-out Julia Child Story." It was, however, too late to stop the piece.

Upset, Ruth wrote to Julia, "This is your story and I am very happy to be part of it in the background. All the publicity belongs to you, Jule. You are the show. You are MORE than the show and nothing you say will make me feel any different."[105] Julia, however, replied in a different vein that she was "Very glad the Smith people refused to cut you out of that story. There'd be no F[rench] C[hef] without our AP, as who could know better than we. And besides, it makes a much better story to have the two of us Smithies together."[106]

As *The French Chef* began to consume more of Julia's time, strengthening the sales of *Mastering the Art of French Cooking*, she came to have two professionals firmly in her court—Bill Koshland and Ruth Lockwood. And they began to have to deal with each other. Ruth first corresponded with Bill Koshland in September 1963, when she honored Julia's request that, during her time abroad, Ruth send Bill tear sheets of her *Boston Globe* articles. Ruth, being Ruth, went beyond to give Koshland the future schedule of programs of *The French Chef* in New York, San Francisco, and Sacramento. She then followed with long, detailed instructions to ensure the cookbook's availability in the California viewing area. She also reminded Koshland of Julia's wish to receive detailed information on the relation of an increase in the book's sales in a city with the advent there of the show. Finally, Ruth added her own request that Koshland get Hammacher Schlemmer to list the cookbook in their next Christmas catalog. Ruth softened these instructions by writing of the greatness of *Mastering*, stating that long before meeting Julia, she had admired not only the content of the book but also Knopf's contribution as its publisher: "the set-up, paper quality, type, and printing." And then she extended an open invitation to Koshland to come and view a taping of the show.[107]

Understanding Bill Koshland's own sense of his importance to both the Knopf publishing house and Julia Child's success, this letter may have put him on guard. He replied in a manner that began kindly, with his thanks, but then responded to its contents with words that let Ruth know his place in the world. Regarding Ruth's letter, he wrote, "I have had a photocopy made of it and sent over to Richard Krinsley of the sales department of Random House, at 457 Madison, and he will carry on as best he can in my absence. I'm off for an extended business trip to Europe. . . . Everything you've written has been duly noted down."[108]

Julia, by contrast, was deeply appreciative when she received a copy of Ruth's letter, informing her that both she and Paul saw it as "a great piece of work." Knowing Bill was traveling, she wrote that she imagined "some one in his office will take care of things." At this point, however, she didn't hold "much real hope that they will do anything specatular [spectacular] for us. If the shows really catch on in New York, they might. We can just hope for the best." Julia conveyed her own affection as she wrote "Dearest Ruth, We were both so glad to get yours of Sept. 21st. You have no idea how we miss our 3 or 4 times daily contact with our AP! But just to read you brings you close, and makes us feel better. Not that we don't feel top-hole, but we miss you."[109]

Ruth seemed to have understood Koshland's intent, however. When she next sent him an article from the *Monitor*, she wrote to Julia, "Isn't it great? I have already sent a copy to Koshland pointing out the wonderful reference to 'The Book.'" With this she enclosed her letter to him, making it clear to Julia that, "I want you to know that I sent a photostat of it to Koshland without any remarks."[110]

Julia, being Julia, tried to smooth things over and make Ruth feel appreciated. Writing from Paris on a trip before she and Paul returned home, she first thanked Ruth for the copies of letters she had sent. Then she wrote, "We saw Koshland in London, and he said he was so glad to get your letters, and hopes to be able to help."[111] In the following year, however, word came indirectly to Julia that Ruth's communications were a burden that Koshland no longer wanted to bear. Writing to Bill, she let him know that she had been told by a mutual friend, "that my dear and ever devoted associate, Ruth Lockwood, has been pestering you to some extent. I'll call her off and henceforth communications will channel only through me. She is a dear girl, but this TV program and 'her' book are passionate interests and she can sometimes be over protective."[112]

During their sojourn abroad Julia and Paul paid a long visit to Simca at Bramafam. The publication of *Mastering*, the successful book launch, and the coming of royalties had dissipated much of the tension between the two women. Once again, they were able to return to the origin of their friend-ship, cooking together. Julia wrote Ruth that in planning a future episode of *The French Chef,* she and Simca had gone "on a mad cooking fest. . . . Every day we have been making croissants, and think we have the recipe taped, so we can do it on the TV. That should be great!"[113]

When Simca gave lessons to the local boulanger on the making of croissants, Paul photographed the two of them. And with that he gave a list to Charlie of the photography work he had done for Julia. Writing with pride in his unposed photographs, Paul related how, in Paris, he had shot Julia working with Chef Bugnard; in San Francisco, cooking with Simca at the City of Paris; in New York, as she worked in the kitchen of the Four Seasons restaurant; and in Cambridge, during the first twenty-six tapings for WGBH.[114] Many of Julia Child's iconic images were Paul's work.

With this return to France, both Paul and Julia began to dream about themselves having a property near Bramafam. In addition to the many pleasures of Provence's land and air, Julia felt she needed to be in France at least every other year "to get again into the good taste and feeling about food." They began looking around, but found that prices of real estate in the region had risen too high for them. As Julia put it, the area was going "through a reel [sic] boom." She wrote to Ruth that while "it has been fun to look, . . . we shall not buy anything, just dream a bit."[115]

Actually, in a long letter from Paul to Charlie, written on Friday of the week prior to Julia's letter to Ruth, Paul let him know that an idea had come to them—that of turning a small structure on the Bramafam property, 150 yards from the big house—into a place for their own use. Their idea was to combine with Simca "financially on this project" in a way that they could begin "using it ourselves, whenever we wanted to." An important advantage would be that Simca and Jean "would do all the contacting & arranging & overseeing." Three days later, after Jean returned, Paul abandoned this idea. Learning that the actual ownership of the property was in the hands of Jean's two sisters, he declared, "I have decided not to invest in any land or property."[116] It didn't take long, however, for the Childs to have a change of mind.

In this same letter Paul offered a glimpse into Julia's relationship with Ruth Lockwood. Listening to Simca, Julia and Paul had decided that Simca needed a business manager to handle the many details of her cooking school. "Ruth Lockwood has been performing the same sort of services for Julia, and believe me it[']s been a blessing. So much easier for Ruth (than for Julie) to say, 'The standard cost for a demonstration-lecture by Julia Child is $250. And I regret to say Madame, that the French Chef Lecture Bureau cannot make any changes in its established costs, even for charitable considerations.'"[117]

The $250 was not for Julia's pocket, but was rather a contribution to WGBH, one that allowed Julia to use part of it to purchase equipment needed for *The French Chef*. When in Paris preparing for the return to the U.S., Julia wrote to Ruth, in anticipation of the $250 for a Smith College club demonstration, "I think I'll buy us a few casseroles and things here in Paris. (PLEASE SEND ME A LIST of anything you want me to buy you when I'm here.)" Following this, Julia made a statement that gave additional evidence of her reliance on Ruth for her performance on *The French Chef*. After she made a request that the crew at WGBH move the set's refrigerator closer to where she prepared the food, Julia wrote, "Or does the movement [Julia's own, from refrigerator to her work area] add a bit of variety?"[118]

Following time at Bramafam, Julia and Paul traveled by car in France and then journeyed to England. Along with visits to friends, Julia met with the editor of the English edition of the cookbook, wrote columns, and prepared scripts for future episodes of *The French Chef*. They had lunch with Bill Koshland, which led Paul to describe him to Charlie as a "Charming, warm feller."[119]

Simca joined them in England, and they were with her again when they took a final trip to Paris. Avis, already in Europe, joined them there. While in Paris, they did a bit of work, lunching with two female editors of *Cuisine et Vins de France*. And, with Simca, they watched in the evening the weekly cooking program on TV featuring Raymond Oliver, the famous head chef of the three-star Parisian restaurant Le Grand Véfour. Paul reported to his brother, "not as good as Our Girl, by gum, making us feel absolutely

GREAT! Now, having seen the 2 best TV cooking shows (London & Paris) in Europe, we feel more confident than ever about ours."[120]

After renewing many old ties with friends and enjoying fine restaurant meals, Paul and Julia packed up their twelve suitcases along with two additional cases of kitchenware from Julia's favorite shop at Les Halles—likely purchased for the show in anticipation of that future $250.[121]

During the weeks of travel, Paul came to understand that they should not have planned for such a long trip, for they had left too little time to resettle before Julia's work was to begin. Once back on Irving Street, he moaned to Charlie, "One should never leave home for three months. And if one does one should never come back!" He wrote all the things that went wrong with the house during their three months away, including the wreck of the garden. Then there was the mountain of mail in the "overflowing laundry-hamper."[122]

When Julia was still in Paris, Ruth Lockwood reported on her own important professional news. In an upbeat letter, she told Julia that "Everything is going beautifully. We are the station's fair-haired boy." After reporting that WGBH accepted her order for a new typewriter with French accents, "I also applied to be put on the staff at $1.00 a year in order to leave the 'volunteer' class and am waiting to hear the verdict. I have finally reached a point where the professional status is important. I don't expect any problems."[123] To this, Julia replied, "Great idea to be a $1. a year woman, much much better than volunteer."[124]

Ruth asked Julia to send her a list of grocery staples to purchase for their return to Cambridge, and Julia responded, "How nice of you to want to stock the fridge." With that list, Julia extended an invitation. On November 13, after their ship landed in New York, she and Paul would drive to Boston, and if all went as scheduled, they would be home around five in the evening. "Why don't you and Arthur come to dinner with us, and you bring the dinner making? Steaks, a veg, a salad, and some fruit? We'll provide drinks, wine, and stove."[125] To that, Ruth quipped, "We shall be waiting for you with the larder ready. I'm glad you are providing the stove. I hate lugging mine around."[126]

Thus after Paul's long complaint to Charlie came these final words: "But Ruth Lockwood (Julia's colleague & Associate Producer in the TV world) was chez nous, with food in the ice-box and a merry smile on her face. A very pleasant sight."[127]

Chapter Eleven

"Julia"

In the fall of 1963, Julia Child's life began to move in two directions. At its base was her increasingly public life as the audience for *The French Chef* expanded to cover much of the U.S. The success of the show was exhilarating, especially as Julia tabulated its rewards in terms of the mounting sales of *Mastering the Art of French Cooking* and her increased royalties. Julia's growing public presence brought many new opportunities, including a stream of invitations to work in New York and thus enjoy the city's pleasures. Nonetheless, the production schedule of *The French Chef* required many weeks lived at an unrelenting pace.

In September 1963, while at Bramafam, Julia and Paul found an alternative path, as they began to imagine an escape valve in the south of France. After learning of the great expense of property in the region, they started thinking of a second home on land that belonged to the family of Simca's husband, Jean Fischbacher. Initially conversations with Jean made it seem impossible. The archival record regarding his change of mind is absent, but the initial bars he had set evaporated. By the November departure of the Childs for the United States, plans to reconstruct a small structure on the property for their use were well underway.

A letter from Simca was waiting for the Childs when they arrived at 103 Irving Street in Cambridge, containing "good news" regarding "the plan of your future Provençal home" developed by the architect they had hired. The existing structure still lacked a name of its own; Simca called it "Bramafam bis," using the French term for a smaller second house on a property. Simca hoped both Julia and Paul would understand the architect's plan and convey any objections to it they might have. Revealing the price Julia and Paul had set, $10,500 (roughly $90,000 at the time of this writing), Simca stated that she had written the architect to check that the plan he delivered at that price covered all elements, including bathroom equipment, electricity, and heating.[1]

As Julia was immediately returning to her intense work on future shows of *The French Chef,* Paul took over the correspondence with Simca, and his judgments likely formed much of their contents. His first response, however, came on the heels of President John F. Kennedy's assassination. Paul wrote Simca that "Julia has cried enough for us both since Friday and we are emotionally exhausted." Paul had admired Kennedy as "an excellent, vigorous, young man, with character, brains and style." In his and Julia's eyes, Kennedy's murder was "a mortal blow to the USA." When Paul turned to the business at hand, he wrote that although he had a few minor changes to suggest, the architect's plans were "Excellent!"[2]

Four days later, with time for both Julia and Paul to heal at least enough to discuss the project, Paul wrote that the architect should proceed. Paul required, however, a breakdown of the costs involved and an agreement from the architect to assume personal responsibility for the work. The one expensive change the Childs sought was the creation of an access road, allowing for turning an automobile around as well as providing for two parking places. (They were Americans, after all.) With that, Paul gave the go-ahead to begin construction. He understood that while there were other significant costs unaccounted for, he trusted Simca and Jean. It was they who would be dealing "directly with the architect and the builders," relaying information on progress and costs to Cambridge. "So, let's get started."[3]

Simca quickly replied that all Paul's "suggestions will be strictly observed." She would have the architect draw up a second plan to confirm these changes, and Jean would immediately hire a contracting firm to build the access road. All this and getting a permit would, however, take some months. Simca then offered a name for the house: "La Pitchoune," a Provençal term meaning "the little one," typically used in reference to a child.[4] It stuck. After completing the last tapings for the season, Julia wrote to Simca, "We are getting so excited thinking about BRAMAFAM PITCHOUNE."[5]

During this time, Paul was facing the fact that Julia's fame would not lift his reputation or bring him income. *House & Garden* was featuring a spread on Julia Child's kitchen. After Paul wrote a description for the piece, he received a letter from the magazine's managing editor. It gave him high praise. As Paul put it, the editor "felt it would be impossible to improve on his story." It was, however, too long, so the published article could only use excerpts. Thus, as he wrote to his brother, "In other words: the article is by me! though of course I get no money for it. Too bad, they were limited in space because the writing is brilliant & the subject is fascinating & human!"[6]

In that same letter, Paul wrote of his fears, a return of his earlier health anxieties. On getting a simple cold, he collapsed. "I knew that I was dying—or merely going into schizophrenia—or both." Nonetheless, unlike in the past, he soldiered on and went to the rehearsal for *The French Chef.* He explained to Charlie that he did so because "if Ruth Lockwood gets a cold & can't rehearse the shows w/ Julia I'll have to take her place, both then and during the actual taping, and I'll have to help work out the stop-watch-timed sections, help plan the idiot-cards, keep an eye on the Floor Manager during the taping to be sure he's feeding-up the right cues at the right times." With that Paul conveyed not only his sense of responsibility, but also the on-site elements of Ruth's job.[7] Paul waited until February 1964 to inform Charlie about La Pitchoune: "Julie and I, with Simca & Jean, have been planning, revising, exchanging ideas, making little drawings & so on; about the small house we plan to build (to have built) on part of the olive tree terraces of the Fischbacher's Bramafan [sic] property."⁸ Coming as this statement did, out of the blue, it mystified Charlie, and Paul explained later in the month that he had kept the Bramafam news quiet because "for a long time we weren't sure it could be brought to pass, due to enormity of entailments vis-à-vis other members of their two families. We wanted to have it so arranged that it would be (legally) not owned by us. . . . The land is theirs. The house will be ours, but revert to them." He continued that he and Julia chose to make these arrangements because of their closeness to Simca and Jean and also because of the French region's "balmy atmosphere at most seasons." While at the time of Paul's writing the project was "very definitely underway," there was "nothing to show yet."⁹

It was at this point that sales of *Mastering the Art of French Cooking*— stimulated by *The French Chef*—were rising significantly, and thus, so were book royalties. In late January 1964 Julia wrote Simca the "good news" of *Mastering*'s latest royalty figure, $7,898.65, and promised to send her two checks, each approximately $3,500 [almost $30,000 at the time of this writing], one for Simca's share of the royalties, the other "for partial payment on BRAMAFAM PARFUMIERE PITCHOUNE." The second check, transferring Julia's royalty payment to Simca, was to cover construction costs and planting expenses at Bramafam, with the remainder to go to Jean in support of his business venture.¹⁰

During the next year, letters flew back and forth over the Atlantic between Simca and Paul, her "frère," about plans, reconstruction, and landscaping. As La Pitchoune came into being, Jean was often at Bramafam, overseeing the work. Simca wrote about the many aspects of construction, including her pleasure in the planting of new trees. Seeing the work of construction and planting was a solace during a very sad time. Simca was facing her mother's fatal illness and ultimate death. Thoughts of a future with Julia and Paul close at hand may have provided Simca with both distraction and hope. Fortunately for both women—whose husbands were no longer the breadwinners—royalty money was now flowing in from the sales of *Mastering*.

In the waning days of 1965, Julia and Paul moved into La Pitchoune. It was the first of the Childs' annual three-month-long winter stays. From that point on, their rhythm of hard work in the U.S. was punctuated by their relatively more relaxed periods living in Provence. In December, as Julia packed up for that first stay, she wrote to Alfred Knopf that soon "we shall be smelling the mimosa and supping garlic soup."[11]

In the fall of 1963, when Julia and Paul returned home from their Europe trip to the labors of their life in Cambridge, those months in the south of France were still in the future. Their spirits were momentarily brightened by Ruth Lockwood as she greeted their arrival "with food in the ice-box and a merry smile on her face."[12] Nonetheless, Cambridge now meant work, hard and unrelenting work. The focus was on Julia, but Paul contributed his important labor. Paul's clearest description of the heavy lifting involved in the production of *The French Chef* came in a letter to Charlie in March 1964, where he included not only Julia's efforts, but also his and that of Ruth Lockwood:

> This has been a busy week, though there is little to report except: up at 5:45, pile car w/ batterie de cuisine & pre-cooked food, drive to Cambridge Electric, walk all the stuff up 2 flights on their fire-escape (quickest access to the kitchen where the shooting is done), unload, lay it out, get all the towels, detergents, spices, casseroles, plastic measuring cups, canned good, bread boards[,] utensils etc.!, out of the 2 locked steel cabinets. Set up two long folding tables, get out heaps of dishes, napkins, table cloths, glass flower vases, candle sticks, furniture, etc., etc [sic] from the store-room (these are on long-time-loan from Design Research and furnish our dining room set.) By about 9 AM this is done and if it's a rehearsal day, I leave for home. Ruth—who has come in [to WGBH] around 8—and Julia,

then begin their long, grinding seige [sic] of rehearsal, using actual
food & performing every act (timed w/ a stop-watch) w/ scrupulous care. I work at home, answer phones, let in gas-men, sharpen
knives, write, carpenter, paint, photo, etc. At 1 P.M. I return to the
Gas & Electric bldg—now & then having done shopping for the two
kitchen-bound women, if they run out of something, or if they've
forgotten something. We lunch together, discuss problems, often
invent a few phrases to use in the openings & closings. Usually they
are not yet finished w/ the first of the two programs they're going
to rehearse. I leave, they go back to work & so do I. I come again
around seven, to wash dishes—they are still hard at it, may stay
till 9 or later. Then everything is packed up, re-stored, re-station
wagoned & taken home. Then PJ [special symbol] have dinner
(usually around 10 P.M.). This happens 4 times a week.

On shooting-days the difference is that once everything is
layed-out [sic] the crew begins to arrive. Cameras are lugged up
the fire-escape in pieces & mounted, cables are hauled in through
windows, light-engineers begin to rig spots, floods, key-lights etc.
Everybody tests everything, re-arranges everything. The place is
an orderly mad-house. Julie & Ruth are rehearsing rough spots,
deciding on last-minute additions & changes, printing-up Idiot cards,
working w/ the floor manager on section-timing & with the switcher
on timing (he gives signals to the floor manager when to flip-up new
I-cards). This is based on the stop-watch-timed sections planned by
Julie & Ruth during rehearsals—very nearly one a minute. There are
not only all those, but now we've worked out a new pattern (last 4
shows) w/ special orange-colored cards for Ruth to use in case Julie
makes a mistake or forgets something—she said "aluminum-covered
steel" in the last show, for instance, instead of "enamel-covered steel"
(!) but it was caught, an orange card was whipped-out and 1 minute
later she corrected herself after the orange card was flashed. The first
show usually has its run-through w/ Russ Morash & the crew, a sort

of dry-run dress-rehearsal, around 10:30 to 11:00, actual shooting by 11:30, lunch from about noon to one, depending upon the variables—second dry-run about 2-3 & finish by 4-5. Everything cleaned up & put away & repacked & stored by 5, 6, 7 or 8, depending. We can often get home by 7 & have a normal dinner.[13]

By early 1964, it was clear that Julia's life (and thus Paul's, as well) had become too hectic. As Paul informed Charlie, "Ruth Lockwood & I are gradually persuading her that no matter how much she loves humanity she must say NO! now and then." Paul gave, as an example, an advertising agency's call to Julia, trying to get her to do a TV commercial. "I took the phone call first, and subsequent ones were handled by Ruth Lockwood, so we were able to head him off." He then enumerated Julia's commitments for the coming spring. "Already lined up for March 1965, a week of public demonstrations at San Francisco Art Museum for fundraising. Also Cleveland. Jim Beard's classes in NY when he is in hospital." From Paul's standpoint, this meant a life "somewhat unbalanced," one that sacrificed both social and cultural life. He hoped it could be "corrected by degrees." All this activity was on top of the rigorous schedule of tapings for *The French Chef* that they were "now up to our ears in." Paul and Ruth seem by this time to have made only a small dent in Julia's willingness to take on more work. Proud as he was of Julia, Paul was finding it hard to catch his breath.[14]

A month later, Paul wrote on a more positive note, conveying that his life held pleasures as well. One was dining with Charlie and Freddie at New York's Four Seasons. After giving the restaurant strong praise, Paul remarked that it was "Too G.D. expensive, though it couldn't be done the way it is for less, unfortunately."[15]

A short break in the taping schedule of *The French Chef* in March allowed Paul and Julia to experience a bit of social life in Cambridge. After Paul listed the guests that Julia and he planned to have over, he wrote to Charlie, "We look forward to it w/ anticipation, not only because of the quality of the guests, but because we've been so Lacoönically tied-up by the TV serpent that it's been ages since we did any entertaining."[16] They cut it close, giving—on the night before the return to rehearsals and taping—what Paul described as a "Splendid dinner party . . . for 10—everything was GO. Last guest departed at 1:15 A.M."[17]

In such freer moments, the Childs expanded their social network as they socialized with Ruth and Arthur Lockwood, and were even hosted by the Lockwoods' friends. At one point, in an interesting and sympathetic manner, Paul mused to Charlie about the Jewish world of the Lockwoods in Boston, contrasted with its counterpart in Cambridge, and tried to frame the difference.

Such quiet moments were becoming ever more scarce, however, as increasingly Julia's life spun in many directions at once. In addition to her WGBH workdays and frequent trips to New York, she wrote a weekly column for the *Globe*, lectured, and gave demonstrations for nonprofit organizations. Despite the efforts of persuasion by Paul and Ruth, Julia typically gave a hearty "yes" to each invitation. Such invitations and acceptances meant that her pace of life continued to speed up rather than slow down.

Julia got her first taste of national publicity on March 20, 1964, when, under the title "How to Sell Broccoli," *TIME* magazine gave favorable attention to her and *The French Chef.* With the show then in thirteen cities, the article emphasized Julia's gestures and popularity, gave quick treatment to her background, and insightfully focused on her enjoyable teaching style. An important lesson to her viewers was the delicious possibilities that could be created with ordinary supermarket ingredients, thus the title. At its close the piece offered broccoli as the true measure of *The French Chef*'s popularity: when featured in the show, broccoli soon sold out in the cities and surrounding areas reached by *The French Chef.*[18] A week later, Paul wrote to his brother, "We too like the TIME piece on Joolie, and felt it was accurate in atmosphere as well as in fact. Couldn't ask for better.[19]

Whatever the personal costs, Julia's work at WGBH was fulfilling to her and held promise for greater sales of *Mastering*. During the summer of 1965, she announced to Bill Koshland, "there is a good chance all educational TV stations will carry the French Chef by the beginning of 1965—and that will mean 80 stations throughout the country!" In earlier years of her show, there was no national organization of public television. At its outset, there was the Eastern Educational Network (EEN), and it fostered sharing of video tapes of *The French Chef* in the region. In 1964, National Educational Television (NET), at that point a clearing house supervising distribution of local programming, reversed its 1962 decision not to distribute Child's show, and thereby made *The French Chef* available to all its network stations.[20] This move allowed the great expansion that Julia was celebrating to Bill. Offering his congratulations, he wrote, "Salutations are due all around to Childs, Lockwoods and all others involved and I think it's terrific."[21] Two days later, he congratulated Ruth directly, "I think it's wonderful what has happened and am really quite overwhelmed." He then asked her to send him the list of the thirty-three cities that were currently on board, and, when available, the ultimate list of eighty-five once *The French Chef* was carried on the network.[22]

Perhaps understanding how safe she was with Bill, Julia was often affectionate in her letters to him. In early August she wrote, "So nice to talk to you today—but wishes, as always, that you were right here, so we could be together and hold hands. Well, we can hope for that sometime in the near future." With that, she went on to write of business.

Bill had likely called to let her know that Bloomingdale's wanted her to give a demonstration. She first accepted with conditions: she did nothing for free, with the money going to WGBH, and "now doing things only through my colleague and agent, Ruth Lockwood."[23] A few weeks later, however, she had second thoughts. She was refining the extra work that she thought appropriate. Writing again to Bill, she declared that regarding "the Bloomingdale business or any other such affair. We've finally come to the conclusion that we shall not do anything quite like that, of a purely commercial nature. For the time being, I shall only do demonstrations for decent charitable organizations such as museums or Smith College, etc., or for something like a gathering of women's page people. I just don't want to be in anyway associated with commercialism (except for selling the book in a dignified way), and don't want to get into the realm of being a piece of property trotting about hither and yon. The line is sometimes difficult to see, but I know where I mean it to be."[24] Julia Child now was clear about her limits, but they were not of time or energy. They were of authorial propriety.

In late November 1964, Julia gave advance word to Simca that the sales were now up to the point that "we should be seeing some $28,000.00 (in total royalties at the next distribution) . . . if my figures are correct W*H*O*O*P*E*E!" At Julia's 45%, this meant an addition of $12,600 (equal to a little over $106,000 at the time of this writing) to the Childs' and Fischbachers' coffers.[25] *The French Chef* was doing its magic.

One major event, long scheduled, involved a series of demonstrations at the San Francisco Museum of Art from March 30 to April 4, 1965. Julia Child was now a famous person—sought after, not seeking. In contrast to the autumn 1961 book tour, invitations surrounding the many-day event came to her, such as a press luncheon, a TV interview, and dinner with the editor of *House & Garden*. And to assist her, Julia brought Ruth Lockwood, along with Paul. In the letter sending this information to Bill Koshland, Julia explained that she fondly remembered Jim Russell, who was now seeking to plan festive signings at bookstores. She nonetheless refused, as she had found such events typically to be "flops." She welcomed, however, the opportunity to "drop in to a number of bookstores with him and sign any number of books, as long as the stores are prepared for the invasion—otherwise (from experience) the whole business is painful for everyone." Russell could arrange this with her contact at the museum and then send dates to Ruth. Unlike other correspondence with Koshland, at the bottom of the letter Julia put in handwriting, "cc: Ruth."[26]

The importance of the San Francisco museum event was underscored by a letter to Julia from Alfred Knopf. Two San Francisco friends, whom he described as gourmets with "charming wives," wished to invite Julia to dinner. Alfred also expressed a hope to come to Boston after Julia's return, "to collect that dinner from you."[27] Clearly, in Alfred Knopf's mind, Julia had become a person of importance. Julia replied that she would be pleased to accept the men's invitation, as long as the dinner could be arranged before the demonstrations began—and the hosts also included Paul and Ruth as their guests. Expressing her hope that Alfred would, as he had suggested, come to Cambridge for a visit, Julia wrote that, in anticipation, she would be "warming up the ovens."[28]

After her return to Cambridge, Julia carefully described to Simca the work involved in San Francisco, where she presented three separate shows at the Museum of Art, each repeated at successive times during the three performance days. "Ruth, Paul and I arrived every morning at about 8:15, set up everything for the first show. . . . Paul did his usual bit of arranging for lighting, water, relations with the women, chopping prunes, and generally doing anything at all that was needed—an homme d'affaires, public relations, and commis [assistant]—and wonderful as always. Ruth did all the set-ups (what dishes where, what comes next, etc. etc.), and also was on the stage with me, unobtrusively cleaning up, and holding up ingredients lists so I wouldn't forget anything." A longtime friend, Rosie Manell, now living in San Francisco, also came to help, doing such chores as peeling ingredients. About five hundred people attended each demonstration. A little shop, "very stylishly furnished," sold cooking utensils and copies of *Mastering*. Over the course of the demonstrations, Julia thought it sold more than a hundred books. When she went around to bookstores with Jim Russell, she found all the bookstores "were full of THE BOOK." Comparing it to their launch visit in 1961, Julia exclaimed to Simca, "Quite a difference from our last trip there! . . . So that was a great satisfaction, I must say."[29]

A few days before writing this report, Julia let Simca know of a new assignment. *The French Chef* was now broadcast over the National Education Network, and WGBH was hosting what Julia described as the organization's "big meeting." She was asked to make a ten-minute tape of preparing a dinner to be shown to the attendees.[30] Reporting a few days later, she conveyed the tape's importance. It was "an experiment in color TV so they and we could see what that was like." For the presentation Julia prepared three dishes: blanquette de veau, salade Niçoise, and tarte aux fraises. She viewed the screening with the NET visitors and wrote, "My, what a difference color makes. In regular TV the greens and reds turn gray, in color you could see every shade of Nicoise, every shade of the otherwise pale Blanquette, and how beautiful were the strawberries!" An instant enthusiast, Julia could now imagine a vivid future in color for *The French Chef*.[31]

Soon afterward, Julia received a personal Peabody Award, given by the National Association of Broadcasters. After calling *The French Chef* an "appetizing program," the citation read, "Julia Child does more than show us how good cooking is achieved; by her delightful demonstrations she has brought the pleasures of good living into many American homes."[32] Judith Jones congratulated her warmly, and then followed with a business-like response, "I understand that you will be sending us the full citation so we can send out a publicity release."[33] In Judith's mind as well as Julia's, *The French Chef* was closely linked to the fortunes of *Mastering*.

Alfred Knopf did come to dinner. As Julia jauntily wrote to Bill, "We did have a royal presence, and it was great fun. Avis came, and a nice couple from San Francisco and New Hampshire, and we ate informally in the kitchen. That is indeed a remarkable and unique presence, and so vigorous!"

She also told Bill the important news that La Pitchoune was almost finished and would be awaiting them when the Childs returned to France in December. She hoped that he might be able to visit them there during their long stay through the month of March and explained that her television work was so exhausting that it required "2 months to pick up the pieces."[34]

Nonetheless, Julia was always adding more to her plate, and four weeks later she wrote Bill of a new plan. James Beard had just paid her a visit, during which he told her of his great success with a paperback book that had sold half a million copies. "This has naturally set me to wondering if we might think of something like this, and take advantage of the French Chef TV shows, [which] are now operating in some 95 cities. It has certainly been the thing that has sold MTAOFC; lots of our audience can't fork up $10., but could let go of a buck." With one more taping to go, there would be 92 shows to select recipes from and "nifty action photos by P. Child." Thus there would be "very little work to do in order to assemble things." She enclosed a small sample of recipes, "so you can see what they look like."[35]

At Julia's request, Bill sent Robert Larsen, WGBH's production manager, a letter describing the rise in sales of *Mastering* as it related to *The French Chef*. "I thought you would be interested in knowing how very well MASTERING THE ART OF FRENCH COOKING by Julia Child (and her two co-authors . . .) has been doing. We are quite convinced that the continuing success of her (and your) program 'The French Chef' has had a lot to do, not so much with keeping the book alive (because it does seem to have a very active life of its own) but rather with having very definitely increased the tempo of its sale. As the program has become more widely shown it seems pretty clear to us that the sales themselves have increased in proportion—maybe almost geometrically rather than arithmetically!" With that he gave the book's recent sales in six-month increments, beginning in 1961, when they were 4,157, to the most recent figure of 20,027 at the beginning of 1965. "I'm sure you know how gratified Julia is at this turn of events; and needless to say, we are not at all displeased either."[36]

Late in October, Julia and Paul were among the honored guests at the gala dinner celebrating the fifty years of the A. A. Knopf publishing house, and Julia was seated next to Bill Koshland. Writing afterwards to both Bill and Judith, Julia let them know of how thrilled both Childs were to be there. With that she sent Judith the recipes from *The French Chef*, making it clear that almost all were from *Mastering*. She did add that she had "a new approach" to the beef Wellington dish—after having recently made it nine times.[37]

In spring 1966 Julia had signed on to be a consultant for the Time Life cookbook series Foods of the World, to be edited by Michael Field. Her role in the project was only to approve or disapprove of a manuscript for the book series.

As she wrote to Simca about traveling to New York to consult, she celebrated being out in the world, temporarily freed of television work. She reported also that she was deeply impressed with the scale of Field's operation, with its big budget and personnel, including Time Life reporters.[38] In a handwritten note to Simca from New York, she wrote that she "Went to Time/Life books: saw brochure. Mention of 'l'ecole des 3 Gs.'" With her own focus on promotion of *Mastering*, Julia seems to have understood that just as the two magazines gave attention to their own books, her service as a consultant for the Time Life series might well pay off in publicity for her own.

The first indication that this might well have been the case was an article in October in *LIFE*, that included six photos by Paul. Julia enclosed a copy to Simca with these words: "It is not much of an article, but no matter, the book is mentioned." Julia also wrote, "there is also to be an article on cooking in the US in Time around the end of November, with perhaps a cover of me! Ye gods! This is all a canny move on their part of build me up for the sale of their cookbook, I suspect. Well, it is all right with me, and I have heard from Avis that Knopf has ordered 40,000 copies for its next printing, rather than the usual 10,000."[39]

In addition, in late November, *The New York Review of Books* published Michael Field's review of three French cookbooks. It began by offering high praise for *Mastering the Art of French Cooking*. After letting readers know of the great difficulty in cooking from the great masters, such as Marie Antoine Carême, Field wrote, that *Mastering* "surpasses every other American book on French cooking in print today. For once, the architectural structure of the French cuisine is firmly and precisely outlined in American terms. And if a number of culinary areas are missed, it is only because the space available has been devoted to doing what is covered superbly. One would wish the book to be at least twice its imposing length."[40]

This review provoked an unusual letter from Alfred Knopf. "When I read a review by Michael Field—I have a good deal of respect for him—of 'Mastering the Art' in the *New York Review of Books* I thought I acquired a new and original idea—namely that you with your associates should write another book as big as 'Mastering the Art' but duplicating it in no respect. Judith however tells me that you are all at work on such a book so all I have to say is good luck and step on the gas."[41] Julia thanked him for the "puffy" in his letter and then let him know in the works was "a big new book to complete our first. The tentative deadline is in two years, though not a word has yet been written!"[42]

Judith also wrote, turning her pleasure in Field's review into an encouragement for Julia to be working on the second volume of *Mastering the Art of French Cooking*. She thanked Julia for sending the material originating with *The French Chef*. She especially liked its recipes posing no conflict with the *Mastering*, ones that were informal and put a dinner on the table in thirty minutes. Thinking (or hoping) about what was for Judith the more important project, she added that Julia's head must now "be bursting" with ideas for volume II.[43]

On Julia's return to the United States in spring 1966 from the first winter season at La Pitchoune came more national recognition of the work she had begun in 1952, work that was made possible by members of her remarkable team. Its six members were still in place. Simca, now at close range for several months a year, was committed to working with Julia on volume II. Paul was at Julia's side and, having supported her in every way, was continuing to photograph her in action and to volunteer his manual labor at WGBH. Avis was nearby, her friendship and support intact. Bill and Judith continued as her mainstays at Knopf. And Ruth remained as Julia's right arm at WGBH. Before the year was out, all their efforts would be amply rewarded.

On May 22, 1966, the National Academy of Television Arts & Sciences honored Julia Child for individual achievement in educational television at their awards ceremony in New York, presenting her with an Emmy. It was the first Emmy for any program on nonprofit television. Then, in November, what served as the most recognizable tribute the U.S. had to offer in the 1960s—the mark of nationwide fame—was bestowed: Julia Child made the cover of *TIME*.

"Julia Child at Emmy awards," Schlesinger Library, Harvard Radcliffe Institute.

It didn't happen by accident. Julia, with her eye on increasing sales of *Mastering the Art of French Cooking*, played a part in bringing it about. Julia agreed to be a consultant on the Time-Life series Foods of the World, organized by Michael Field. While this brought in some income, more importantly, her commitment to the series was, by her own account, strategic, a move on her part to build publicity to grow sales for *Mastering the Art of French Cooking*. In early October 1966, when she wrote to Judith Jones that LIFE's article was "locked up," certain to appear, she added that *TIME* was planning to do an article on her to appear around Thanksgiving, but it could "still be in the air." With this she explained, "My reluctant acceptance of being a consultant for the Time-Life French cookbook has paid off—as they will be launching it, I think at about that time." She continued, "I am giving you warning of this just in case it may (we hope) increase our book sales, and I hope there will be plenty available."[44]

When late in October, Julia wrote Judith again, she conveyed this news: "We are engulfed, at this moment with Time-Life books and Time Magazine. They are going to do a special article to appear just before Thanksgiving, with me on the cover (!)—that will be the day!" With that Julia wrote of the week she would have to give to cooking and conversations with TIME writers and sitting for Boris Chaliapin, as he painted her portrait for the cover. "So there's a good week out of Vol. II, but I trust this will be worth while [sic] for Vol. I's sales so I shall not begrudge a moment."

In addition, she was going to have to take more time from the next volume's work to review the drafts of the Time-Life book, and at a later time, the book's recipes. With this came Julia's telling words in parentheses: "Have to pay them back for all the free publicity, obviously." As she contemplated future work for the series, she wrote, "So I am caught in a fox trap of my own devising, but feel in view of everything that it has been worth while."[45]

In many ways, the article inside the magazine on Julia is a period piece, reminding us that 1966 was an era different from today. The piece begins with her culinary skill: "The TV camera zooms in for close up and focuses on her hands. She may be dicing an onion, mincing a garlic clove, trussing a chicken. Her fingers fly with the speed and dexterity of a concert pianist." The text then quickly moves to her entertaining television personality: "Even her failures and faux pas are classic." Giving the example of a potato pancake that fell on the worktable, it stated that as Julia put it back in the pan, "she bats her big blue eyes at the camera and advises, 'Remember, you're all alone in the kitchen and no one can see you.'" Both male and female viewers "watch her every move, forgive her every gaffe and, in a word, adore her."

"Chaliapin paints Julia," Schlesinger Library, Harvard Radcliffe Institute, copyright: Julia Child Foundation.

Written in the early days of Women's Liberation, the article may have celebrated a woman, but it did so with a whiff of the publication's machismo. Before presenting Julia's French recipe for Thanksgiving turkey, the magazine wrote of the significant male audience of *The French Chef*: "So good is she that men who have not the slightest intention of going to the kitchen for anything but ice cubes watch her for pure enjoyment." Julia was quoted as saying: "A man in a chef's apron is a fine sight. . . . They are marvelous. They're more daring, while women are often timid and tend to get bogged down in detail. I think one can see from history that the great creators are men." These words, coming from Julia, a successful professional woman, demonstrate that the desire to please can be found in the most surprising places.

In its many pages, the article sketched her biography with light hands: Smith College, for example, appeared primarily as the place where Julia's six-foot-two height led the institution to change its basketball rules. Kind words, however, were written of Paul as the "cookbook's official photographer," who recorded her every step as preparation for future sketches to appear in print; he had also designed her "kitchen laboratory" and was the artist "whose paintings, wood carvings and social engravings decorate the rest of the house." Ruth Lockwood was mentioned as the show's producer, but only when she was quoted regarding "Julia's goofs." Simca was ignored, with the exception of the report that after Thanksgiving, Julia and Paul were going "to winter in the house that the book built, next door to Simone Beck," where Julia would be working with her on the second volume of *Mastering*. As for those whose work was behind the scenes in both Cambridge—Avis DeVoto—and in New York at Knopf—Judith Jones and Bill Koshland—there was no mention at all.

In summing up her appeal, *TIME* stated that "Julia Child's TV cooking shows have made her a cult from coast to coast and put her on a first name basis with her fans."[46]

Julia Child had now become "Julia." The recognition that came to her with TIME's cover story was all hers. Except for a complimentary nod to Paul, a single mention of Simca, and a quote from Ruth, her team was invisible.

One wonders how each of the six experienced this moment of Julia's fame. Unfortunately the written record is incomplete, for Paul was at her side, and it is likely that, rather than writing, Avis DeVoto and Ruth Lockwood—both living nearby—picked up the phone to call. It would also have been characteristic of Judith Jones and Bill Koshland to telephone Julia right away from their Knopf offices.

When Koshland did write to Julia at a later time, he focused on what the *TIME* cover story meant for sales of the book, clearly something Julia wanted to know. He reported that "the issue of Time went on the stands on Monday November 21, and for the three days of that week (we did not bill on Thanksgiving Day or the following Friday) orders received totaled 722 copies, for the following week 5902, for the week following that 7843, and for three days of this week 2290 copies. Wow! Please see that you put Henry Luce on your Christmas list."[47]

It took the distant member of Julia's team to express her emotions on paper. Away in France, Simca wrote, "I showed everyone: Gourmettes, in Paris, and students of the Cours, thus everyone. . . . TIME, and the article in France-Soir, published last night, where you are in a photo (reproduction of TIME) with the title, 'an American made herself famous by revealing the secrets of French cuisine on TV,' and further, Julia Child has become the object of a true cult, and the supreme consecration: the cover of TIME, that grants her an article of 9 pages!!! I will save this article, which is sensational, but not as much as TIME, naturally, and that I reread and reread, it gives me the impression of 'drinking milk,' as one says in France, when we read or have heard something that gives immense pleasure, and this is the case."[48]

From this author's perspective, in *TIME*'s portrayal of Julia Child's success, the magazine missed out on a key element, and this neglect has largely continued to this day. Yes, much came from Julia's buoyant personality, hard work, and talent. But equally important was her capacity for friendship and collaboration. Julia Child never worked alone, and by 1966 she had gathered a team of six, working—with the possible exception of Simca—largely outside the limelight—Paul Child, Simone Beck, Avis DeVoto, William Koshland, Judith Jones, and Ruth Lockwood.

These six became her essential co-workers on her long journey from 1952 to 1966. All contributed their time, labor, and varied talents. Their support and assistance helped put Julia Child on that "first name basis" with her American readers and audience by 1966. Together, they aided her in ways that made it possible for Julia Child to be known and remembered simply as "Julia."

Endnotes

All quoted materials cited from the Julia Child Materials are copyrighted as follows: Julia Child Materials © 2021, Julia Child Foundation for Gastronomy and the Culinary Arts.

ABBREVIATIONS FOUND IN ENDNOTES:
JC: Julia Child
PC: Paul Child
CC: Charles Child
FC: Freddie Child
SB: Simone Beck
AD: Avis DeVoto
JJ: Judith Jones
WAK: William A. Koshland
RL: Ruth Lockwood
DdeS: Dorothy de Santillana
AAK: Alfred A. Knopf

ADP: Avis DeVoto Papers, Schlesinger Library, Harvard Radcliffe Institute
SBP: Simone Beck Papers, Schlesinger Library, Harvard Radcliffe Institute
JCP: Julia Child Papers, Schlesinger Library, Harvard Radcliffe Institute

INTRODUCTION
1   Laura Shapiro, *Julia Child: A Life* (New York: Viking Penguin, 2007), 2.
2   Justin Spring, *The Gourmands' Way: Six Americans in Paris and the Birth of a New Gastronomy* (New York: Farrar, Straus and Giroux, 2017) offers a compelling portrayal of the influence of his six subjects in Paris, including Julia Child. Here I draw from 26–44; quote, 30.

CHAPTER 1: ASSEMBLING THE TEAM
1   Bob Spitz, *Dearie: The Remarkable Life of Julia Child* (New York: A. A. Knopf, 2012), 117–20.
2   Alex Prud'homme, *The French Chef in America: Julia Child's Second Act* (New York: Anchor Books, 2017), 147–48. Jennet Conant, *A Covert Affair: Julia Child and Paul Child in the OSS* (New York: Simon & Schuster, 2011). Conant describes it as "an extension course at Columbia College," 14. Another source has Paul at Columbia for

two years: Cynthia Zarin, "Portrait of a Marriage: Julia Child Captured in Paul Child's Shimmering Photographs," *New Yorker*, December 2, 2017. Prud'homme states that "Paul was given tuition for one year at Columbia" (148). Spitz, *Dearie*, does not mention any college education for Paul, writing instead that when Charlie went to Harvard, "Paul went to work" (120).

3   Alex Prud'homme and Katie Pratt, *France Is a Feast* (New York: Thames and Hudson, 2017), 189.

4   PC to CC, January 15, 1951, box 5, folder 66, JCP.

5   Julia's drawing, JC to CC and FC, Jan. 10, 1951, box 5, folder 66, JCP.

6   Simone Beck with Suzanne Patterson, *Food & Friends: Recipes and Memories from Simca's Cuisine* (New York: Penguin Books, 1991).

7   Beck, *Food & Friends*, 3–11.

8   Beck, *Food & Friends*, 27–36, passim.

9   Beck, *Food & Friends*, 43–46.

10   Beck, *Food & Friends*, 65–69, quote, p. 68.

11   Beck, *Food & Friends*, 80–81.

12   Beck, *Food & Friends*, 81–82.

13   Beck, *Food & Friends*, 91–97.

14   Beck, *Food & Friends*, 129–32, quote, 132.

15   Beck, *Food & Friends*, 141–43; quotes, 142, 143.

16   Beck, *Food & Friends*, quotes, 151, 159.

17   Beck, *Food & Friends*, quote, 160.

18   Beck, *Food & Friends*, quote, 161.

19   Beck, *Food & Friends*, 161–63, quotes, 162, 163.

20   JC to JJ, "Cooking Biography," box 33, folder 427, JCP.

21   JC to CC family, January 10, 1951, box 5, folder 66, JCP.

22   JC, January 11, 1951 appointment book, MC 660, 139.8, additional papers, JCP.

23   Beck, *Food & Friends*, quote, 163.

24   Beck, *Food & Friends*, quote, 226.

25   JC to FC and family, April 7, 1951, box 5, folder 66, JCP.

26   JC to FC and family, April 7, 1951, box 5, folder 66, JCP.

27   PC to CC, PC diary, December 12, 1951, box 5, 66, JCP.

28   "Gourmandes" in its French meaning are persons who take pleasure in good food.

29   PC to CC, January 17, 1952, box 5, folder 67, JCP.

30   JC, "Ecole des Trois Gourmandes," March 18, 1952, box 41, folder 514, JCP.

31   "Informal Lessons in French Cuisine," *Embassy News*, June 20, 1952, box 41, folder 514, JCP.

32   JC to FC, February 4, 1952, box 5, folder 67, JCP.

33   JC to FC, "about mid-April, 1952," box 5, folder 67, JCP.

34   JC to FC, "about mid-April, 1952," box 5, folder 67, JCP.

35   JC to FC, likely late winter 1952, box 5, folder 67, JCP.

36   JC appointment book, August 28, 1952. Additional papers of Julia Child, M660, 139, Schlesinger Library, Harvard Radcliffe Institute.

37   PC to CC, PC diary, August 29, 1952, box 6, folder 68, JCP.

38   PC to CC, PC diary, November 23, 1952, box 6, folder 68, JCP.
39   PC to CC, PC diary, December 7, 1952, box 6, folder 68, JCP.
40   PC to CC, PC diary, January 7, 1953, box 6, folder 69, JCP.
41   PC to CC, PC diary, March 17, 1951, box 5, folder 66, JCP.
42   PC to CC, PC diary, April 20, 1951, box 5, folder 66, JCP.
43   PC to CC, November 3, 1951, underlined in original, box 5, folder 66, JCP.
44   PC to CC, PC diary for December 9, 1951, December 14, 1951, box 5, folder 66, JCP.
45   PC to CC, PC diary for January 30, 1952, February 2, 1952, box 6, folder 67, JCP.
46   PC to FC, PC diary, February 5, 1952, box 6, folder 67, JPC.
47   JC to FC, February 4, 1952, box 6, folder 67, JCP.
48   JC to FC, "about March 22, 1952" [in PC's hand], box 6, folder 67, JCP.
49   JC to FC, February 4, 1952, box 6, folder 67, JCP.
50   PC to CC, PC diary fragment, 1952, box 6, folder 67, JCP.
51   PC to CC, PC diary fragment, April 1, 1952, box 6, folder 67, JCP.
52   PC to CC, PC diary fragment, September 6, 1952, box 6, folder 68, JCP.
53   PC to CC, PC diary, October 9, 1952, box 6, folder 68, JCP. Paul was referring here to the work of Alfred Korzybski.
54   PC to CC, PC diary, October 9, 1952, box 6, folder 68, JCP.
55   PC to CC, PC diary, October 11, 1952, box 6, folder 68, JCP.
56   PC to CC, PC diary, October 29, 1952, box 6, folder 68, JCP.
57   JC appointment book, 1951. Additional papers of Julia Child, 1890–2004 (inclusive), 1950–2001 (bulk), MC 660, 139. Schlesinger Library, Radcliffe Institute.
58   PC to CC, PC diary, January 6 and 7, 1953, box 6, folder 69, JCP.
59   PC to CC, PC diary, January 13, 1953, box 6, folder 69, JCP.

CHAPTER 2: AVIS COMES ABOARD

1   AD to JC, April 3, 1952, box 7, folder 71, ADP.
2   JC to AD, May 5, 1952, box 7, folder 72, ADP.
3   JC to AD, May 5, 1952, box 7, folder 72, ADP.
4   AD to JC, May 30, 1952, box 7, folder 71, ADP; Joan Reardon, ed., *As Always, Julia: The Letters of Julia Child and Avis DeVoto* (Boston: Houghton Mifflin Harcourt, 2010), 12–15. (Hereafter, cited as Reardon.)
5   Alfred A. Knopf, the publisher, later to be important in Julia's life. AD to JC, October 3, 1952, box 7, folder 71, ADP.
6   PC to CC, PC diary, November 8, 1952, box 6, folder 68, JCP.
7   The ellipsis is in the original letter. JC to AD, December 15, 1952, box 7, folder 72, ADP.
8   AD to JC, December 25, 1952, box 7, folder 71, ADP; Reardon, 18–20.
9   PC to CC, PC diary, December 31, 1952, box 6, folder 86, JCP.
10   JC to SB and LB, December 29, 1952, box 7, folder 72, ADP.
11   JC to AD, December 30, 1952, Reardon, 20–22; not found in Schlesinger collection.
12   AD to JC, January 2, 1953, box 7, folder 71, ADP; Reardon, 24–27.
13   AD to JC, January 4, 1953, box 7, folder 71, ADP; Reardon, 27–28.
14   AD to JC, January 13, 1953, box 7, folder 71, ADP; Reardon, 41.
15   JC to AD, January 19, 1953, Reardon, 42–48; not found in Schlesinger collection.

16 JC to AD, February 12, 1953, Reardon, 68–72 (quotes, 70, 72); not found in Schlesinger collection.
17 JC to AD, February 12, 1953, Reardon, 71; not found in Schlesinger collection.
18 AD to JC, February 23, 1953, box 7, folder 71, ADP; Reardon, 79.
19 AD to JC, February 8, 1953, box 7, folder 71, ADP; Reardon, 66.

CHAPTER 3: MARSEILLE
1 PC to CC, PC diary, March 1, 1953, box 6, folder 69, JCP.
2 PC to CC, PC diary, March 24, 1953, box 6, folder 69, JCP. A tumbril is a two-wheeled cart, here on cobblestones.
3 PC to CC, PC diary, April 8, 1953, box 6, folder 69, JCP.
4 PC to CC, PC diary, April 8, 1953, box 6, folder 69, JCP.
5 PC to CC, PC diary, April 19, 1953, box 6, folder 69, JCP.
6 PC to CC, PC diary, April 23, 1953, box 6, folder 70, JCP.
7 JC to AD, March 6, 1953, Reardon, 98–100]; not found in Schlesinger collection.
8 AD to JC, March 20, 1953, box 7, folder 71, ADP; Reardon, 107.
9 AD to JC, March 20, 1953, box 7, folder 71, ADP; Reardon, 107.
10 AD to JC, March 20, 1953, box 7, folder 71, ADP; Reardon, 116.
11 AD to JC, March 20, 1953, box 7, folder 71, ADP; Reardon, 108.
12 AD to JC, March 20, 1953, box 7, folder 71, ADP; Reardon, 116–17.
13 AD to JC, undated, but follows September 24, 1953, box 7, folder 71, ADP.
14 PC to CC, April 10, 1953, box 5, folder 69, JCP.
15 JC to AD, April 24, 1953, Reardon, 121; not found in Schlesinger collection.
16 AD to JC, April 28, 1953, box 7, folder 71, ADP.
17 PC to CC, April 24, 1953, box 5, folder 69, JCP.
18 PC to CC, PC diary, April 29, 1953, box 6, folder 69, JCP.
19 AD to JC, April 28, 1953, box 7, folder 71, ADP.
20 AD to JC, April 10, 1953, box 7, folder 71, ADP.
21 AD to JC, April 10, 1953, box 7, folder 71, ADP.
22 JC to AD, April 24, 1953, Reardon, 120–21; not found in Schlesinger collection.
23 AD to JC, undated fragment, likely written after receiving JC's letter of April 24, 1953, box 7, folder 71, ADP.
24 SB to JC, likely 1956, MC 432, folder 83, SBP.
25 JC to SB and LB, October 25, 1953, box 7, folder 77, AD.
26 JC to SB, October 29, 1953, box 7, folder 77, ADP.
27 JC to SB, November 2, 1953, box 7, folder 77, ADP.
28 JC to SB, November 6, 1953, box 7, folder 77, ADP.
29 JC to SB, October 29, 1953, box 7, folder 77, ADP.
30 JC to SB, November 6, 1953, box 7, folder 77, ADP.
31 JC to SB and LB, October 25, 1953, box 7, folder 77, ADP.
32 JC to SB, November 6, 1953, box 7, folder 77, ADP.
33 JC to SB, April 3, 1954, MC 432, folder 76, SBP.
34 JC to SB, January 25, 1954, MC 432, folder 74, SBP.
35 JC to SB, January 28, 1954, MC 432, folder 74, SBP.

36   JC to LB, January 29, 1954, MC 432, folder 74, SBP.
37   PC to CC, PC diary, May 2, 1953, box 6, folder 69, JCP.
38   PC to CC, PC diary, April 11, 1953, box 6, folder 69, JCP.
39   JC to FC, April 10, 1953, box 6, folder 69, JCP.
40   PC to CC, PC diary, September 22, 1953, box 6, folder 70, JCP.
41   PC to CC, PC diary, May 1, 1953, box 6, folder 67, JCPC.
42   PC to CC, PC diary, May 2, 1953, box 6, folder 67, JCP.
43   JC to AD, June 3, 1953, Reardon, 123–26.
44   AD to JC, September undated, box 7, folder 71, ADP.
45   AD to JC, September 12, 1953, box 7, folder 71, ADP.
46   AD to JC, September 30, 1953, box 7, folder 71, ADP; Reardon, 13.
47   Copy of letter from DdeS, November 3, 1953, in JC to SB and LB, November 11, 1953, box 7, folder 77, ADP.
48   JC to AD, November 23, 1953, Reardon, 149, 150; not found in Schlesinger collection.
49   AD to JC, February 22, 1954, Reardon, 157–58; not found in Schlesinger collection.
50   AD to JC, February 27, 1954, Reardon, 160–65; not found in Schlesinger collection.
51   PC to CC, PC diary, July 20, 1953, box 6, folder 70, JCP.
52   PC to CC, PC diary, August 1, 1953, box 6, folder 70, JCP.
53   PC to CC, PC diary, September 4, 6, 9, 1953, box 6, folder 70, JCP.
54   PC to CC, PC diary, September 21, 1953, box 6, folder 70, JCP.
55   AD to JC, February 22 and 27, 1954, Reardon 156–164; not found in Schlesinger collection.
56   SB to JC, March 1, 1954, MC 432, folder 74, SBP.
57   JC to SB, March 9, 1954, MC 432, folder 74, SBP.
58   JC to SB, May 3, 1954, MC 432, folder 76, SBP.
59   PC to CC, PC diary, September 21, 1953, box 6, folder 70, JCP.
60   JC to SB, March 2, 1954, MC 432, folder 74, SBP.
61   JC to SB, May 16, 1954, MC 432, folder 76, SBP.
62   JC to SB, May 16, 1954, MC 432, folder 76, SBP.
63   JC to SB, July 1, 1954, MC 432, folder 76, SBP.

CHAPTER 4: HOME LEAVE AND GERMANY

1   JC to AD, July [27], 1954, Reardon, 177; not found in Schlesinger collection.
2   AD to JC, July 31, 1954, Reardon, 184; not found in Schlesinger collection.
3   JC to SB, August 1, 1954, MC 432, 77a: 1–2, SBP.
4   JC to SB, August 1, 1954, MC 432, folder 77, SBP.
5   AD to JC, August 20, 1954, box 7, folder 73, ADP; Reardon, 187.
6   JC to AD, August 23, 1954, Reardon, 190; not found in Schlesinger collection.
7   JC to SB, post August 18, 1954, MC 432, folder 77, SBP. Here I give special thanks to Carol Rigolot, who enabled me to understand what Julia intended to state.
8   JC to SB, post August 18, 1954, MC 432, folder 77, SBP.
9   JC to SB, September 2, 1954, MC 432, folder 77, SBP.
10   JC to SB, September 27, 1954, MC 432, folder 77, SBP. Julia was referring to Fannie Farmer, *Boston Cooking-School Cook Book*, 1896.

11   JC to SB, September 27, 1954, MC 432, folder 77, SBP.
12   JC to SB, undated, in sequence, when Julia was in New York City between September 29 and October 10, 1954, MC 432, folder 77, SBP.
13   JC to AD, September 21, 1954, box 7, folder 74, ADP; Reardon, 192.
14   JC to AD, September 21, 1954, box 7, folder 74, ADP; Reardon, 193.
15   JC to AD, September 21, 1954, box 7, folder 74, ADP; Reardon, 194.
16   AD to JC, September 27, [1954], box 7, folder 73, ADP.
17   JC to AD, April 11, 1954, Reardon, 166–67; not found in Schlesinger collection.
18   JC to AD, October 1, 1954, Reardon, 195; not found in Schlesinger collection.
19   AD to JC, October 7, [1954], box 7, folder 73, ADP.
20   JC to SB, November 1, 1954, MC 432, folder 77, SBP.
21   JC to SB, March 2, 1954, MC 432, folder 74, SBP.
22   Julia's full draft with Simca's changes, JC and SB, November [no date], 1954, MC 432, folder 77, SBP.
23   AD to JC, November 1, [1954], box 7, folder 73, ADP. Reardon provides a partial version of this letter, 201–04, without suggesting deletions.
24   AD to JC, January 13, 1955, Reardon.
25   AD letter copied, JC to SB, December 23, 1954, MC 432, folder 78, SBP.
26   AD to JC, January 13, 1955, Reardon, 224; not found in Schlesinger collection; JC to SB quotes the relevant passage, January 17, 1955, MC 432, folder 79, SBP.
27   JC to SB, January 17, 1955, MC 432, folder 79, SBP.
28   JC to SB, April 2, 1955, MC 432, folder 80, SBP.
29   JC to SB, January 7, 1955, MC 432, folder 79, SBP.
30   JC to SB, December 13, 1954, MC 432, folder 78, SBP.
31   JC to SB, January 12, 1955, MC 432, folder 79, SBP.
32   JC to SB, January 17, 1955, MC 432, folder 79, folder SBP.
33   JC to SB, January 25, 1955, MC 432, folder 79, SBP.
34   Jennet Conant, *A Covert Affair: Julia Child and Paul Child in the OSS* (New York, Simon & Schuster, 2011), 10–23.
35   JC to AD, April 14, 1955, box 7, folder 74, ADP; Reardon, 237.
36   JC to SB, July 13, 1955, MC 432, folder 80, SBP.
37   JC to SB, October 13, 1955, MC 432, folder 82, SBP.
38   AD to JC, undated, immediately following December 7, 1955, box 7, folder 73, ADP.
39   CC to PC, November 13, 1955, box 7, folder 73, ADP.
40   JC to SB, December 19, 1955, MC 432, folder 82, SBP.
41   JC to SB, December 19, 1955, MC 432, folder 82, SBP.
42   JC to SB, December 28, 1955, MC 432, folder 82, SBP.
43   JC to SB, December 19, 1955, MC 432, folder 82, SBP.
44   SB to JC, undated but in sequence at beginning of 1956, MC 432, folder 83, SBP.
45   JC to SB, January 17, 1956, MC 432, folder 83, SBP.
46   JC to SB, March 3, 1956, MC 432, folder 83, SBP.
47   AD to JC, February 21, 1956, box 7, folder 73, ADP.
48   AD to JC, June 16, 1956, box 7, folder 73, ADP.
49   AD to JC, February 11, 1956, box 7, folder 73, ADP.

50 AD to JC, February 13, 1956, box 7, folder 73, ADP; Reardon, 266–67.
51 JC to SB, February 23, 1956, MC 432, folder 83,: 16, SBP.
52 JC to SB, April 23, 1956, MC 432, folder 83, SBP. Ellipses are in the original letter.
53 JC to SB, June 5, 1956, MC 432, folder 84, SBP.
54 JC to SB, June 25, 1956, MC 432, folder 84, SBP.
55 JC to SB, August 13, 1956, MC 432, folder 84, SBP.
56 JC to SB, September 7, 1956, MC 432, folder 84, SBP.
57 JC to SB, October 3, September 7, 1956, MC 432, folder 84, SBP.
58 JC to SB, October 15, 1956, MC 432, folder 84, SBP.

CHAPTER 5: WASHINGTON

1 JC to SB, November 27, 1956, MC 432, folder 84, SBP.
2 AD to JC, April 28, [1955], box 7, folder 73, ADP.
3 JC to SB, November 27, 1956, MC 432, folder 84, SBP.
4 JC to SB, December 21, 1956, MC 432, folder 84, SBP.
5 JC to AD, February 25, 1957, box 7, folder 76, ADP.
6 JC to AD, March 22, 1957, box 7, folder 76, ADP.
7 AD to JC, March 20 and 21, 1957, box 7, folder 75; November 29, 1957, box 7, folder 75, ADP.
8 JC to SB, January 28, 1957, MC 432, folder 85, SBP.
9 JC to SB, January 28, 1957, MC 432, folder 85, SBP.
10 JC to AD, early March [date obscured], 1957, box 7, folder 76, ADP.
11 JC to AD, March 22, 1957, box 7, folder 76, ADP.
12 https://clickamericana.com/topics/culture-and-lifestyle/scenes-from-grocery
   -stores-supermarkets-of-yesteryear. A good way to visualize this are supermarket ads
   from the period available to view.
13 JC to SB, January 1, 1957, MC 432, folder 85, SBP.
14 JC to SB, April 10, 1957, MC 432, folder 85, SBP. Cambridge (in the Boston area)
   clearly had advantages unknown in my mid-size Louisiana city.
15 JC to SB April 22, 1957, MC 432, folder 84, SBP.
16 AD to SB, May 7, 1957, box 8, folder 85, ADP.
17 AD to JC and PC, January 21, 1957, box 7, folder 75, ADP.
18 AD to JC, April 5, 1957, box 7, folder 75, ADP.
19 JC to AD, May 2, 1957, box 7, folder 76, ADP.
20 AD to JC, May 10, 1957, box 7, folder 75, ADP.
21 JC to AD, June 12, 1957, box 7, folder 76, ADP.
22 AD to JC, April 30, 1957, box 7, folder 75, ADP.
23 "Efficiency report," August 1957, MC 644, box 6, folder 72, JCP.
24 JC to AD, June [no date], 1957, box 7, folder 76, ADP.
25 JC to AD, June 12, 1957, box 7, folder 76, ADP.
26 JC to AD, June 20, 1957, box 7, folder 76, ADP.
27 JC to AD, July 28, 1957, box 7, folder 76, ADP.
28 JC to AD, June 12, 1957, box 7, folder 76, ADP.
29 JC to AD, June 20, 1957, box 7, folder 76, ADP.

30   JC to AD, August 3, 1957, box 7, folder 76, ADP.

31   JC to SB, August 6, 1957, MC 432, folder 86, SBP.

32   JC to SB, August 19, 1957, MC 432, folder 86, SBP.

33   JC to SB, August 1, 1957, MC 432, folder 86, SBP.

34   JC to SB, August 29, 1957, MC 432, folder 86, SBP.

35   JC to SB, August 19, 1957, MC 432, folder 86, SBP.

36   JC to SB, July 15, 1956, MC 432, folder 86, SBP.

37   JC to SB, August 1, 1957, MC 432, folder 86, SBP.

38   JC to SB, undated [likely late 1957], MC 432, folder 87, SBP.

39   DdeS to JC, November 19, 1957, MC 432, folder 87, SBP.

40   JC to DdeS, November 22, 1957, MC 432, folder 87, SBP.

41   JC to AD, June 20, 1957, box 7, folder 76, ADP.

42   AD to JC, June 24, 1957, box 7, folder 75, ADP.

43   AD to JC and PC, July 9, 1957, box 7, folder 75, ADP.

44   JC to SB, November 30, 1957, MC 432, folder 87, SBP.

45   JC to SB, December 4, 1957, MC 432, folder 87, SBP.

46   JC to SB, December 15, 1957, MC 432, folder 87, SBP.

47   JC to SB, December 15, 1957, MC 432, folder 87, SBP.

48   JC to SB, copy of D. De Santillana to JC, December 11, 1957, MC 432, folder 87, SBP.

49   JC to SB, copy JC to DdeS, December 13, 1957, MC 432, folder 87, SBP.

50   JC to AD, January 12, 1958, box 7, folder 79, ADP. Ellipsis by JC.

51   AD to JC, January 17, 1958, Reardon, 307–08.

52   JC to AD, February 2, 1958, box 7, folder 79, ADP; Reardon, 310.

53   JC to AD, February 2, 1958, box 7, folder 79, ADP.

54   JC to AD, February 10, 1958, box 7, folder 79, ADP.

55   AD to JC, February 10, 1958, box 7, folder 78, ADP.

56   JC, "Ecole de Trois Gormandes," March 18, 1952, box 41, folder 514, JCP.

57   JC to AD, March 12, 1958, box 7, folder 79, ADP.

58   AD to JC, March 14, 1958, box 7, folder 78, ADP; Reardon, 312.

59   JC to AD, undated, box 7, folder 79, ADP.

60   AD to JC, March 25, 1958, box 7, folder 78, ADP; Reardon, 314–15.

61   JC to SB, Copy of de Santillana to JC, March 21, 1958, MC 432, folder 88, SBP.

62   Copy of JC letter to DdeS, "Managing Editor," sent to SB, March 27, 1958, JC to SB, MC 432, folder 88, SBP.

63   AD to JC, undated, box 7, folder 78, ADP.

64   JC to AD, April 6, 1958, box 7, folder 79, ADP.

CHAPTER 6: SHIFTING GEARS

1   JC to SB, July 30, 1958, MC 432, folder 89, SBP.

2   JC to AD, July 26, 1958, box 7, folder 79, ADP.

3   JC to AD, July 31, 1958, box 7, folder 79, ADP.

4   JC to SB, August 5, 1958, MC 432, folder 90, SBP.

5   AD to JC, July 29, 1958, box 7, folder 78, ADP.

6   JC to SB, August 7, 1958, MC 432, folder 90, SBP.

7   JC to SB, September 9, 1958, MC 432, folder 90, SBP.
8   AD to JC, July 29, 1958, box 7, folder 78, ADP.
9   AD to JC, October 6, 1958, box 7, folder 78, ADP.
10   JC to SB, October 20, 1958, MC 432, folder 91, SBP.
11   AD to JC, October 6, 1958, box 7, folder 78, ADP.
12   AD to JC, January 25, 1959, box 7, folder 78, ADP.
13   JC to SB, December 7, 1958, MC 432, folder 93, SBP.
14   AD to JC, December 10, 1958, box 7, folder 78, ADP.
15   JC to AD, January 23, 1959, box 7, folder 79, ADP.
16   JC to Dorothy de Santillana, May 6, 1958, copy to SB, MC 432, folder 88, SBP.
17   JC to SB, May 6, 1958, MC 432, folder 88, SBP.
18   SB to JC, May 13, 1958, MC 432, folder 88, SBP.
19   JC to SB, July 13, 1958, MC 432, folder 89, SBP.
20   JC to SB, July 13, 1958, MC 432, folder 89, SBP.
21   JC to SB, July 13, 1958, MC 432, folder 89, SBP.
22   JC to SB, July 22, 1958, MC 432, folder 89, SBP.
23   SB to JC, July 25, 1958, MC 432, folder 89, SBP.
24   JC to SB, July 30, 1958, MC 432, folder 89, SBP.
25   JC to SB, August 5, 1958, MC 432, folder 90, SBP.
26   JC to SB, July 13, 1958, MC 432, folder 89, SBP.
27   JC to SB, July 13, 1958, MC 432, folder 89, SBP.
28   SB and JC correspondence, mid-May to early June 1958, MC 432, folder 88–89; quote; SB to JC, July 10, 1958, folder 89, SBP.
29   JC to SB, November 23, 1958, MC 432, folder, 92, SBP.
30   JC to SB, November 24, 1958, MC 432, folder 92, SBP.
31   JC to SB, September 15, 1958, MC 432, folder 90, SBP.
32   SB to JC, September 19, 1958, MC 432, folder 90, SBP.
33   JC to SB, December 6, 1958, MC 432, folder 93, SBP.
34   JC to SB, December 6, 1958, MC 432, folder 93, SBP.
35   JC to SB, December 6, 1958, MC 432, folder 93, SBP.
36   SB to JC, January and February 1959, MC 432, folders 94–95, SBP.
37   JC to SB, March 4–23, 1959, MC 432, folder 96, SBP.
38   JC to SB, March 30, 1959, 432, folder 96; JC to SB, April 1, 1959, MC 432, folder 96, SBP.
39   SB to JC, November 19, 1958, MC 432, folder 92, SBP.
40   SB to JC, November 22, 1958, MC 432, folder 92, SBP.
41   SB to JC, March 27, 1959, MC 432, folder 96, SBP. Réveillon is the traditional festive meal in France on the eves of Christmas and New Years, taken after midnight.
42   JC to SB, April 19, 1959, box 7, folder 80, ADP.
43   JC to Dorothy de Santillana, April 9, 1959, copy JC to SC, MC 432, folder 96, SBP.
44   Dorothy de Santillana to JC, April 27, 1959, box 7, folder 80, ADP.
45   PC to CC, July 16, 1959, MC 644, box 6, folder 73, JCP.
46   JC to "Fam," July 14, 1959, MC 644, box 6, folder 73, JCP.
47   JC to "Fam," July 14, 1959, MC 644, box 6, folder 73, JCP.
48   PC to CC, July 6, 1959, MC 644, box 6, folder 73, JCP.

49   PC to CC, PC diary, July 19, 1959, MC 644, box 6, folder 73, JCP.

50   PC to CC, August 2, 1959, MC 644, box 6, 73, JCP.

51   PC to JC, August 15, 1959, MC 644, box 6, 73a: 16, JCP.

52   JC to SB, September 8, 1959, box 7, folder 80, ADP.

53   Copy of Dorothy de Santillana letter, JC to SB, September 22, 1959, box 7, folder 80, ADP.

54   JC to SB, September 25, 1959, box 7, folder 80, ADP.

55   JC to SB, copy of letter to Dorothy de Santillana, October 1, 1959, box 7, folder 80, ADP.

56   PC to CC, October 10, 1959, MC 644, box 6, folder 73, JCP.

57   PC to CC, November 7, 1959, MC 644, box 6, folder 73, JCP.

58   Paul Brooks to JC, November 6, 1959, copy, box 7, folder 80, ADP.

59   JC to SB and AD, undated but before November 22, 1959, box 7, folder 80, ADP. Ellipses in original. Julia also enclosed a copy of the letter from Brooks.

60   JC to SB and AD, undated but before November 22, 1959, box 7, folder 80, ADP. The reference to Donon is to Joseph Donon, *The Classic French Cuisine* (New York: Knopf, 1959).

61   AD to JC, November 11, 1959, box 7, folder 81, ADP.

CHAPTER 7: WAITING

1   Although Koshland is mentioned in biographies of Julia Child, he is typically a minor figure. Two important exceptions are Laura Shapiro, *Julia Child: A Life* (London: 2007) and Calvin Thompson, "Cooking with Julia Child," *The New Yorker*, December 23, 1974, https://www.newyorker.com/magazine/profiles/1974/12/23/good-cooking.

2   WAK travel journal, 1922, 19, Archives, Phillips Exeter Academy, Exeter, New Hampshire.

3   WAK, travel journal, 7.

4   WAK, Harvard application, 1924, Harvard University Archives.

5   *Harvard 1928, Sexennial* Report (Cambridge, MA: printed for the class, 1934), 113.

6   "The American Jewish Committee Twenty-Eighth Annual Report, 1935," *The American Jewish Year Book*, vol. 37 (September 28, 1935 to September 16, 1936): 5696.

7   As seen online in photographs of the American Jewish Joint Distribution Committee's press announcements, for example, June 7, 1939. https://archives.jdc .org/topic-guides/the-story-of-the-s-s-st-louis/. Accessed January 7, 2022.

8   Paid obituary, *New York Times*, May 9, 1997, announcing Koshland's death from cancer on May 7, 1997.

9   *Harvard Class of 1928, Vicennial Report* (Cambridge, MA, 1948), 196 (photo 35); Wolfgang Saxon, "William A. Koshland, 90, Former Knopf President, Dies," *New York Times*, May 9, 1997.

10   In the early 1960s, Sinton frequently visited the cousin he called "Billy" in his Madison Avenue apartment in New York. It was a home he shared with a man known only by the cousin as Max.

11   Finding aid, Alfred A. Knopf, Inc. Records, Manuscript Collection MS-00062, Harry Ransom Center, University of Texas at Austin. (Hereafter, Knopf Coll., Harry Ransom Center.)

12   Wolfgang Saxon, "William A. Koshland, 90, Former Knopf President, Dies," *New York Times*, May 9, 1997.

13   *Harvard Class of 1928 Fiftieth Anniversary Report* (Cambridge, MA, Printed for the University, 1978), 402–03.

14 AD to JC and PC, July 9, 1957, box 7, folder 75, ADP.
15 AD to JC, November 19, 1958, box 7, folder 78, ADP.
16 John Sinton, phone conversation with author, May 6, 2020.
17 Quotes from AD to JC in JC to SB, November 14, 1959, box 7, folder 80, ADP.
18 WAK to AD, November 18, 1959, box 7, folder 81, ADP.
19 AD to JC, November 19, 1959, box 7, folder 81, ADP.
20 WAK to AD, November 18, 1959, box 7, folder 81, ADP.
21 WAK to AD, November 10, 1959, Knopf Coll., Harry Ransom Center.
22 AD to JC, December 5, 1959, box 7, folder 81, ADP; Reardon, 339.
23 AD to JC, December 27, 1959, Reardon, 341–42.
24 AD to JC, February 18, 1960, box 7, folder 81, ADP; Reardon, 354–56.
25 JC to SB, February 1960, JC to SB, MC 432, folder 97, SBP.
26 JC to SB, February 23, 1960, box 8, folder 83, ADP.
27 AD to JC, March 5, 1960, box 7, folder 81, ADP.
28 AD to JC, March 13, 1960, box 7, folder 81, ADP.
29 AD to JC, March 13, 1960, box 7, folder 81, ADP.
30 JC to SB, March 1, 1960, box 8, folder 83, ADP.
31 AD to JC, April 9, 1960, box 7, folder 81, ADP; Reardon, entire letter, 360–63.
32 AD to JC, April 9, 1960, box 7, folder 81, ADP.
33 AD transcription of JJ notes for JC, April 9, 1960, Reardon, 361–62.
34 AC notes, AD transcription for JC, April 9, 1960, Reardon, 362–63.
35 AD to JC, April 9, 1960, box 7, folder 81, ADP.
36 AD to JC, April 9, 1960, box 7, folder 81, ADP.
37 AD to JC, April 9, 1960, box 7, folder 81, ADP; Reardon, 361.
38 AD to JC, April 9, 1960, box 7, folder 81, ADP; Reardon, 361.
39 AD to JC, April 9, 1960, box 7, folder 81, ADP.
40 AD to JC, April 9, 1960, box 7, folder 81, ADP.
41 AD to JC, April 17, 1960, box 7, folder 81, ADP.
42 JC to AD, April 20, 1960, box 8, folder 82, ADP.
43 AD to JC, April 23, 1960, Reardon, 364.
44 JC to SB, April 30, 1960, box 8, folder 83, ADP.
45 PC to CC, April 30, 1960, box 7, folder 74, ADP.

CHAPTER 8: THE HOUSE OF KNOPF
1 A night letter is a telegram sent at night to be delivered the following morning. AD to JC, May 9, 1960, Reardon, 368.
2 AD to JJ, telegram, May 9, 1960, Knopf Coll., Harry Ransom Center.
3 Anne Frank was interned in the Bergen-Belsen concentration camp, where she died of typhus in 1945.
4 Judith Jones, *The Tenth Muse* (New York, Anchor Books, 2007), 45–46.
5 JJ to JC, May 10, 1960, MC 644, box 33, folder 427, JCP
6 JC to JJ, May 14, 1960, Knopf Coll., Harry Ransom Center.
7 JC to CC and FC, May 15, 1960, MC 644, box 7, folder 74, JCP.
8 SB to JC, May 16, 1960, MC 432, folder 97, original in French, SBP.

9   JC to SB, May 15, 1960, box 8, folder 83, ADP.

10   JC to SB, May 15, 1960, box 8, folder 83, ADP.

11   JC to AD, June 16, 1960, box 8, folder 82, ADP.

12   JC to AD, October 20, 1960, box 8, folder 82, ADP.

13   JC to AD, May 3, 1960, Reardon, 367; not found in Schlesinger collection.

14   JC to AD, May 24, 1960, box 8, folder 82, ADP. (My copy of *Mastering*, the 1963 fifth edition printing, does have in its lengthy recipe for cassoulet, among the variations on page 404, "Preserved Goose," written with the instruction, "It can usually be bought in cans from one of the food-importing stores."

15   PC to CC, May 14, 1960, MC 644, box 7, folder 74, JCP.

16   JC to CC and FC, June 23, 1960, MC 644, box 7, folder 74, JCP.

17   PC (and JC) to CC, June 26, 1960, MC 644, box 7, folder 74, JCP.

18   Here I am aware of the limits of correspondence and my own research for this project. I cannot know what Paul experienced beyond his archived letters or any he wrote after 1966.

19   AD to JC, May 29, 1960, box 7, folder 81, ADP.

20   JC to SB, August 21, 1960, box 8, folder 83, ADP.

21   JJ to JC, May 27, 1960, MC 644, box 33, folder 427, JCP.

22   JJ to JC, June 1, 1960, MC 644, box 33, folder 427, JCP.

23   JJ to JC, June 1, 1960, MC 644, box 33, folder 427, JCP.

24   JJ to JC, June 1, 1960, MC 644, box 33, folder 427, JCP.

25   JC to JJ, July 16, 1960, Knopf Coll., Harry Ransom Center.

26   JJ to JC, July 18, 1960, MC 644, box 33, folder 427, JCP.

27   JC to JJ, July 21, 1960, Knopf Coll., Harry Ransom Center.

28   JC to AD, June 16, 1960, box 8, folder 82, ADP.

29   JC to SB, July 27, 1960, box 8, folder 83, ADP.

30   JC to SB, July 28, 1960, box 8, folder 83, ADP.

31   JC to SB, July 28, 1960, JC to SB, box 8, folder 83, ADP.

32   AD to JC, May 29, 1960, box 7, folder 81, ADP.

33   JC to JJ, July 21, 1960, Knopf Coll., Harry Ransom Center.

34   AD to JC, July 19, 1960, box 7, folder 81, ADP.

35   WAK to JC, August 10, 1960, MC 644, box 33, folder 427, JCP.

36   PC to CC, July 25, 1960, MC 644, box 7, folder 74, JCP.

37   JJ to JC, August 16, 1960, MC 644, box 33, folder 427, JCP.

38   JC to JJ, July 21, 1960, Knopf Coll., Harry Ransom Center.

39   JJ to JC, August 16, 1960, MC 644, box 33, folder 427, JCP.

40   WAK to JC, August 10, 1960, MC 644, box 33, folder 427, JCP.

41   JC to WAK, August 15, 1960, MC 644, box 33, folder 427, JCP.

42   WAK to JC, August 18, 1960, MC 644, box 33, folder 427, JCP.

43   JJ to JC, "NOTES" ON PART I OF FRENCH COOKBOOK," August 18, 1960, MC 644, box 33, folder, 427, JCP.

44   JJ "NOTES," folder 427, JCP.

45   JJ "NOTES," folder 427, JCP.

46   JJ "NOTES," folder 427, JCP.

47   JJ "NOTES," folder 427, JCP.

48   JJ "NOTES," folder 427, JCP.
49   JJ "NOTES," folder 427, JCP.
50   JJ "NOTES," folder 427, JCP.
51   JJ "NOTES," folder 427, JCP.
52   JJ "NOTES," folder 427, JCP.
53   JJ "NOTES," folder 427, JCP.
54   JJ "NOTES," folder 427, JCP.
55   JJ "NOTES," folder 427, JCP.
56   JJ "NOTES," folder 427, JCP.
57   JJ "NOTES," folder 427, JCP.
58   JJ "NOTES," folder 427, JCP.
59   JJ "NOTES," folder 427, JCP.
60   JJ "NOTES," folder 427, JCP.
61   JJ "NOTES," folder 427, JCP.
62   SB to JC, May 3, 1961, MC 432, folder 101, SBP.
63   JJ "NOTES," folder 427, JCP.
64   JC to SB, August 21, 1960, box 8, folder 83, ADP.
65   JC to SB, August 27, 1960, box 8, folder 83, ADP.
66   JJ to JC, August 31, 1960, MC 644, box 33, folder 427, JCP.
67   JJ to JC, August 31, 1960, MC 644, box 33, folder 427, JCP.
68   JJ to JC (with JC comment), August 31, 1960, MC 644, box 33, folder 427, JCP.
69   JC to SB, September 12, 1960, box 8, folder 83, ADP.
70   JC to AD, October 20, 1960, box 8, folder 82, ADP.
71   JC to SB, August 4, 1960, box 8, folder 83, ADP.
72   JJ to JC, November 18, 1960, Knopf Coll., Harry Ransom Center.
73   WAK to JC, November 18, 1960, Knopf Coll., Harry Ransom Center.
74   JC to CC and FC, December 5, 1960, MC 644, box 7, folder 74, JCP.
75   JC to AD, February 7, 1961, box 8, folder 82, ADP.
76   PC to CC and FC, May 15, 1960, MC 644, box 7, folder 74, JCP.
77   JJ to JC, July 18, 1960, MC 644, box 33, folder 427, JCP.
78   JC to JJ, July 16, 1960, Knopf Coll., Harry Ransom Center.
79   JC to SB, October 26, 1960, box 8, folder 83, ADP.
80   WAK to JC, November 18, 1960, Knopf Coll., Harry Ransom Center.
81   JJ to JC, November 18, 1960, Knopf Coll., Harry Ransom Center.
82   JC to WAK, November 27, 1960, Knopf Coll., Harry Ransom Center.
83   JJ to JC, January 10, 1961, MC 644, box 33, folder 429, JCP.
84   JC to JJ, January 13, 1961, MC 644, box 33, folder 427, JCP.
85   JJ to JC, February 13, 1961, MC 644, box 33, folder 427, JCP.
86   JJ to JC, February 16, 1961, MC 644, box 33, folder 427, JCP.
87   JC to JJ, February 20, 1961, MC 644, box 33, folder 427, JCP.
88   JJ to JC, February 28, 1961, MC 644, box 33, folder 427, JCP.
89   JC to JJ, March 4, 1961, MC 644, box 33, folder 427, JCP.
90   JJ to JC, March 6, 1961, MC 644, box 33, folder 427, JCP.
91   JC to JJ, March 8, 1961, MC 644, box 33, folder 427, JCP.

92   JC to JJ, March 19, 1961, MC 644, box 33, folder 427, JCP.

93   JJ to JC, April 14, 1961, MC 644, box 33, folder 427, JCP.

94   JC to JJ, April 18, MC 644, box 33, folder 427, JCP.

95   SB to JC, April 25, 1961, MC 432, folder 100, SBP.

96   JC to SB, April 28, 1961, box 8, folder 84, ADP.

97   JC to AD, April 28, 1961, box 8, folder 82, ADP.

98   JC to SB, May 1, 1961, box 8, folder 82, ADP.

99   Avis's notes on visit to Bramafam, December 17, 1966–January 9, 1967, A-167, 2-32, **ADP**.

100   JC to JJ, April 24, 1961, MC 644, box 33, folder 427, JCP.

101   JC to JJ, May 8, 1961, MC 644, box 33, folder 427, JCP.

CHAPTER 9: THE LAUNCH

1   Mark DeVoto interview of his mother Avis DeVoto, n.d., Knopf Coll., Harry Ransom Center.

2   JJ to JC, August 16, 1960, Knopf Coll., Harry Ransom Center.

3   JC to JJ, September 6, 1961, MC 644, box 34, folder 428, JCP.

4   JJ to JC, September 13, 1961, MC 644, box 34, folder 428, JCP.

5   JC to SB, September 11, 1961, box 8, folder 84, ADP.

6   JC to SB, September 13, 1961, box 8, folder 84, ADP.

7   JC to JJ, September 13, 1961, MC 644, box 34, folder 428, JCP. Julia Child Papers, Schlesinger, Library.

8   JC to SB, September 15, 1961, box 8, folder 84, ADP.

9   SB to JC, September 19, 1961, MC 432, folder 101, SBP.

10   JC to SB, September 15, box 8, folder 84, 15–16, ADP.

11   JC to WAK, September 29, 1961, MC 644, box 34, folder 428, JCP.

12   WAK to JC, September 29, 1961, MC 644, box 34, folder 428, JCP. (These are the dates written on the two successive letters, despite the seeming impossibility of instant written communication in 1961.)

13   JC to Harding Lemay, October 3, 1961, MC 644, box 34, folder 428, JCP.

14   JC to Harding Lemay, October 15, 1961, MC 644, box 34, folder 428, JCP.

15   JJ to JC, August 11 [c/o Avis] MC 644, box 34, folder 428, JCP.

16   AD to JJ, July 23, 1961, Series I, Knopf Coll., Harry Ransom Center.

17   JJ to AD, August 28, 1961, Series I, Knopf Coll., Harry Ransom Center.

18   AD to JJ, August 14, 1961, Series I, Knopf Coll., Harry Ransom Center.

19   JJ to AD, August 29, 1961, Series I, Knopf Coll., Harry Ransom Center.

20   SB to JC, October 9, 1961, MC 432, folder 101, SBP.

21   JC to SB, October 13, 1961, box 8, folder 84, ADP.

22   The narrative of the launch in New York City is based on Julia Child's 1961 appointment book, MC 660, JCP.

23   *Julia Child: The Last Interview and Other Conversations*, introduction by Helen Rosner (Brooklyn, NY: Melville House Publishing, 2019), 3–32.

24   JC to JJ, January 13, 1961, MC 644, box 33, 427g: 7, Julia Child Papers, Schlesinger Library.

25   JC to SB, October 13, 1961, box 8, 84d: 6, ADP.

26 The narrative of the book tour relies on Julia Child's 1961 appointment book, MC 660, 139, JCP, and "ITINERARY. Simone Beck, and Paul and Julia Child, November 5, 1961 to Dec. 16," MC 644, box 34, folder 429, JCP.

27 JC to JJ, November 9, 1961, MC 644, box 34, folder 428, JCP.

28 PC to AD, November 22, 1961, A-167, box 1, folder 13, 81–88, ADP. Paul's following narration comes from this source.

29 Paul here exaggerated her role, given her own statement in Simone Beck, with Suzanne Patterson, *Food & Friends: Recipes and Memories from Simca's Cuisine* (New York: Penguin Books, 1991), 132.

30 JC Itinerary, cc to JJ, November 5–December 16, 1961, MC 644, box 34, folder 429, JCP.

31 JC to JJ, November 1, 1961, MC 644, box 34, folder 428, JCP.

32 JJ to JC, November 9, 1961, MC 644, box 34, folder 428, JCP.

33 JJ to JC, November 9, 1961, MC 644, box 34, folder 428, JCP.

34 The basis of this narrative is the long letter that Paul wrote to Avis of the trio's time in California, A-167, box 1, folder 13, ADP.

35 JC to JJ, November 22, 1961, MC 644, box 34, folder 428, JCP.

36 PC to AD, November 22, 1961, A-167, box 1, folder 13: 82–83, ADP.

37 Charlotte Jackson to WAK, November 18, 1961, Knopf Coll., Harry Ransom Center.

38 PC to AD, November 22, 1961, A-167, box 1, folder 13, ADP.

39 PC to AD, November 22, 1961, A-167, box 1, folder 13, ADP.

40 JJ to JC, November 20, 1961, MC 644, box 34, folder 428, JCP.

41 JC to JJ, November 22, 1961, MC 644, box 34, folder 428, JCP.

42 PC to AD, November 22, 1961, A-167, box 1, folder 13, ADP.

43 JC to JJ, November 22, 1961, MC 644, box 34, folder 428, JCP.

44 JC to JJ, November 29, 1961, MC 644, box 34, folder 428, JCP.

45 PC to AD, December 2, 1961, A-167, box 1, folder 13, ADP.

46 JC to JJ, December 2, 1961, MC 644, box 34, folder 428, JCP.

47 PC to AD, December 2, 1961, A-167, box 1, folder 13, ADP.

48 JC Itinerary, cc to JJ, November 5–December 16, 1961, MC 644, box 34, folder 429, JCP.

49 JJ to AD, November 29, 1961, Knopf Coll., Harry Ransom Center.

50 Quotes from Julia Child, interview, https://www.youtube.com/watch?v=VTY1oT-uekc (viewed October 6, 2021).

51 JC to SB, December 18, 1961, box 8, 84, ADP.

52 JC to SB, December 18, 1961, box 8, 84, ADP.

53 SB to JC and PC, December 20, 1961, and December 26, 1961, MC 432, folder 101, SBP.

CHAPTER 10: THE FRENCH CHEF

1 JC to SB, January 17, 1962, box 8, folder 85, ADP.

2 AD to SB, February 17, 1962, box 8, folder 82, ADP.

3 PC to CC, [February 24, 1962], MC 644 box 7, folder 77: 17, Julia Child Papers, Schlesinger Library.

4 Braude, too, had come under political scrutiny, but unlike Paul, she was fired as a security risk. Beatrice Braude obituary, *Washington Post*, October 21, 1988.

5   JC to Dave Davis, August 8, 1962, MC 644, box 38, 486a: 8, Julia Child Papers, Schlesinger Library.

6   JC to SB, March 3, 1962, JC to SB, box 8, folder 85, ADP; CPI Inflation Calculator.

7   PC to CC, March 6, 1962, MC 644, box 7, folder 77, JCP.

8   JC to SB, October 8, 1962, box 8, folder 85, ADP.

9   JC to SB, November 15, 1963, box 8, folder 85, ADP.

10   PC to CC, March 6, 1962, report on February 7, 1962, MC 644, box 7, folder 77, JCP.

11   JC to FC, March 14, 1962, MC 644, box 7, folder 77, JCP.

12   Dana Polan provides an excellent guide to *The French Chef* in his *Julia Child's The French Chef* (Durham and London: Duke University Press, 2011).

13   PC to CC, March 17, 1962, MC 644, box 7, folder 77, JCP.

14   PC to CC, May 29, 1962, MC 644, box 7, folder 77, JCP.

15   PC to CC, March 17, 1962, MC 644, box 7, folder 77, JCP.

16   JC to WGBH, April 26, 1962, MC 644, box 38, folder 486, JCP. The following discussion relies on this document.

17   JC to FC, March 14, 1962, MC 644, box 7, folder 77, JCP.

18   PC to CC, March 17, 1962, MC 644, box 7, folder 77, JCP.

19   JC to SB, April 27, 1962, box 8, folder 85, ADP.

20   JC, 1962 appointment book, MC 644, box 139, JCP.

21   JC to SB, May 13, 1962, box 8, folder 85, ADP.

22   Beatrice Braude[?] to JC, May 24, [1962], MC 644, box 38, folder 486, JCP.

23   JC to SB, May 25, 1962, box 8, folder 85, ADP.

24   PC to CC, May 14, 1962, MC 644, box 7, folder 77, JCP. Paul's "stoogensis" likely referred not only to the hidden hand doing the work but also to the then-popular comedy team, the Three Stooges.

25   JC to SB, June 6, 1962, box 8, folder 85, ADP.

26   PC to CC, November 7, 1959, MC 644, box 6, folder 73, JCP.

27   PC to CC, May 25, 1962, MC 644, box 7, folder 77, JCP.

28   JC, 1962 appointment book, MC 644, box 139, JCP.

29   JC to SB, July 27, 1962, box 8, folder 85, ADP.

30   JC to SB, August 2, 1962, box 8, folder 85, ADP.

31   PC to CC, August 6, 1962, MC 644, box 7, folder 77, JCP.

32   PC to CC, May 14, 1962, MC 644, box 7, folder 77, JCP.

33   JC to JJ, July 7, 1962, box 34, folder 430, ADP.

34   Ellipses are in the original letter. PC to CC, August 22, 1962, MC 644, box 7, folder 77, JCP.

35   PC to CC, September 27, [1962], MC 644, box 7, folder 77, JCP.

36   JC to Dave Davis, August 8, 1962, MC 644, box 38, folder 486, JCP.

37   Arthur Lockwood, http://cinematreasures.org/chains/1043/previous became an important civic figure in Boston and was a founder in 1948 (and later head) of the Jimmy Fund at the Dana-Farber Cancer Institute.

38   Response to email query to Boston University answered by "Kate," July 20, 2020: "Based on our records, it appears as though this MA thesis was written in 1958."

39   JC to WAK, August 10, 1962, MC 644, box 34, folder 430, JCP.

40   WAK to Krinsley, memo, October 11, 1962, Knopf Coll., Harry Ransom Center.
41   JC to WAK, JJ, October 6, 1962, MC 644, box 34, folder 430, JCP.
42   WAK to JC, October 11, 1962, MC 644, box 34, folder 430, JCP.
43   WAK to DK, October 17, 1962, Knopf Coll., Harry Ransom Center.
44   PC to CC, November 19, 1962, MC 644, box 34, folder 77, JCP.
45   PC to CC, November 19, 1962, MC 644, box 34, folder 77, JCP.
46   PC to CC, November 19, 1962, MC 644, box 7, folder 77, JCP.
47   WAK to JC, November 29, 1962, MC 644, box 34, folder 430, JCP.
48   WAK to JC, November 29, 1962, MC 644, box 34, folder 430, JCP.
49   JC to SB, November 15, 1962, box 8, folder 85, ADP.
50   JC to SB, December 6, 1962, box 8, folder 85, ADP.
51   JC to SB, December 18, 1962, box 8, folder 85, ADP.
52   PC to CC, December 12, 1962, MC 644, box 7, folder 77, JCP.
53   PC to CC, December 12, 1962, MC 644, box 7, folder 77, JCP.
54   WAK to JC, November 29, 1962, MC 644, box 34, folder 430, JCP.
55   JC to SB, November 23, 1962, box 8, folder 85, ADP.
56   JC to SB, December 18, 1962, box 8, folder 85, ADP.
57   JC to Robert Larsen, December 18, 1962, on GBH Facebook page, August 5, 2019, https://www.facebook.com/WGBHBoston/photos/as-it-is-every-day-it-was-a-brisk-63-degrees-in-the-wgbh-media-library-archives-/10162704871645455/, accessed 7/20/20.
58   RL to RM, December 24, 1962, MC 644, box 38, folder 486, JCP.
59   JC to SB, January 26, 1963, box 8, folder 86, ADP.
60   WAK to JC, January 3, 1963, Knopf Coll., Harry Ransom Center.
61   WAK to JC, January 11, 1963, MC 644, box 34, folder 431, JCP.
62   JC to WAK, January 14, 1963, MC 644, box 34, folder 431, JCP.
63   WAK to JC, January 17, 1963, MC 644, box 34, folder 431, JCP.
64   JC to SB, December 6, 1962, box 8, folder 85, ADP.
65   JC to WAK, January 19, 1963, MC 644, box 34, folder 431, JCP.
66   PC to CC, January 26, 1963, MC 644, box 7, folder 78, JCP. Ben Thomson, the founder of Design Research in Cambridge, was an architect and one of the founders of the firm Architects Collaborative.
67   PC to CC, February 9, 1963, MC 644, box 7, folder 78, JCP.
68   JC to SB, February 10, 1963, box 8, folder 86, ADP.
69   PC to CC, February 9, 1963, MC 644, box 7, folder 78, JCP.
70   PC to CC, February 9, 1963, MC 644, box 7, folder 78, JCP.
71   WAK to Krinsley, January 7, 1963, Knopf Coll., Harry Ransom Center.
72   WAK to Krinsley, January 7, 1963, Knopf Coll., Harry Ransom Center.
73   Polan, *Julia Child's The French Chef,* 201.
74   JC to WAK, January 9, 1963, Knopf Coll., Harry Ransom Center.
75   JC to WAK, February 11, 1963, MC 644, box 34, folder 431, JCP.
76   JC to WAK, February 24, 1963, MC 644, box 34, folder 431, JCP.
77   JC to WAK, March 7, 1963, MC 644, box 34, folder 431, JCP.
78   JC to SB, April 2, 1963, box 8, folder 86, ADP.
79   JC to SB, March 2, 1963, box 8, folder 86, ADP.

80   PC to CC, June 15, 1963, MC 644, box 7, folder 78, JCP.

81   Julia Child quoted, Polan, *Julia Child's The French Chef*, 189.

82   PC to CC, May 4, 1963, MC 644, box 7, folder 78, JCP.

83   Email correspondence between author and a representative of The Julia Child
      Foundation for Gastronomy and the Culinary Arts, May 3, 2021.

84   WAK to JC, undated, MC 644, box 34, folder 431, JCP.

85   JC to WAK, March 16, 1963, MC 644, box 34, folder 431, JCP.

86   JC to WAK, March 16, 1963, MC 644, box 34, folder 431, JCP.

87   WAK to JC, with PC annotations, March 19, 1963, MC 644, box 34, folder 431, JCP.

88   PC to CC, March 2, 1963, MC 644, box 34, folder 78, JCP.

89   JC to WAK, March 24, 1963, MC 644, box 34, folder 431, JCP.

90   JC to WAK, April 19, 1963, MC 644, box 34, folder 431, JCP.

91   JC to WAK, May 11, 1963, MC 644, box 34, folder 431, JCP.

92   JC to WAK, June 10, 1963, MC 644, box 34, folder 431, JCP.

93   JC to WAK, June 24, 1963, MC 644, box 34, folder 431, JCP.

94   PC to CC, July 27, 1963, MC 644, box 34, folder 78, JCP.

95   JJ to JC, August 5, 1963, MC 644, box 34, folder 431, JCP.

96   JC to WAK, August 21, 1963, MC 644, box 34, folder 431, JCP.

97   WAK to JC, August 23, 1963, MC 644, box 34, folder 431, JCP.

98   WAK to WAK memo, August 29, 1963, Knopf Coll., Harry Ransom Center.

99   PC to CC, August 23, 1963, MC 644, box 34, folder 78, JCP.

100   PC to CC, August 23, 1963, MC 644, box 7, folder 78, JCP.

101   RL to JC and PC, September 3, 1963, MC 644, box 20, folder 262, JCP.

102   RL to JC, September 10, 1963, MC 644, box 20, folder 262, JCP.

103   JC to RL, September 15, 1963, MC 644, box 20, folder 262, JCP. Schlesinger Library.

104   RL to JC, September 21, 1963, MC 644, box 20, folder 262, JCP.

105   RL to JC, October 1, 1963, MC 644, box 20, folder 262, JCP.

106   JC to RL, October 10, 1963, MC 644, box 20, folder 262, JCP.

107   RL to WAK, September 16, 1963, MC 644, box 34, folder 432, JCP.

108   WAK to RL, September 18, 1963, copy, MC 644, box 34, folder 432, JCP.

109   JC to RL, September 28, 1963, MC 644, box 20, folder 262, JCP.

110   RL to JC, October 23, 1963, MC 644, box 20, folder 262, JCP.

111   JC to RL, October 29, 1963, MC 644, box 20, folder 262, JCP.

112   JC to WAK, August 31, 1964, MC 644, box 34, folder 432, JCP.

113   JC to RL, September 28, 1963, MC 644, box 20, folder 262, JCP.

114   PC to CC, September 20, 1963, MC 644, box 7, folder 78, JCP.

115   JC to RL, September 28, 1963, MC 644, box 20, folder 262, JCP.

116   PC to CC, September 20, 1963, MC 644, box 7, folder 78, JCP.

117   PC to CC, September 20, 1963, MC 644, box 7, folder 78, c: 5–6, JCP.

118   JC to RL, October 10, 1963, MC 644, box 20, folder 262, JCP.

119   PC to CC, October 21, 1963, MC 644, box 34, folder 78, JCP.

120   PC to CC, November 4, 1963, MC 644, box 34, folder 78, JCP.

121   PC to CC, November 6, 1963, MC 644, box 7, folder 78, JCP.

122 PC to CC, November 17, 1963, MC 644, box 34, folder 78, JCP.
123 RL to JC and PC, October 25, 1963, MC 644, box 20, folder 262, JCP.
124 JC to RL, October 29, 1963, MC 644, box 20, folder 262, JCP.
125 JC to RL, October 29, 1963, MC 644, box 20, folder 262, JCP.
126 RL to JC, penciled date, November 4, [1963], MC 644, box 20, folder 262, JCP.
127 PC to CC, November 17, 1963, MC 644, box 34, folder 78, JCP.

CHAPTER 11: "JULIA"
1 SB to JC, November 15, 1963, MC 432, folder 103, SBP.
2 PC to SB, November 25, 1963, MC 432, folder 103, SBP.
3 PC to SB, November 29, 1963, MC 432, folder 103, SBP.
4 SB to PC, December 6, 1963, MC 432, folder 103, SBP.
5 JC to SB, December 16, 1963, box 8, folder 86, ADP.
6 PC to CC, December 7, 1963, MC 644, box 7, folder 78, JCP.
7 PC to CC, December 7, 1963, MC 644, box 7, folder 78, JCP.
8 PC to CC, February 15, 1964, MC 644, box 7, folder 79, JCP. In this instance Paul misrepresented La Pitchoune, because construction involved an adaptation of an existing structure on the Bramafam property.
9 PC to CC, February 27, 1964, MC 644, box 7, folder 79, JCP.
10 JC to SB, January 23, 1964, box 8, folder 86, ADP.
11 JC to AAK, December 12, 1965, MC 644, box 34, folder 433, JCP.
12 PC to CC, November 17, 1963, MC 644, box 7, folder 78, JCP.
13 PC to CC, HLH paragraph insertion, March 21, 1964, MC 644, box 7, folder 79, JCP.
14 PC to CC, February 2, 1964, MC 644, box 7, folder 79, JCP.
15 PC to CC, March 10, 1964, MC 644, box 7, folder 79, JCP.
16 PC to CC, March 10, 1964, MC 644, box 7, folder 79, JCP.
17 PC to CC, March 15, 1964, MC 644, box 7, folder 79, JCP.
18 "Television: How to Sell Broccoli," *TIME*, March 20, 1964, online edition, http://content.time.com/time/subscriber/article/0,33009,940374,00.html, viewed October 26, 2021.
19 PC to CC, March 28, 1964, MC 644, box 7, folder 79, JCP.
20 Dana Polan, *Julia Child's The French Chef* (Durham and London, Duke University Press, 2011), 201, 205.
21 WAK to JC, July 21, 1964, MC 644 box 34, folder 432, JCP.
22 WAK to RL, July 23, 1964, MC 644, box 34, folder 432, JCP.
23 JC to WAK, August 5, 1964, MC 644, box 34, folder 432, JCP.
24 JC to WAK, August 31, 1964, MC 644, box 34, folder 432, JCP.
25 JC to SB, November 27, 1964, box 8, folder 86, ADP.
26 JC to WAK, January 25, 1965, MC 644, box 34, folder 433, JCP.
27 AAK to JC, March 11, 1965, MC 644, box 34, folder 433, JCP.
28 JC to AAK, March 18, 1965, MC 644, box 34, folder 433, JCP.
29 JC to SB, April 14 and 15, 1965, box 8, folder 87, ADP.
30 JC to SB, April 11, 1965, box 8, folder 87, ADP.
31 JC to SB, April 15, 1965, box 8, folder 87, ADP.

32   "Personal Award: Julia Child For 'The French Chef,'" Peabody: Stories that Matter, http://www.peabodyawards.com/award-profile/personal-award-julia-child -the-french-chef, viewed November 26, 2020.

33   JJ to JC, May 3, 1965, MC 644, box 34, folder 433, JCP.

34   JC to WAK, June 2, 1965, MC 644, box 34, folder 433, JCP.

35   JC to WAK, June 29, 1965, MC 644, box 34, folder 433, JCP. Julia Child's *The French Chef Cookbook* was published by Knopf in 1968.

36   WAK to Mr. Larsen, copy, July 23, 1965, MC 644, box 34, folder 433, JCP.

37   JC to JJ and WAK, November 5, 1965, MC 644, box 34, folder 433, JCP.

38   JC to SB, April 16, and after April 21, 1966, box 8, folder 88, ADP.

39   JC to SB, October 24, 1966, box 8, folder 88, ADP.

40   Michael Field, "The French Way," *New York Review of Books*, November 1965.

41   AAK to JC, November 30, 1965, MC 644, box 34, folder 433, JCP.

42   JC to AAK, December 12, 1965, MC 644, box 34, folder 433, JCP.

43   JJ to JC, November 29, 1965, MC 644, box 34, folder 433, JCP.

44   JC to JJ, Oct. 2, 1966, MC 644, box 34, folder 434, JCP.

45   JC to JJ, Oct. 27, 1966, MC644, box 34, folder 434, JCP.

46   "Food: Everyone's in the Kitchen," *TIME*, November 25, 1966, Text: 74–87 passim; quotes, 74, 80, 87. Although I read the article at the Ransom collection and photographed it, online access is available: https://time.com/4230699 /food-everyones-in-the-kitchen/.

47   WAK to JC and PC, December 14, 1966, box 434, JCP.

48   SB to JC, November 25, 1966, MC 432, folder 106, SBP (Translated by the author from the French).

Acknowledgments

Two archives enabled this study, the Schlesinger Library of the Harvard Radcliffe Institute in Cambridge, Massachusetts and the Harry Ransom Center on the campus of the University of Texas in Austin. I am grateful for these repositories for preserving and organizing the papers of Julia Child and members of her team, the helpfulness of their staffs, and for the pleasure of working in their pleasant reading rooms. The Schlesinger is also the repository of the photographs by Paul Child that illustrate this book. A special thanks to Diana Carey for her online guidance regarding these images during the difficult period of the pandemic's lockdown. In addition I benefited from records at the Harvard University Archives and, through the helpfulness of Leonard Egan, from materials at the Archives and Special Collections of Phillips Exeter Academy.

I wish to thank The Julia Child Foundation for Gastronomy and the Culinary Arts, the holder of the copyright for the words of Julia and Paul Child, for permission to quote from their letters.

For help on legal issues, especially copyright, I relied the firm Frankfurt Kurnit Klein + Selz. I am grateful for the advice of partner Maura J. Wogan, specialist in intellectual property.

I wish to thank Jessica Case of Pegasus Books for her care and attention to language in editing the manuscript. In addition, I am grateful to those at the press who aided in the production of this book.

After writing the manuscript's first draft, I reread Laura Shapiro's *Julia Child* and found that she had referred to a number of my central figures as comprising Julia's "team." I hadn't remembered this, but it was likely playing in my unconscious as I began exploring Julia Child's correspondence at the Schlesinger Library. Laura also gave an important reading to an early draft. Her encouraging me to explore more fully the lives and concerns of those who contributed to Julia's life and work proved important to the manuscript's development.

I am grateful to the family members of three members of Julia's team, who offered information at various stages of this book: Mark DeVoto, the son of Avis DeVoto; John Sinton, a cousin of William Koshland; and Susan Lewinnek, the daughter of Ruth Lockwood. In the case of this book, research and writing was no lonely enterprise, but turned out to bring these good people into my world.

Because of Covid, necessitating a return to home base, I could not, as planned present my early work at the "Scholars Seminar" at the Huntington Library in California, but I relied on two key colleagues for their long-distance help. After reading an early draft, Jane Smith encouraged me to think more fully about Julia's business sense. Carol Rigolot helped me improve a late draft of the manuscript by her careful reading and attention to word usage and grammar. I am truly grateful to both of them.

Two others read the manuscript and gave me important feedback. I took to heart the many valuable suggestions of historian Lynn Dumenil. Sherie Cheung, a physician with a strong interest in cooking, was an important reader who gave me very useful reactions and suggestions as she responded to the text.

And finally there was Daniel Horowitz—historian, writer, and beloved spouse—who listened and advised throughout as I researched and wrote. Dan also offered thoughtful comments on an early draft. Woven into our long life together, the many months of Covid lockdown proved to be fruitful ones for the two of us.

Illustration Credits

p. xxi: "Julia and Paul at Their Wedding," ©Schlesinger Library, Harvard Radcliffe Institute, HOLLIS: 8001251303

p. xiv: Paul Child, "Julia Child and Chef Bugnard," ©Schlesinger Library, Harvard Radcliffe Institute, HOLLIS: 12694681

p. 10: Paul Child, "Simca, close up," ©Schlesinger Library, Harvard Radcliffe Institute, MC660-1-91; 577885

p. 15: Paul Child, "Group portrait of Simone Beck, Julia Child, and Louisette Bertholle seated at a wooden table chopping vegetables," ©Schlesinger Library, Harvard Radcliffe Institute, Hollis: 002673216

p. 28: Paul Child, "Avis DeVoto seated outdoors eating," ©Schlesinger Library, Harvard Radcliffe Institute, Image ID 31071211

p. 31: Paul Child, "Trial shot of Julie reading letter," ©Schlesinger Library, Harvard Radcliffe Institute, HOLLIS: olvwork578218

p. 42: Paul Child, "Rompillion," ©Schlesinger Library, Harvard Radcliffe Institute, Hollis: 577821

p. 49: Paul Child, "Julia Child silhouetted in Marseille apartment window with boats in the background," Schlesinger Library, Harvard Radcliffe Institute, Hollis: 631178, ©Julia Child Foundation.

p. 81: Paul Child, "Paris; Chez Gourmette's school, [Avis and Julia]," ©Schlesinger Library, Harvard Radcliffe Institute, Hollis: 581329

p. 82: Paul Child, "Portrait of Julia Child and Avis DeVoto seated outdoors [Rouen]," ©Schlesinger Library, Harvard Radcliffe Institute, Hollis: 533481

p. 87: Paul Child, "Lumberville; Sacramento delta [Christmas, Julie singing carols] Julie singing carols," ©Schlesinger, Harvard Radcliffe Institute, Hollis: 581371

p. 88: Paul Child, "Erica's Wedding [four people in kitchen during cake decorating]," ©Schlesinger Library, Harvard Radcliffe Institute, Hollis: 12694681

p. 105: Paul Child, "Julia and Paul Child seated indoors reading at a table. Lopus [Lopaus], ME," ©Schlesinger Library, Harvard Radcliffe Institute, Hollis: 631179, ©Julia Child Foundation.

p. 108: Paul Child, "103 Irving St.", ©Schlesinger Library, Harvard Radcliffe Institute, Hollis: 584725, [original in color].

Index

A

Across the Wide Missouri, 26
Anne Frank: The Diary of a Young Girl,
    142–143
Arden, Elizabeth, 186, 203
Artamonoff, George, 7–9, 11
awards, x, 247, 250–251, *251*

B

Bacon, Martha, 94–96
Baker, Evangeline, 186
Ball, George, 179
Ball, Mrs. George, 179
Beard, James, 109, 178, 182, 192–193, 201,
    206, 209–212, 224, 242, 247
Beck, Maurice, 3, 4, 5
Beck, Simone (Simca)
    birth of, 3
    book tour with, xv, 173–177, 183–195
    in California, 184–191
    in Cambridge, 98–99, 182–183, 192–193
    career of, 5–24, 34–52, 57–61, 66–82,
        90–91, 94–95, 97–98, 109–115,
        120–122, 134–136, 163–165
    in Chicago, 192
    cookbook manuscript and, 145–149,
        151–152, 155, 158–163, 168–171
    cookbook sales and, 193–196, 223
    cooking school of, 13–25, 29, 42–43, 68,
        99, 183, 197
    cooking show and, 202, 204
    in Detroit, 99, 183–184
    early years of, 3–5
    education of, 5
    health concerns of, 66, 83, 97, 110, 151
    manuscript rejection and, 99–102
    marriages of, 4–5
    in Marseille, 53, 59
    meeting Avis DeVoto, 79–80, 91
    meeting Julia Child, 3, 7–9
    new roles for, 69–82, 90–91
    in New York, 181–182
    parents of, 3–4, 239
    in Paris, 4–24, 34–52, 57–61, 66–74
    photos of, *10*, *15*, *190*
    as teacher, 68
    as team member, ix–x, xv, 8–24, 34–52,
        57–61, 66–82, 173–177, 183–195, 250,
        254–255
    in United States, 98–102, 173–177,
        181–193
    visits with, 231–233, 236–237, 254
    in Washington, 100–102, 192
Bertholle, Louisette
    concerns about, 68–69
    cookbook manuscript and, 146
    cookbook sales and, 193–196, 223
    cooking school of, 13–24, 29, 42–43, 68,
        99, 183, 197
    meeting Avis DeVoto, 71–72
    new roles for, 69–73, 83
    photo of, *15*

as teacher, 68

as team member, 6–8, 10–18, 34–39, 43–44, 49–50, 53

Book of the Month Club, 7, 44, 209, 213, 215–216, 222–223

book promotions, xv, 173–195, 200–201, 209, 215–219, 223–224, 251–252

book tour, xv, 173–177, 183–195

Boston Globe, 180, 211, 213, 224, 228, 230, 243

Boston Herald, 180

Bouquet de France, 37

Branson, Katharine, x, 186

Braude, Beatrice, 195, 198, 202, 207–208

Brooks, Paul, 121–122

Bugnard, Max, *xiv*, 12–13, 52, 68, 73, 80–81, 232

Bundy, Mrs. McGeorge, 179

C

Cameron, Angus, 132–133, 136–137, 139, 144

Carême, Marie-Antoine, xiv, 73, 102, 249

Cassiot, Aimée, 7

Cavalcade of Books, 190

Cercle des Gourmettes, 6–11, 19, 52, 68, 76, 80–81, 95, 113, 255

Chaliapin, Boris, 252, *253*

Challiol, Marcelle, 116

Chancellor, John, 182

Chappell, Warren, 167–168

Chicago Tribune, 192

Child, Bertha Cushing, 2

Child, Charles Tripler, 1

Child, Charles (Charlie)

correspondence with, xi–xiii, 1–2, 13, 17–24, 32–34, 42–47, 53–54, 57–58, 88, 93, 145–148, 154, 164, 195–206, 210–212, 217, 222, 226, 232–235, 238–243

telegram from, 76

visits with, 45–47, 64, 90, 242

Child, Frederika (Freddie)

correspondence with, xi–xiii, 12–13,

16–17, 20–23, 43–47, 54, 145, 148, 164, 197, 200

visits with, 45–47, 64, 90, 242

Child, Julia

as "agent," 155–156, 193–196

article on, x, xvi, 229–230, 243, 250–255

awards for, x, 247, 250–251, *251*

background of, ix–xvi, 1–2

birthday of, 119

business sense of, ix, xv, 20, 31–35, 74, 80, 113–115, 155–156, 173, 193–196

in California, 64, 184–192

in Cambridge, 62–66, 85–89, 107–109, *108*, 172–250

in Chicago, 192

column by, 224–226, 228, 243

cooking demonstrations by, 174, 184–187, 190–192, 196–198, 209–212, 222, 227, 233, 242–247

cooking school of (L'École des Trois Gourmandes), 13–25, 29–30, 42–43, 68, 94, 99, 183, 197

cooking show of, x, xv–xvi, 194–233, 236–253

cover story on, x, xvi, 243, 250–255

in Detroit, 183–184

early career of, x–xvi, *xiv*, 1–24

early years of, x–xi, 2

education of, x, xiv–xv, 12

fame for, ix–x, 201–256

in Germany, 66–83

home leave for, 60, 62–67

inspiration for, xiii–xiv

in Maine, 65

manuscript rejection and, x, 99–102, 122–123

marriage of, ix, xi–xii, 2–3

in Marseille, 41–61

Mastering the Art of French Cooking launch and, 172–193

Mastering the Art of French Cooking manuscript of, x, xvi, 10–61, 73–171, 248–250

Mastering the Art of French Cooking promotions and, xv, 173–195, 200–201, 209, 215–219, 223–224, 251–252

Mastering the Art of French Cooking royalties and, xv, 60, 68, 144–146, 167, 194–197, 202, 221–225, 231, 236–240, 245

Mastering the Art of French Cooking sales and, 173, 184–188, 193–196, 200–202, 213–226, 230, 236, 239–248, 251–255

Mastering the Art of French Cooking tour of, xv, 173–177, 183–195

meeting Avis DeVoto, x, 62–64

meeting Paul Child, xi, 2

meeting Simca Beck, 3, 7–9

new roles for, 69–82

in New York, 67, 171, 181–182

in Norway, 114–171

parents of, x–xi, 200, 203

in Paris, xiii–xiv, 2–40, 75, 79–80, 83–84

photos of, *xii, xiv, 15, 31, 42, 49, 81–82, 87–88, 105, 119, 143, 190, 215, 251, 253*

publicity campaigns and, xv, 173–195, 200–201, 209, 215–219, 223–224, 251–252

radio interviews, 181–192

second home of, 236–240, 247

shifting gears, 103–123

"signature" of, *228*

success of, ix–x, 201–256

team of, ix–x, xv–xvi, 1–82, 131–146, 149–256

television appearances, x, xv–xvi, 181–182, 194–233, 236–253

as translator, 49–50

in United States, 62–67, 85–102, 171

vacation of, 226–234, 240

in Washington, 66–67, 85–102, 192

wedding of, *xii*

Child, Paul

birth of, 1

book tour with, xv, 173–177, 183–195

business sense of, 21–23

in California, 64, 184–192

in Cambridge, 62–66, 85–89, 107–109, *108,* 172–250

career of, xii–xiii, 2–3, 13, 21–23, 42, 53–54, 57–61, 66–70, 75, 88–94, 103–105, 139–140, 147–148, 153–154, 165, 196, 202–203, 205–206, 222, 232, 240–242, 249–250

in Chicago, 192

cooking school and, 13–25, 29, 42–43

cooking show and, 196–198, 203–205, 213–223, 240–242, 246–247

designs by, 21–22, *22*

in Detroit, 183–184

early years of, 1–2, 22–23

education of, 2, 22–23

in Germany, 66–83

health concerns of, 86, 103–104, 115, 121, 139–140, 147–148, 238

in Maine, 65

marriage of, ix, xi–xii, 2–3

in Marseille, 41–61

meeting Julia Child, xi, 2

in New York, 67, 171, 181–182

in Norway, 114–171

parents of, 1–2

in Paris, xiii–xiv, 2–40, 83–84

photos of, *xii, 42, 88, 105, 119*

reassignment of, 60–61

resignation of, 148, 153, 195–196

second home of, 236–240, 247

as team member, 1–41, 196–256

in United States, 62–67, 75, 85–102, 171

vacation of, 226–234, 240

in Washington, 66–67, 75, 85–102, 192

wedding of, *xii*

City in History, The, 192

Claiborne, Craig, 177–178, 181, 184, 188, 193

Classic French Cuisine, The, 131

"Cooking Biography," 8

cooking demonstrations, 174, 184–187, 190–192, 196–198, 209–212, 222, 227, 233, 242–247

cooking equipment, 37–39, 45, 56, 65–66, 90, 137, 157–158, 196, 218, 229, 240, 246

cooking school, 13–25, 29–30, 42–43, 68, 94, 99, 183, 197
Cordon Bleu, xiv, 5, 12–13, 30
Coryn, Sidonie, 153, 167
Course of Empire, The, 26, 33, 47
Cousins, Dorothy (Dort), 3, 8, 185, 215
Cousins, Ivan, 3, 8, 185
Cuisine et Vins de France, 77, 95, 163–164, 233
Cuisinière Provençale, 44
Curnonsky, 39, 44

D
Davis, David, 206
de Gaulle, Charles, 112–113
de Santillana, Dorothy, 26–27, 33–38, 44, 55–57, 63–64, 79, 85–86, 96–102, 109–123, 130–131, 135
Deane, Martha, 181
Detroit News, The, 183
DeVoto, Avis
  as assistant, 44–47, 50–51, 54–57, 66
  birth of, 25
  career of, 26–31, 76–79, 91–92, 98–102, 106, 132–133
  children of, 26, 45, 70–71, 92, 210
  cookbook launch and, 178–179
  cookbook manuscript and, 130–139, 141–142, 145–148, 152–153, 170–171
  cookbook sales and, 223
  death of husband, 76
  description of, 46, 64–66
  early life of, 26–31
  health concerns of, 71, 134
  manuscript rejection and, 99–102
  marriage of, 26
  meeting Bill Koshland, 96, 130
  meeting Julia Child, x, 62–64
  meeting Louisette Bertholle, 71–72
  meeting Simca Beck, 79–80, 91
  in New York, 136–138
  in Paris, 79–80, 91
  photos of, *28*, *81–82*
  promoting Paul Child, 89
  shifting gears, 106–123
  as team member, 24–41, 44–47, 54–57, 66, 250, 255
  visits with, 62–64, 67, 85, 91–92, 105–106, 172–173, 204, 206, 209–210, 233
  in Washington, 91–92, 99
DeVoto, Bernard, 26–33, 62–64, 76
DeVoto, Gordon, 26, 45, 70–71, 92
DeVoto, Mark, 26, 45, 210
Die Meistersinger, 126
Dione Lucas's Gourmet Club, 182
Dior, Christian, 96
Donon, Joseph, 123, 131, 137
Duhamel, Albert, 196, 207

E
Eastern Educational Network (EEN), 220, 244
"Easy Chair, The," 26–27
Edinberg, Ruth Jeanne, 207
Embassy News, 14
Emmy Award, x, 250–251, *251*
Escoffier, Auguste, xiv, 52–53, 73–74, 95, 102, 111
Etlinger, Paulette, 11

F
Fairbank, Ben, 204, 206
Fairbank, Ginny, 206
Field, Michael, 248–251
Filene, Edward, 2
Fischbacher, André, 187
Fischbacher, Jean, 5–7, 17, 74, 81, 98–99, 115–116, 187, 195, 232, 236–239
Fischbacher, Simone Beck, 3, 13, 17, 98–99, 236–237. *See also* Beck, Simone (Simca)
Fish, Dick, 229
Fisher, Dorothy Canfield, 7, 11, 44–45
Food & Friends, 3, 7, 9
Foods of the World series, 248–249, 251–252
Foreign Service, 22, 60, 75, 85, 93, 148, 153, 206, 217
Frank, Anne, 142–143
French Chef, The, x, xv–xvi, 194–233, 236–253

descriptions of, 196–198, 203–205,
  213–223, 240–242, 246–247, 252–254
first airings, 196–198, 202–205
launching, x, xv–xvi, 201–205
proposal for, 198–201
success of, 202–253
French Cooking in the American Kitchen, 70
French Home Cooking, 32
Frost, Robert, 205–206

G
Galbraith, Kenneth, 179
Galbraith, Mrs. Kenneth, 179
Goldberg, Jacob, 207
Goodhart, Charles, 198
Goodhart, Margaret (Miffy), 198
Gordon, Louis H., 207

H
Haas, Walter, 126
Hale, Nancy, 179
Harper's, 26–27
Harper's Bazaar, 44, 94–96, 98, 110, 164
Harrap's French and English Dictionary, 23
Harvey, Peggy, 192
Herald Tribune, 219
Hitler, Adolf, 128
Holiday, 88–89
Holocaust, 67
House & Garden, 94, 164, 181, 194, 238,
  245

I
I've Been Reading, 196–198

J
Jackson, Charlotte, 187
Jacobs, Sidney, 135–137, 139
James, William, 107
Jarlauld, Jacques, 4
Jones, Evan, 142–143, 177
Jones, Judith
  background of, 141–143
  congratulations from, 247

cookbook manuscript (pre-publication),
  x, 131–138, 141–146, 149–193
Mastering the Art of French Cooking,
  166–193
meeting with, 136–139
photo of, *143*
as team member, 131–139, 141–146,
  149–193, 250–255
visits with, 225–226
Joy of Cooking, The, 23, 65, 132, 144
Julia Child Foundation for Gastronomy and
  the Culinary Arts, 222

K
KCBS, 187
Kennedy, Bob, 206
Kennedy, Edith, 2, 109
Kennedy, John F., 179, 237
Kennedy, Mary, 206
kitchen equipment, 37–39, 45, 56, 65–66,
  90, 137, 157–158, 196, 218, 229, 240, 246
KNBC, 186
Knopf, Alfred A., x, 8, 32, 79, 100–101,
  126–131, 138–139, 141–171, 245–249
Knopf, Blanche, 101, 128–129, 132, 137, 139
Knopf, Pat, 100–101, 139
Koshland, Abraham, 126
Koshland, Simon, 126
Koshland, Steven, 127
Koshland, William (Bill) A.
  background of, 123–132, 207
  Mastering the Art of French Cooking launch
    and, 176–177, 180, 185–189, 194
  Mastering the Art of French Cooking
    manuscript and, x, xvi, 101, 129–137,
    141–144, 153–158, 163–166, 248–249
  Mastering the Art of French Cooking print
    runs and, 200–201, 209, 215–216,
    222, 225
  Mastering the Art of French Cooking
    sales and, 185–188, 194, 200–201,
    213–226, 230, 243–248, 254–255
  meeting with, 136–139, 209–210
  newspaper column and, 224–226

photo of, *125*
as team member, 176–180, 185–201,
    213–230, 243–248, 250, 254–255
visits with, 96, 130, 210–212, 220–221,
    225–226, 233, 248
Krinsley, Richard (Dick), 185, 209–210,
    218–219, 226, 230

L

La Bonne Cuisine de Madame E. Saint-Ange,
    xv, 52
Ladies' Home Journal, 94
Larousse Gastronomique, xv, 44
Larsen, Robert, 201–202, 214, 224, 248
Le Grande, Alexandre, 3
L'École des Trois Gourmandes, 13–25, 29,
    42–43, 68, 80, 99, 110, 163–164, 183, 197
LeMay, Harding, 176–177, 181, 189
Lewinnek, Susan, 207–208
LIFE magazine, 249, 252
Lockwood, Arthur H., 207–208, 227, 229,
    234, 243
Lockwood, Ruth
    article on, 229–230
    background of, 206–208, 214–215
    The French Chef and, x, 214–218,
        220–222, 254
    daughter of, 207–208
    education of, 207–208
    marriage of, 207–208
    photos of, *208, 215*
    as team member, x, xvi, 206–208, 214–218,
        226–235, 240–246, 250, 254–255
    visits with, 243
Lucas, Dione, 30, 57, 66, 78, 178, 182, 184,
    188–189, 193, 198, 201

M

MacVicar, Avis, 25–26. *See also* DeVoto,
    Avis
Martha Deane radio show, 181–182
Mastering the Art of French Cooking, x,
    xv–xvi, 8, 11–12, 27, 124, 165–166, 172–
    195, 200–202, 209–225, 229–254

cookbook launch, 172–193
cookbook manuscript, x, xvi, 10–61,
    73–171, 248–250
cookbook manuscript acceptance,
    141–142
cookbook manuscript rejection, x,
    99–102, 122–123
cookbook manuscript title, 165–166
cookbook print runs, 200–201, 209,
    215–216, 222, 225, 249
cookbook promotions, xv, 173–195,
    200–201, 209, 215–219, 223–224,
    251–252
cookbook royalties, xv, 60, 68, 144–146,
    167, 194–197, 202, 221–225, 231,
    236–240, 245
cookbook sales, 173, 184–188, 193–196,
    200–202, 213–226, 230, 236,
    239–248, 251–255
cookbook tour, xv, 173–177, 183–195
McBaine, Jane, 187
McCarthy, Joseph, 57, 75
McWilliams, Dorothy (Dort), 3, 8, 185, 215
McWilliams, John, xi, 200, 203
McWilliams, Julia, xi, 2. *See also* Child,
    Julia
McWilliams, Julia (mother), xi
McWilliams, Phila, 189, 200, 203
Mills, Marjorie, 180
Moffat, Don, 35
Monitor, 231
Moore, John L., 153
Morash, Russ, 206, 214, 222, 241
Morgenthau, Henry, 195
Morgenthau, Henry, III, 198
Mumford, Louis, 192
Mussolini, Benito, 207

N

National Academy of Television Arts & Sci-
    ences, 250
National Association of Broadcasters, 247
National Educational Television (NET),
    244, 246–247

NBC, 182
New York Review of Books, The, 249
New York Times, 177–178, 222
newspaper column, 224–226, 228, 243

O

Office of Strategic Services (OSS), xi, 2, 10, 18, 73, 195
Oliver, Raymond, 233

P

PBS, xv
Peabody Award, 247
Perkins, Elliot, 106, 133
Platt, June, 100–101
Prospects of Mankind with Eleanor Roosevelt, 195, 208
Prud'homme, Anthony, 181, 205
Prud'homme, Erica Child, *88,* 205
Prud'homme, Rachel, 181
publicity campaigns, xv, 173–195, 200–201, 209, 215–219, 223–224, 251–252
Putnam, Sumner, 10–11, 34–35

R

radio interviews, 181–192
Raney, William (Bill), 99, 101
Réalités, 95
Reboul, Jean-Baptiste, 44
Ripperger, Helmut, 11
Rocky Mountain Herald, 179
Rombauer, Irma, 132, 137, 144
Roosevelt, Eleanor, 195, 207–208
Royce, Josiah, 107
Russell, Jim, 185–187, 245–246
Russell, Madeline Haas, 186–187

S

Sailland, Maurice Edmond, 39
Saint-Ange, Madam, xv, 52, 73, 111
San Francisco Chronicle, 185, 187
San Francisco Examiner, 186
Sheeline, Paul, 35–38, 146, 148
Sinton, John, 125

Smith Alumnae Quarterly, 229
Stevenson, Adlai, 32, 63
Stöckli, Albert, 211
Strauss, Levi, 126
Swan, Marshall, 148

T

team members, ix–x, xv–xvi, 1–82, 131–146, 149–256
television appearances
cooking demonstrations, 196–198, 222
cooking show, x, xv–xvi, 194–233, 236–253
proposal for, 198–201
for publicity, 181–182, 195
Thillmont, Claude, 18, 24, 52–53, 59, 68, 73, 75, 81, 83
Thompson, Lovell, 33, 36–37, 86–87, 97
TIME magazine, x, xvi, 243, 250–255
Time-Life series, 248–249, 251–252
Today show, 181–182
Tyree, Lucille, 6, 99, 175, 183

U

Ullman, Allan, 215, 223

V

Vogue, 44, 95, 164, 181

W

Weinstock, Herbert, 89, 101
WGBH, x, xv, 195–210, 213, 216–218, 220–234, 240, 243–248, 250
What's Cooking in France, 6, 11, 35, 69
Wile, Julius, 184, 188–189
Wilson, Jose, 182
Woman's Day, 64, 66
Woods, Jean, 186
World War I, 3
World War II, xi, 2, 5, 67